Stephanie Stocker
Caste and Equality

Culture and Social Practice

*To my grandfather Luis Stocker (*1923)*

Stephanie Stocker (PhD) is a research fellow for Cultural Anthropology at the University of Tübingen, Germany. Her research interests include modernity, education, friendship and youth in South Asia.

Stephanie Stocker

Caste and Equality

Friendship Patterns among Young Academics in Urban India

[transcript]

This thesis was accepted as a dissertation in fulfillment of the requirements for the degree of Doctor of Philosophy (Dr. phil.) by the Faculty of Humanities at Eberhard Karls University of Tübingen in 2016.

Bibliographic information published by the Deutsche Nationalbibliothek
The Deutsche Nationalbibliothek lists this publication in the Deutsche Nationalbibliografie; detailed bibliographic data are available in the Internet at http://dnb.d-nb.de

Cover concept: Kordula Röckenhaus, Bielefeld
Cover illustration: © Stephanie Stocker, 2017
Printed by Majuskel Medienproduktion GmbH, Wetzlar
Print-ISBN 978-3-8376-3885-1
PDF-ISBN 978-3-8394-3885-5

Table of contents

Notes | 7
Introduction | 9

PART I: FRIENDSHIP IN INDIA – A 'SOCIAL PHENOMENON OF MODERNITY'?

1. Anthropological accounts of modernity | 25
1.1 Modernity in India: Modern and ritual spheres | 31
1.2 "In between"? Locating the educated middle class | 35

2. Research question: Peer groups among Tamil graduate students | 43
2.1 Education, modernity and "college culture" | 46
2.2 The concept of conviviality | 53
2.3 Region and design | 57

PART II: MAKING AND MAINTAINING FRIENDSHIP

3. Exposure and status on campus | 75
3.1 Accessing Madurai Kamaraj University | 78
3.2 The campus | 80
3.3 Peer groups | 83
3.4 (Boy)friend and (girl)friend: gendered identities on campus | 86
3.5 "Like my relative": Ties, ranks and boundaries | 94
3.6 Conclusion | 102

4. Beyond the campus: Among friends in the domestic sphere | 105
4.1 *Paṭiccavaṅka*, an ambivalent image | 106
4.2 Peers as support, sponsors and patrons | 111
4.3 'University' and 'village' friends | 116
4.4 Conclusion | 120

Part III: Just a friend? Ritual implications

5. "Key site of cultural contestation"? Youth, education and marriage | 127

5.1 Marriage in South India | 131

5.2 Kin or non-kin marriage: Conflicting status aspirations in Tamil Nadu | 137

6. Reflections on compatibility: The students' perspective | 143

6.1 "No siblings please" – social and familial concerns | 149

6.2 Education, career and dowry | 153

6.3 Good looking or pretentious? Ideals of beauty and physical compatibility | 163

6.4 Astrological compatibility: The significance of horoscopes and jōtiṭar | 165

6.5 Conclusion | 171

7. Peers as mediators in matchmaking and pre-wedding ceremonies | 173

7.1 Delayed marriage and remedy rituals | 174

7.2 First encounters | 185

7.3 Evaluating the spouse: *Poṉṉu pārkka* and *māppiḷḷai vīṭu aṟiya* | 194

7.4 Finalizing the match: *Pū cūṭṭu viḻā* and *niccayatārttam* | 201

7.5 Conclusion | 205

8. Peers in wedding ceremonies | 213

8.1 Status and 'hidden' support on stage | 216

8.2 Inclusion and exclusion in wedding meals | 223

8.3 *Kūṭṭu naṭpu* in beauty parlors: Women's groups | 227

8.4 Representation of non-kin friends in marriage media | 231

8.5 Friends, courtship and love marriage | 244

8.6 Conclusion | 259

9. Conclusion and outlook | 263

References and literature | 273

Illustrations, tables and maps | 283

Abbreviations | 285

Glossary | 287

Acknowledgements | 299

Notes

Double quotation marks (i.e. "college culture") denote original quotes from authors or conversation partners as well as translations. Sources of quoted words, phrases or paragraphs are indicated in the same passage in the text. A complete register of literary sources is provided at the end of the thesis. Specifications of statements from the participants in my research include their names, which are partly changed, in addition to relevant information, such as the date, place of living, age or occupation.

Comments and expressions denoted by single quotation marks (i.e. 'backward') I employ under reserve. They pertain to disputed expressions, which usually appear in narratives and public discourses. Those terms are largely extracted from anonymous conversations, inquiries or literature. Principally, they present generalized or subjective views, stereotypes and associations.

Italics (i.e. *distinctive, India Today, kūṭṭu naṭpu*) are used for accentuations, but also titles of literary sources, films, institutions and personal names. Further, they designate Tamil and other Indian expressions, either when they appear for the first time in the text or after a longer passage. Depending on the usage by the actors, they are spelled in the colloquial or written form. An alphabetic list is provided as a final glossary, with the exception of titles or adopted terms from other authors, which will be explained within the text. Not noted in Tamil script are names of informants, gods or geographical places as well as expressions that I collected from further literary sources.

Introduction

> Kātalai tāṇṭiyum uḷḷa paṭi – eṉṟum naṭputāṉ uyarntatu pattu paṭi
> ("Friendship is one step beyond love – and it is worth ten times more than love")

This slogan is an excerpt from the soundtrack of the movie *Nanban* ("friends"), a Tamil blockbuster, released in 2012. The film depicts the friendship between three male students, made in the campus of an engineering college in Chennai. Their relationship transcends the campus borders when two of them begin to search for their lost companion by recounting shared experiences, including common future aspirations, conflicts with parental authorities and professors or their first romantic encounters. Nanban was voted the "most expected film" through an online survey by the weekly magazine *Ananda Vikatan* in 2011. This great echo outside the country which, according to the magazine *India Today*, attracted international audiences in the United States, Malaysia and Singapore, brings me to the core of the thesis: egalitarian friendships among peer groups as a product of the educational regime in India.

While anti-hierarchical relations have existed throughout several periods in India, the ideal of a 'pure' and 'unrestricted' bond beyond established barriers constitutes a comparatively recent phenomenon. Evidently, such configurations have been a product of modernization, urbanization and the reservation politics of the Indian government which enhanced a new understanding of local hierarchies. Especially within the urban context, social boundaries as organizing principles continue to dissolve, become reformulated and reemerge in an altered mode (Bate 2009; Gorringe 2005; Kolenda 1978; Sekine 2001). These changes in established social relations will be analyzed through the example of students, graduates and alumni of Madurai Kamaraj University (MKU) in the southeast Indian state of Tamil Nadu. Illuminating those transformational processes from the perspective of India's young generation, the thesis investigates the following central question: do peer groups of university graduates present an external, anti-hierarchical configuration, structured and defined by the principles of modern public education or do they appear to be organized by the ordering system of Tamil caste society?[1]

Madurai provides a rewarding ethnographic setting for this inquiry, since its social structure is strongly influenced by local boundaries between and within adjacent, scattered villages. Apart from fragmented and localized caste and kinship segregations as well as rigid gender norms, a peculiar adherence to social standing and family reputation (*māṉam*) characterizes the population immediately surrounding the groups investigated. In Indian village society, the experience of friendship largely takes place within one's own caste or kin (Mandelbaum 1970: 355). My neighbor Navaneethan, a 63 year-old former MKU student, described to me the friendship patterns during his own college days, in the mid-1970s: "In previous generations, we lived in our native villages and towns. At that time, we acted according to the customs of our caste. For us, there was no chance of having friendship with other community members. Friends and cousins were the same." If students forged alliances in the academic context beyond caste or kin, they usually took the form of political relationships, in which 'friends' acted as party comrades.[2] It is exactly that regulated structure which motivated me to conduct my research in the Madurai region, a social scenario where only in the course of a growing migration and city agglomeration, youngsters formed friendships 'for their own sake'. Such configurations do not merely reveal a functional character but emotional content. *Kūṭṭu naṭpu* ("togetherness"/ "friendship"), a term used to define relationships among peers, is a concept coined to celebrate common activities and distinctive forms of communication and has emerged in recent literature, lyrics and blockbusters.

In social anthropology, the significance and impact of friendships have been comparatively neglected, considering the range of kinship studies in this discipline. This gap in research proves particularly astonishing since across time periods and cultures friendship constitutes a fundamental form of socialization – from amicable liaisons in ancient Greece to spiritually motivated unions in the Middle Ages and virtual connections in global internet platforms today. Relevant philosophical and historical thought circle around the following questions: What makes friendship a special form of relationship in contrast to other constellations? In which way is friendship shaped by historical epochs and cultural influences? Do gender-specific connotations exist, and how do children and youngsters acquire the capacity to form friendships?

---

1 For an outline of the caste system in India and Tamil Nadu see section 2.3.2.

2 I am grateful to Navaneethan and Professor Thamburan Dharmaraj for these insights.

One of the earliest friendship ideals dates back to Greco-Roman antiquity, when Aristotle articulated his idea of friendship as a necessary prerequisite for good life in the 3rd century BCE. In his Nicomachean Ethics, he distinguishes three types of friendships: friendships of "utility", based on advantages, friendships of "pleasure" marked by sociability and finally "pure" or "complete" friendships, based on goodness (1972: 230ff.). While the philosopher expresses a skeptical view of the first two forms, for they are merely attributed to external purposes, the last type of friendship enjoys the highest regard and manifests itself as a perfect symmetrical bond (Eichler 1999: 33ff.). A similarly high appreciation for friendship was expressed by Epicurus for whom "a life without friends is a life diseased, pained, and in need of succor" (Mitchell 2001: 1). Three centuries later, the roman politician and philosopher Cicero wrote in his letters to Atticus "who banished the friendship from life, away from the world the sun" – a statement which portrays friendship as a voluntary and reciprocal union, an end in itself (Eichler 1999: 56-57)

A spiritual component is introduced in the medieval period when Thomas Aquinas conceptualized friendship as a religious union. Focusing principally on a bond between men and God, the theologist regarded friendships as a feature of Christian Western civilization (Devere 2005: 844ff.).[3] Michel de Montaigne superseded that restricted conceptualization by postulating a model of friendship involving an affectionate and self-chosen alliance. In his essay "Of friendship" (1909-14), he recounts his ideal bond of mutual knowledge and understanding. In contrast to heterosexual relations, where both men and women merely take advantage of the arrangement, he postulated that a friendship between men is grounded on reliability, openness, solidarity and stability.

During the utilitarianist era of Elizabethan and Jacobean England, skeptical views of friendship emerged. According to Francis Bacon, egoism and utility dominate the relationship between males while a 'pure' and 'true' friendship rarely proves possible. David Hume summarizes that attitude by pointing out that friendship mainly results out of pretence and fraud (Eichler 1999: 110ff.). The most cynical perspective on the alleged amity, however, was formulated by Arthur Schopenhauer through his well-known slogan: "A friend in need, as the saying goes, is rare. Nay, it is just the contrary; no sooner have you made a friend than he is in need, and asks for a loan" (2015).

The critical rationalism of the Enlightenment era in the late 18th century serves as the traditional counter pole to the utilitarian tradition. Its main representative, Immanuel Kant, defines friendship as a union created and maintained out of mutual and equal affection. Importantly, this affection is not

3 For friendship ideals in other religious systems see Devere 2005.

'irrational' but based on reason and free choice (Eichler 1999: 127ff.). As a new and essential aspect of friendship, the German philosopher introduces the term of 'sincere and pure sentiment' ("aufrichtige, reine Gesinnung") (ibid: 133), a concept which encompasses consideration, appreciation and respect. In that sense, friendship not only requires mutual attraction but also implies *distance.* By respecting the other person, one has to measure his own demands and not harass his friend with personal debauchment, indulgences and weakness. Though helpfulness constitutes a central element for the Kantian model of friendship, he attributed an auxiliary rather than exhaustive character to that kind of support. Friendship therefore, is based on mutual attraction and decent detachment alike.

Against the background of loosening family ties throughout the last century, academic interest in relationships among non-kin has grown considerably. Global demographic trends like migration, urbanization and digitalization worldwide increased the significance of friendships as an analytical social category, complementary to established familial bonds (Tenbruck 1964: 450). In addition to altered family structures, current fields of interest have investigated the impacts of gendered practices. This aspect has remained neglected over a long period of time, as the above-mentioned philosophical debates about friendship almost exclusively concentrated on relationships between men.[4] Following contemporary social and psychological studies, however, women prove to be more open and approachable for amicable bonds while men appear the 'retiring' and 'diffident' sex. Moreover, *cross-gendered* constellations have emerged and increasingly gained recognition. So far, alliances between men and women have largely been considered an intermediate state to a sexual liaison. Related studies, however, revealed that to a certain extent, male respondents attribute a higher quality to friendships with women where they experience openness and less rivalry than to those among their own sex.[5]

Regardless of the variety in research interests, contemporary approaches of social theory analyze friendship as a "social phenomenon of modernity" (Brandt 2013: 25) since that constellation composes an outcome of internal processes of differentiation in 'modern' Western society. Following respective approaches, friendships appear as an advanced model and expression to overcome social segregation – despite critical voices that it is precisely such a differentiation which impedes cohesion (ibid). Focusing on cross-cultural relationships between Māori and Pākehā in Aotearoa New Zealand, Agnes Brandt therefore evaluates

4 Few exceptions can be found in Brandt (2013: 24).

5 Broadcasted in the radio program "Eine Seele in zwei Körpern" by Dr. Michael Conradt on 17/12/2014 (http://www.br.de/radio/bayern2/wissen/radiowissen/freundschaft-seele-koerper100.html).

the variety of contemporary alliances as "flexible forms of sociality that allow the actors to actively construct, de- or reconstruct existing boundaries" (ibid: 16).

The idea of friendship as a 'modern' phenomenon becomes relevant in the Indian context, where actors from different social backgrounds increasingly form friendships that emerge in a non-familial milieu, external to their original social group. Those constellations appear as a recent category and a result of wider social transformations in contemporary India. Central issues of my research include conditions and limits of egalitarian friendship constellations with respect to prevalent notions of social boundaries on the one hand and current developments that blur established barriers on the other. Based on the following observations, I ask: on which grounds do friendships exist and how are they constructed in different socio-cultural situations? Analyzing the experience of friendship from an inter-cultural point of view turned out to be a fairly complicated endeavor: in social anthropology, friendships have found only marginal interest while kinship systems prevail as the main structuring principle in ethnographic settings. The reason for this lack of research lies in the difficulty to define 'friendship', a concept which, in contrast to kin designations, is dynamic and context-related. Not only does this term signify something different among and within several cultures, it is consistently reformulated across actors, eras and situations. Moreover, the notion and ideal of friendship is not limited to one constellation but may be attached to other forms of relationships. It appears among kin, within political contexts or as part of a romantic liaison. Following Brandt, we deal with a concept, which comprises a "relational phenomenon, i.e., the meaning of friendship is acquired in the process of engagement between actors" (2013: 36). Though the reluctance for studying friendships seems to be evident, its topicality cannot be denied. The challenge for the anthropological discipline therefore lies in approaching the term by emic categories, explanation patterns and practices.

Aware of the conceptual complexity, I refrain from grasping an 'indigenous' notion of friend in absolute terms but limit my scope to *peer groups* in a higher educational stage as an accessible focus. Murugesh, a 29 year-old PhD student described the peculiar amity among such campus relationships at Madurai Kamaraj University: "After the completion of UG, we have PG. Here, the atmosphere will be different and the friendship circle will be different." Peer group as a sociological phenomenon was first introduced by the American sociologist Charles Cooley (1929). Originally, it designates a group of persons of similar age, origin or sex. According to ethnographic studies, peer groups constitute a distinctive referential system to a prevailing dominant social structure. In an autobiographic outline on masculine values, David Jackson describes how peers perform that distinction by behavioral norms and an egalitarian structure. Common examples include mutual sharing or teasing: "The tightly organized network of male bonding […] effectively polices the boundaries of what counts as masculinity through 'norm-enforcing mechanisms' (like joking, bantering and swearing)" (Jackson 1990: 170f.). Considering its growing social relevance in many parts of the world, most related studies explore how those constellations get incorporated in different socio-cultural contexts: How do peers situate friendships in a domestic or ritual environment? Do local hierarchies become reproduced or do friendships serve to circumvent local boundaries? Such an analysis requires an examination of the foundation for maintaining intimate ties. How do actors cultivate their connections and which meaning do they attribute to their friendships? Which topics appear and which taboos persist in those cohesive circles?

While most studies in Tamil Nadu have conceptualized peer groups in terms of a transitional stage of adolescence (Nakassis 2013), my research predominantly refers to groups of young adults, notably MKU-graduate students from their mid-1920s until early 1930s. Exploring common stages to acquire adulthood and maturity, I intend to illustrate that friendships and alliances, made in the educational context, constitute *more* than a temporary constellation which is restricted to the campus. Instead, I will show that those groups do have an integrative function in wider social and ritual events. Hence, the point of interest lies in the status and significance of peer groups, an anti-hierarchical constellation shaping the realm of experience for degree holders.

In Indian society, other studies exist on egalitarian clusters, mainly in the urban space using the example of business partners, syndicates or political associations. With reference to caste, kinship and gender categories, principle interest circulated around the question of whether a 'modern' environment, notably a site where such segregations are subverted, produces an altered understanding of the ritual order. Christopher J. Fuller's anthology *Caste today* provides one representative account: André Béteille accesses what he describes as "modern occupations" (1996: 150), namely, an assigned middle or upper class composed of academics, lawyers or journalists. On the basis of their everyday practices, explanation patterns and interactions, the author explores the extent to which those groups adhere to the Indian caste order and which sanctions continue to persist. Béteille finds an ambivalent and unstable view, in the sense that his informants alter their attitude towards caste differences according to the situation. While intellectuals emphasize a shrinking role of social barriers as part of a nationalist discourse that proclaims progressive ideals, in other situations, caste rules appear in a 'curtailed' form, which the author describes as "a truncated system" (1996: 161).

Ethnographic and sociological studies on sectors of society such as the 'middle class', 'academics' or the 'urban population' are generally confronted with the problematic task of defining a clear-cut social category. Aware of that methodological difficulty, my research accesses peer groups as an analytical focus, which I understand as a class-phenomenon, related to a distinctive 'modern' category. The supposition that cross-caste and cross-gendered friendships require an environment to come into view, a space in which 'modern' ideals such as the value of equality remain prevalent, forms the foundation for this approach. In other words, the types of friendships in my study formed according to the local understanding of 'modernity'. Moreover, these constellations principally occur among social groups of the population that one could categorize as the 'middle class'. Such a classification is certainly projected, yet by no means arbitrary. In fact, studies on class mobility in urban areas of South India have defined friendships across different backgrounds as 'indicators of modernity' (Dickey 2010: 198).

The following chapters are divided into three parts: an outline on the purpose and structure of the study, containing relevant theoretical approaches (part I), examinations of friendships created and maintained within and outside the campus (part II) and niches for cultivating those constellations in the ritual marriage context (part III). Using the example of several peer groups at different stages in life, I employ a diachronic perspective on how egalitarian friendships, as an embodied form of a proclaimed value of equality, are stabilized or altered throughout different social environments.

Certainly, utilized terms such as 'modernity' or 'middle class' appear imprecise and need to be reconsidered and placed in the research context. Part one begins by specifying the theoretical approaches to examining 'modernity' in the anthropological discipline. Aside from terminological clarifications, chapter one highlights that not one but many different forms of modernity exist. Indeed, a range of global developments – industrialisation, democratization or digitalization – take place in several parts of the world, but contain a similar intention and agenda. At the same time, the impacts of those trends may considerably differ from one another at the local level. Such variations can only become understood by taking into account the role of cultural practices that model the immediate configuration of 'modern' influences. 'Modernity' therefore does not necessarily signify a 'loss of culture', but offers an opportunity for new formations that emerge from the interplay between large-scale impacts and local principles. Global flows of ideas, products and people as well as inter-cultural linkages of events occur within the framework of normative imaginations and systems.

Assuming a heterglossic and culture-specific form of modernity, I turn to its elaboration in an Indian context. Based on historical outlines, contemporary trends and related academic approaches, I move forward defining a distinctive realm of experience as a *modern compartment.* That sphere appears in the form of educational institutions, companies or technologies which predominantly emerged in the postcolonial era proclaiming ideals of equality, individual choice or women's empowerment. Characterized by standardized principles that span the entire state, modern compartments compose a countervailing power vis a vis local mechanisms of inclusion and exclusion. The topicality of modern processes calls for a reexamination of existing boundaries in South Tamil Nadu where, according to the Indian scholar Rajan Krishnan, recent developments are shaping the "tamil psyche, which is torn between the threatening pre-modern assertation of caste and 'egalitarian' and free modern market space of the modern individual" (2008: 141). This tension most affects the Indian middle class, which represents the social category with which nearly all of my informants identify themselves despite heterogeneity within the group with respect to other characteristics. 'Middle class' presents another problematic term that finds itself consistently rearticulated among and within different cultures. Therefore, in a subsequent section, I elucidate how class identity becomes constructed and acted out in the Madurai region. In doing so, I do not concentrate exclusively on aspirations, lifestyle and modes of distinction; with reference to the interplay between global trends and prevailing social norms, I point out the peculiar position "in between" conflicting demands.

Having clarified central concepts of 'modernity', 'Indian modernity' and 'middle class', the second chapter gives those reflections a more concrete form with the example of peer groups of Indian students and graduates. The research question about the significance of such friendship constellations will be placed within the wider ethnographic debate about whether those groups display a 'modern' and countervailing structure that is maintained within encompassing social principles in Tamil Nadu. A range of classic approaches adheres to Louis Dumont's theory that a foundational element of Indian society consists in a hierarchical precept, based on a pure-impure divide. Beyond caste segregations, that principle determines other domains including marriage circles and daily interactions in public (Skoda 2002: 143). Though that debate was initiated more than half a century ago, it continues even today and has gained relevance against the background of recent social developments: while the population, particularly in the surrounding villages, mainly identifies with the local community, the urban context exhibits several recently formed networks that transcend caste principles and related restrictions. Typically, the educational realm delineates the above-defined 'modern compartment' so that related accounts of social transformations assess "how a particular kind of modern subject gets created [...] by the technologies of the school" (Kumar 2007: 221). Precisely, the educational sphere functions as a transmitter of models and ideas of the modern nation state, including democracy, equality, justice and development (Alex 2009: 141, Jeffery 2005: 13). I argue that peer groups produce an embodiment of that 'modern' state discourse by retaining the value of equality. Hence, they turn into egalitarian constellations that subvert established boundaries of the South Tamil caste society – a phenomenon defined as "college culture" (Osella & Osella 1998: 191). The concept of *conviviality* ("Konvivium"), introduced by Christian Strümpell, provides one recent approach to explaining such constellations. It posits egalitarian friendships and gatherings as temporary phenomena, which find acceptance in specific spheres, particularly in modern compartments. However, in domains where the ritual order prevails, convivial configurations remain unseparated from a hierarchical caste order. Having outlined that argumentation in great detail, the analytical challenge of this paper lies in reviewing whether that approach can be applied to the case study at hand.

The research is based on one year of fieldwork from October 2011 until September 2012. Rather than researching conventional middle class milieus, often associated with populated metropolises, I carried out my study in a geographical setting in which a segregated social structure determines interactions within the population more so than in other Tamil regions. I approached peculiar concepts of 'friendship', 'modernity' or 'educated behavior' not only through my contacts to the graduate students, but also living with a host family in the outskirts of Madurai. In this setting, I had the opportunity to experience first-hand how the exposure to a different system translates into behavioral responses directly, negotiated or in a newly articulated fashion in the domestic and ritual context. Those insights proved indispensable for my research, the methodology for which I present in detail in the second part of this chapter.

Part II turns to the ethnographic material, pursuing the question about how friendships are made and maintained in the educational sphere and beyond. Chapter 3 assesses the campus of Madurai Kamaraj University as a crucial setting for egalitarian peer groups: aspirations of students reveal that education promises more than mere prospects for a successful career. Due to their educated background, students and graduates acquire a distinctive status of *paṭiccavaṅka* ("educated person"). On this ground, they turn into networks, based on a distinctive social position. Observing everyday interactions and activities of a selected sample of Master students (MA) and doctoral candidates (PhD) between 20 and 29 years of age, I investigate whether those constellations effectively constitute an 'external' model that counteracts South Tamil caste society. In fact, a closer look reveals internal strategies of both inclusion and exclusion. In addition to gender provisions, campus friendships exist within a framework of ranking one another and reveal superior and inferior positions within the group. Differing relationships, attitudes or courtesy point to multiple forms of friendships, the quality of which is determined by kinship designations. Finally, I will turn to the significance of caste differences. While students negate caste-based discrimination amongst themselves, they do refer to community identity for rationalizing characteristics, behavior and achievements of their friends.

Chapter 4 analyzes how friendship constellations are entrenched within Tamil society and everyday life: observing the behavior of peer groups in several adjacent home villages, I point out that students not only acquire an elaborated status as *paṭiccavaṅka* but succeed in maintaining egalitarian clusters. Such networks commonly function as a support system along their path toward living secular lives. As college friends, they constitute a category separated from local village friends, often acquaintances from the same community or kin. Yet, college friends do not confront established norms in Tamil village society: as a vivid feature of peer groups, I highlight its potential for reinterpreting networks and the extent to which these individuals adjust their interaction in line with social restrictions in a domestic context.

The dynamic character of friendship patterns finds full consideration in the *ritual* framework. Part III turns to the designated stage of life subsequent to graduation, namely that of marriage, which presents the central life event for every Tamil person and demarks entrance into maturity by asserting the ritual status. During the remaining chapters, the principal focus lies on educational influences through an analysis of the graduates' view on marriage and its significance for egalitarian friendships. To date, the ritual context has been commonly assumed a *limit* to anti-hierarchical formations. Yet, when I gave a presentation on networks and friendships between academics from different social backgrounds on the 43rd Annual Conference on South Asia in Madison, Wisconsin, the audience raised the objection that anti-hierarchical constellations may coexist within the ritual sphere. Indeed a valid comment, considering the involvement of non-familial friends in marriage practices. In particular in the view of the young brides and grooms, support from friends is perceived as an essential part of this life stage. Indirect and overt engagement of non-kin friends will be highlighted by the example of several case studies, including networks of former MKU students in an advanced age.

Ethnographies principally regard marriage as a "key site of cultural contestation" between the young generation on the one hand and parental authorities on the other. Chapter 5 therefore presents an outline of theoretical accounts on marriage as a converging zone for negotiating inter-generational worldviews. Kimberly Hart assumes the conventional view of most ethnographic works when she defines marriage as a "site where the politics of gender, ideologies of modernity, and economy intersect with young people's desire for emotional fulfillment" (2007: 347). Against this academic backdrop, I present recent changes in Tamil middle class weddings, particularly the transition from consanguineous to non-kin marriages. Reviewing the wide range of academic accounts of marriage in India, I place the focus on its significance for the young middle class generation in South India. Observations of matchmaking strategies make apparent why family members of bride and groom invest a large portion of their capital into a suitable alliance. While related ethnographies argued that, within the ritual context, egalitarian friendships fade, my findings suggest increasing influence and a cocreation of non-familial contacts. Their experience and shared views throughout principal stages of matchmaking and ceremonial happenings consolidates the bond of anti-hierarchical friendships. Spouses, siblings and friends act as 'agents' to introduce 'modern' principles into an arranged marriage – including the value of equality, participation of the younger generations, codes of conduct, but also an elaborated taste for and the integration of romantic feelings and desires. The crucial role of non-kin friends has increasingly been adopted in a sometimes embellished way in Tamil media. *Kadhalil sodhappuvadhu yeppadi* ("How to destroy love"), a 2012 romantic comedy film, which highlights the participative role of friends in approving or destroying courtships and alliances, exemplifies this phenomenon. In contrast to aforementioned ethnographies, however, I argue that this form of involvement does not oppose but takes place *in accordance* with established social norms.

Chapter 6 turns to students' and graduates' narratives about compatibility between spouses, considering familial, economic, physical and astrological aspects. In the case of non-kin alliances between unacquainted families, professional assemblers guide the matchmaking process, monitor the search for a spouse and introduce additional standards and criteria for compatibility. Based on graduates' ideal of a *companionate* marriage (Fuller & Narasimhan 2008: 752), I point out how pertinent profile data are rationalized by applying acquired 'modern' ideals of equality, individual choice or a strengthened position of the woman. During this section, I follow the recommendation of Henrike Donner "to challenge simplistic assumptions about the way new 'modern' selves are constructed in relation to social institutions like marriage and to analyze generalizing concepts like intimacy and companionate marriage through an anthropological reading of specific ideas and social relations" (2008: 89). This chapter rejects the assumption that marriage negotiations are consistently determined by parental authorities and rather highlights the space for my conversation partners to articulate their own desires in line with culture-specific boundaries.

Notwithstanding divergent formulations of conjugal ideals, cross-generational consent about the crucial importance of marriage remains. Peers therefore not only urge each other to start a family, but establish personal contacts between the spouses and work to make the bride and groom attractive to each other. That engagement beyond the family-initiated search for a spouse is demonstrated in chapter 7, which provides a meticulous description of principal matchmaking rituals – from first encounters between in-law families until the finalization of the match. Recent progressive trends have led to growing uncertainties among wife givers and takers alike, an increasing demand for remedy rituals and creative strategies of inquiry. I highlight inter-generational views on the right procedure, an area where non-familial networks increasingly become activated. The case examples suggest that peers or other actors external to the family take on a crucial role as mediators (*terintavaṅka*) in matchmaking.

The status and function of non-ritual friends will be further disclosed during the section on wedding rituals (*kalyāṇam*). Chapter 8 provides insights into recent trends in the conducting of the ceremonial event. Mushrooming halls and the large variety of decoration, style, music and other features transform the ritual into a platform for displaying and strengthening social standing. Based on several extracts from the marriage ceremony, I point out in which way university friends become incorporated into or excluded from the ritual activities. Observation of their interaction in beauty parlors, during procedures on stage and the wedding meal reveal different forms of support before, throughout and after the event. Moreover, I take account of ritual moments in which egalitarian constellations appear inauspicious. For elucidation, I turn to the visual representation in printing and audio media, such as invitation cards, wedding albums and videos. A digression on courtships and self-chosen unions defines non-familial friends and peers as main actors. Having presented the delicate implication of 'love marriage' (as opposed to a companion marriage) in Tamil society, I illuminate with the help of a case study the function of peers as key organizers – from initiating formalities to ensuring the proper exertion of ceremonial events.

The final conclusion brings together previous strands of argumentation: reviewing peer behavior throughout the chapters, this thesis demonstrates how Tamil students, graduates and postgraduates creatively navigate across differing systems. This section directs the reader's attention to the actor's ability to adjust his or her mode of interaction with the prevailing social environment. Based on these considerations, I discuss the flexible character of Tamil friendship ideals that exist side by side. To enrich the debate on caste, status and anti-hierarchy in Tamil Nadu, I pose the question of whether the concept of conviviality can be applied to social networks among academics. While I largely find this approach useful for my own case study, I also propose alternative thoughts and highlight previously neglected aspects.

My ethnography traces the experience of a representative section of the young, middle class generation at the beginning of their career and entry into family life. Against this background, the thesis allows inferences into emerging issues in social anthropology with respect to local notions of "modernity", "education" and "distinction" as well as implications of changing ritual practices. It inquires into how modern state discourses, promoted by higher education, may succeed or fail in influencing local practices. In a concrete sense, it asks to what extent new professional prospects and a changed social composition in the academic context produce a transformation of established boundaries. Such concerns build on a plethora of broadly conceived research investigating whether educational regimes reproduce or undermine embedded social, cultural and economic inequalities.

Finally, I highlight remaining inconsistencies. A first discrepancy concerns the conceptual approach of 'egalitarian' groups. Certainly, one cannot assume such constellations as a clear-cut category. Interactions, boundaries, activities and quality of peer groups vary across parameters, including gender, caste, class and age and those factors lead to differing viewpoints among individual peer group members with regard to their experience of friendship. In fact, despite expressing a high regard for and displaying actual behavior in favor of equality, the educational sphere generates caste-based inequalities, typically through the revitalization of political movements (see section 3.5). Yet, the participants in my study form clusters in a domain where secular ideals are specifically enhanced. Therefore, I argue that particularly those constellations, more than others in South Tamil society, are distinctly marked by ideals such as irrational love, intimacy, and emotions resisting social barriers.

Second, a definite confrontation of 'university friends' towards other forms of relationships appears to be artificial (see chapter 3.3): at times, the discursive construction of the notion of 'friend' is ambivalent and contradictory, which makes it impossible to define this concept in unambiguous terms. It must be conceded that a friendship ideal exists among kin, neighbors or close family acquaintances. Aware that this form of friendship might occur in other social contexts as well, I adhere to the example of peers as an analytical cluster.

A third clarification refers to the lack of a common understanding of terms like 'modern', 'backward' or 'educated'. In search of a comprehensive interpretation, this thesis risks evoking the impression of an attempt to lump together deviating opinions and experiences into a consistent picture. Moreover, concepts vary across different layers, especially on semantic, institutional or personal levels. For a differentiated analysis, the data set includes institutionalized actions, narratives and deviating interpretations alike. Other neglected aspects and prospects for future studies are presented in the conclusion.

Part I: Friendship in India – a 'social phenomenon of modernity'?

> And what if we had never been modern? Comparative anthropology would then be possible. The networks would have a place of their own.
>
> BRUNO LATOUR (1993: 10)

Regarding social transformation in the context of higher education, I begin this thesis by pursuing the question: how does social anthropology deal with the term 'modernity'? Such an outline seems topical, considering that for a long time the discipline objected to drawing a rather static picture of the 'far' and 'cultural' other that is rooted in its tradition and isolated from 'Western modernity'.[1] Throughout the first chapter, I demonstrate the challenge for anthropologists to reflect on complexities, processes and understandings of modernity and modernization across the globe. According to classical approaches, modernity implies a notion of social change and the surmounting of what is deemed 'tradition'. This idea suggests that modernity can be conceptualized within a static framework, irrespective of social and cultural conditions. However, cultural theorists have rendered those approaches obsolete, claiming that modernity must be related to a particular cultural context. Introducing the theory of an "alternative" or "multiple" modernity, recent accounts have postulated a

1 Arjun Appadurai and Carol A. Breckenridge highlight the increasing attention in social sciences, stating that "what is distinctive about any particular society is not the fact or extent of its modernity, but rather its distinctive debates *about* modernity, the historical and cultural trajectories that shape its appropriation of the means of modernity, and the cultural sociology [...] that determines who gets to play with modernity and what defines the rules of the game" (Appadurai & Breckenridge 1996: 16).

more dynamic and pluralistic image of this term and point to a plethora of historical examples in which social transformations have existed on their own, decoupled from historical or geographical constrains. That debate will be situated in the Indian context: referring to crucial historical milestones, I provide an insight into how the concept of modernity has been implemented in a culture-specific way. Rather than offering a linear development from tradition to a modern state, two parallel systems emerged: one sphere stems from social realities within a particular locality while a second 'modern' realm of experience is characterized by a pan-Indian "oneness" – a term which Peter Berger and Frank Heidemann (2013: 2) regard as an abstract product of scientific or political discourses. Regarding the juxtaposition of both systems, I will end this section with the inter-located position of India's middle class, which constitute the representative group in my research.

India's public education presents a vivid paradigm for this 'modern' system, as it enhanced a separate platform for anti-hierarchical constellations and constitutes an alteration to existing cultural barriers. In the second section, I turn to the research focus of this thesis, notably friendships and peer groups at university and other educational institutions. The campus is conceptualized as an environment that adheres to progressive ideals of equality. Within this setting, the perspectives of university-educated students and professionals, who find themselves exposed to two opposing value systems, lie at the center of this research project. One of these systems acknowledges the value of equality within the university realm and a second respects established boundaries and norms of South Tamil society. The concept of 'conviviality', which I subsequently outline, provides a potential analytical framework for explaining these perspectives.

The relevance and topicality of this study become apparent with the introduction of the social environment for my research setting. I thereby take account of classic academic works in Madurai as well as current demographic changes and recent debates. Against this ethnographic background, the chapter concludes by elucidating my own fieldwork, including structure, strategies and difficulties.

1. Anthropological accounts of modernity

What is modernity? Though there has been a wide range of accounts of this term focusing on aspects of culture (Latour 1993), institutions (Giddens 1990) or mentalities (Bhargava 2001), all definitions assume a significant transformation of society and its institutions within a certain passage of time. Anthony Giddens provides an often cited and comprehensive definition when he writes: "'Modernity' refers to modes of social life or organization which emerged in Europe from about the 17th century onwards and which subsequently become more or less worldwide in their influence" (1990: 1). His association of modernity "with a time period" and "with an initial geographical location" (ibid) is adopted in Latour's consideration, as he relates this term to "a new regime, an acceleration, a rupture, a revolution in time" (1993: 10). Attaching modernity to developmental and temporal stages evoked the idea of a contrasting 'tradition' formulated as "an archaic and stable past" (ibid). Throughout the 21th century, a binary opposition of those two exclusive terms prevailed and was applied as an evaluation criterion for cultural states, practices and mentalities (Kaviraj 2005: 501; Giddens 1990: 36).

At the beginning of the 1980s, however, the idea of tradition as a rigid and enclosed system was strongly called into question. The ahistorical construct of a static cultural model was impugned by an imagination that "tradition resembles less an artifactual assemblage than a process of thought – an ongoing interpretation of the past" (Handler and Linnekin 1984: 274). Decisive is not only the rejection of 'tradition' as an anti-thesis to 'modernity', but the acceptance of an intentional examination of such categories. Margaret Jolly therefore argues for a stronger conscience of scholars for the "self awareness of culture", emphasizing that "rather than presenting our accounts as real pasts, Western scholars might look more carefully and comparatively at the encoding of past present relations in the variety of symbolic constitutions of tradition" (1992: 63f.). Recent approaches have therefore conceptualized 'modern' practices as new manifestations of the old. Paul Rabinow enriched the debate with the theoretical foundation of the "anthropology of the contemporary" (Rabinow 2008). He emphasizes the need to avoid the dualism of 'tradition' and 'modernity' and highlights the flexible and compatible character of both phenomena as well as their linkage that constitutes a sphere of "contemporary" (ibid: 2f.). As a vivid example for that approach, Bate (2009) identifies the recourse of Tamil political speakers to archaic language forms as a feature of modernity. This observation suggests that "modernity is not the mere succession of tradition, rather [...] the production of tradition is a primary modality of modernity" (ibid xvii). The academic controversy with respect to modernity and modernization produced a wide range of further approaches across the arts and other disciplines related to cultural and humanities. Assuming a cross-cultural focus, anthropologists have largely illuminated the question of whether modernization processes developed in a homogenous or in a multi-faceted and culture-specific way.

The idea of a linear transition from tradition to modernity has been adopted by those anthropological approaches which Rajeev Bhargava (2001: 10) summarizes under the concept of "acultural theories" as they regard modernity as a unitary procedure across culture and space. The "European theory of modernity" (Kaviraj 2005: 497) provides the theoretical foundation for the view that due to their common social past, Western countries including Canada, America and Australia have followed a homogenous trajectory of modernization. Supported by this historical approach, classical social scientists developed the idea of Europe as the center of modernity while they considered other countries as lagging behind, but predestined to finally track a similar course of development.

Accordingly, the "theories of transition" (ibid: 489), one position among the aculturalists, regard any modernization processes as an orientation toward the institutional forms of European history of the 19th century. That assumption presents the starting point for the "common theory" (ibid: 502), an approach which conceptualizes modernity in terms of a historically unique event in Europe, distinct from any previous social changes. The Marxist assumption that the establishment of a capitalistic economy produces a similar pattern of a commoditized social structure across several European countries forms the principal socio-economic foundation for this approach (ibid).

Regardless of their particular orientation, acultural approaches draw on a functionalist view, i.e. the assumption that defined elements exist in every society that developed in relation to each other. Such elements include: "capitalist industrialization, the increasing centrality of the state in the social order [...], urbanization, sociological individuation, secularization in politics and ethics, the creation of a new order of knowledge, vast changes in the organization of family and intimacy, and changes in the fields of artistic and literary culture" (Kaviraj 2005: 508). Though remaining disconnected, those elements operate in relation to others and shape the process of modernization in a similar way, regardless of the cultural context. In other words, once one element undergoes change, other elements will operate in dependence to that first one or to none of them. Applied to European society, new modes of production and a capitalist economy triggered similar changes in legal, political and ideological structures. Since the rest of modernity is assumed to follow one technological impetus, modernization appears to proceed in a parallel and symmetrical fashion in every culture across the world, as Kaviraj emphasizes: "By the functional connection, through which different elements of the modernist paradigm support and reinforce each other, after a time, when most of the essential elements are put in place, modern societies tend to look very similar" (ibid: 509).

The concept of modernity as a standardized course has been strongly opposed by approaches presuming a more complex understanding of the term. The principle critique is directed to the Western "'hegemony' of modernity as an analytic category" as formulated by John Tomlinson, who rejects the application of a Western category and "its strategic role in the maintenance of western cultural dominance [...] its universalizing tendencies [...] and its deployment as a sort of diversionary discourse masking the aggressive advance of global capitalism" (Tomlinson 1999: 33). Similar concerns gained attention alongside a new understanding of modernization, which considers different forms and indigenous notions of modernity unrelated to the West. Mark Liechty (2003: 250) regards any facets of social change that appear in the form of "cultural homogenization, Americanization, Westernization [as] all variants of a myth and a cultural narrative." Despite his Eurocentric orientation, Giddens (1990: 175) has admitted that modernization processes exceed the mere dissemination of occidental institutions when he states that new forms of world interdependency and planetary conscience contain concepts based on non-occidental institutions.

Approaches that contradict aculturalists and their idea of a standardized pathway of modernity have been subsumed under the category of "cultural theory" (Bhargava 2001: 13). The designation of this academic direction derives from the objective to relate processes of modernization to a particular culture. Cultural theorists assume that "all practices [...] are partly constituted by beliefs [...] which refer directly or implicitly to values that give these practices a normative direction" (ibid). Their position strongly opposes the historically grounded view that modernity is merely set up by a distinctive incident in industrialized Europe. Instead, culturalists argue that despite similar impulses across European countries such as the capitalist system, different implications, configurations and consequences of modernity exist. Adherents to the cultural approach destabilize the functional theory of the aculturalists by questioning a distinctive interplay of technological developments on the one hand and cultural institutions on the other, which constitute a point of departure for modernization (ibid). The "sequential view", outlined by Kaviraj (2005: 510ff.) for instance, offers a rather heterodox picture. Drawing on political practices and popular struggles, its supporters argue that even in early stages of modernization, isolated elements, including capitalism and democracy opposed each other and therefore evolved at different temporary stages. Thus, features of modernization are not necessarily related functionally to each other. Instead, in every society a cultural and normative system exists that encompasses technological change. Furthermore, this direction supposes that different successions and combinations of social developments determine the nature of modernity. Culturalists therefore have successfully pointed out several discrepancies in the acultural theory in regard to the incomparability of modernity across societies. As a consequence, each society should employ its own internal concepts for analysis. At the same time, a cultural view proved to be problematic since it renders a comparative discussion of the term 'modernity' and its elaboration nearly impossible.

Both aculturalist and culturalist theories maintain the assumption that people have lived isolated from any contact to cultural alternatives and that globalization and the adoption of Western cultural elements signify the breakdown of native culture. Throughout recent decades however, cultural diffusion and intercultural communication have been recognized not as sudden alterations that appear at a certain point in time but rather as continuous adaptations to different options across the globe. While culturalists risks abandoning any greater capacity for defining an applicable theory of modernity, recent anthropologists have concentrated on the contact zones between new or foreign and indigenous systems. This set of theories is united by a common quest for an alternative to the persisting notion of modernity as a "Western project" (Giddens 1990: 174).

The anthology "Alternative Modernities", published in 2001, offers one of the most representative theoretical foundations of these contemporary accounts. Editor Dilip Gaonkar calls for the acceptance of the plurality of different cultural realities and the overcoming of a homogenous concept of one, singular Western modernity. His introduction stresses the orientation of all contributors, notably that "modernity today is global and multiple and no longer has a governing centre or master narrative to accompany it" (Gaonkar 2001: 14). The author proposes a dialectic approach, elucidating the acceptance or rejection of Western modernity in line with local circumstances. Thus, he assumes a dual, "Janus-like" (ibid: 9ff.) character of modernity, as he distinguishes between two processes of modernization: societal modernization and cultural modernity. The former refers to cognitive and institutional transformations, particularly the improvement of material conditions and the adoption of ideas expressed by the Enlightenment philosophers. The second process describes an aesthetic component, such as cultivation and care of the individual self and enhances different aspects including lifestyle or class consciousness.

This approach finds a particular echo within the Indian context.[1] Bhargava has adopted and complemented this concept by clarifying that "a change in its traditional structure and an equally significant difference from Western modern institutions is critical for an alternative modernity to exist" (Bhargava 2001: 20f). He applies the idea of Alternative Modernities to the configuration of the caste system and secularism in India. Referring to the first paradigm, the author demonstrates that caste hierarchy proved immovable in the face of European influence, which three developments make evident: the control by Portuguese and British colonialists, education and contemporary social change. While colonialism and the practice of assigning specific occupations and posts in administrative service according to caste only strengthened caste identity, modern education, which transports ideals of equality and individualism, did not undermine caste differences. Finally, he highlights the significance of caste in contemporary India from an indicator within a hierarchical system towards a symbol of cultural identity and a "potent resource for mobilization in an egalitarian political democracy" (ibid). Secularism offers a second example for the concept of Alternative Modernities, which reiterates that the Western concept of reformism is not applicable in an Indian context (ibid: 22). In order to elaborate his argument, Bhargava characterizes the religious scenery in India by four facts. Firstly, different religious communities coexist together in India. Secondly, Hinduism is followed more in practice than in belief. Thirdly, external institutions often serve as reformers of religiously motivated practices. Fourthly, the lack of a central establishment like the church complicates such a

1 Its relevance within the country has been especially formulated by Kaviraj's statement: "To recognize the unfamiliar behavior of Indian democracy, the unfamiliar evolutions of the Indian state, the un-Western urbanity of our cities, and surprisingly unaccustomed twists in economic behavior, we required a theory of modernity that could cut itself from its points of origin in European history and conceive of these trends as modern" (Kaviraj 2005: 501).

reformation of current practices. Based on those particularities, he finds that secularism in a Western form turned out to be inadaptable to Indian society, since it advocates religious freedom of the individual, the value of equal citizenship and a strict separation of state and religion. These two cases of colonialism and secularism intend to illustrate the central argument underlying the idea of Alternative Modernities, notably that "modernity could have sprouted at different places either simultaneously or at different times" (ibid: 15).

While the concept of Alternative Modernities and its application to the Indian context presumes a dualistic view, Marshall Sahlins argues for a harmonization of *etic* and *emic*[2] perspectives. His concept of an "indigenization of modernity" (2000) points to an interactive development of the native cultural conceptualization together with external factors. In other words, actors create their own forms of local modernization by incorporating selected foreign influences, cultural images and practices. Such a perspective comes close to Gaonkars articulation of a "creative adaptation", which describes "a site where people 'make' themselves modern, as opposed to being made modern by alien and impersonal forces and where they give themselves an identity and a destiny" (2001: 18).

Reviewing that outline of different arguments, it can be concluded, that ethnographic methods do not assume a singular notion of modernity but opt for a plural sense of the term. Accordingly, Gaonkar's contention subsumes the present state of anthropological research on modernity which "is an incomplete project and necessarily so" (2009: 21) and the realization that "people [...] everywhere, at every national or cultural site, rise to meet it, negotiate it, and appropriate it in their own fashion" (ibid). Following this brief review on the most relevant intellectual approaches in the discipline of anthropology, the manifold configurations of 'modernity' shall be applied within the Indian context.

2 The *emic* view considers the perspective from 'within', following the categories of the actors. This term stands in contrast to the *etic* view which represents the perspective from 'outside', following the categories of the academic observer.

1.1 MODERNITY IN INDIA: MODERN AND RITUAL SPHERES

In India, modernization is largely linked to a comprehensive sphere that emerged as part of foreign influences and internal movements oriented towards a common value system beyond established local structures and boundaries. In their anthology *The modern Anthropology of India,* Peter Berger and Frank Heidemann (2013) conceptualize Indian modernity by contrasting two societal realities in the country: a "pan-Indian knowledge" that forms ideas of modern values and regional particularities. The first reality comprises a political landscape, including centralized administrations and government schemes, economic developments, such as industrialization and consumer trends. National sports or the cultural scene comprise a significant realm, exemplified by the Bollywood industry, which formed fan clubs across the entire country. In short, this level is marked by cross-state institutions, movements and associations which unite common ideals beyond local configurations of Indian society and "propagate nationalist ideas, family values and messages against the rigidity of caste" (ibid: 2). The second reality takes the shape of regional peculiarities, including dialects or local caste-, kinship- and gender relations. It represents a domain that according to Heidemann seems to "have greater relevance for day-to-day interactions" (ibid).

For better understanding, those two analytical categories shall be henceforth distinguished by the designations 'modern' and 'ritual' sphere. While this thesis regards education as a field belonging to the first realm, marriage constitutes a key event of the second. Because this separation carries greater relevance for my argumentation, I provide a detailed account of the implication for both realms of experience in the subsequent part.

Historically, modernity in India is linked to three key episodes: the British colonial rule from the mid 18th century until 1947, the formation of the Indian nation state after its independence and the economic liberalization in the early 1990s. Each epoch has been academically analyzed in its own right.

Based on the principles of the Pax Britannica, the designation for the politics of the British Empire, the colonialists introduced an external system that set up a distinction between a modern sphere and local structures. By the establishment of a foreign administration and educational institutions of science, art and law, they consolidated a state-wide scheme next to configurations of Indian caste society: the idea of humanitarianism found dissemination through schools, welfare institutions and hospitals and the new legal system independent of local hierarchies and gender relations promoted an equal society (Berger & Heidemann 2013: 2ff.).

British influence and its interaction or resistance in Indian society drew particular attention among Indian scholars[3] who worked on issues of social change and modernity. The sociologist M.N. Srinivas (1966) defined the term "Westernization" as a new form of social elevation introduced into Indian society during British rule. Both the custom to eat at the table and the ritual significance of purifying cow dung serve as typical examples of a change in attitudes toward "look[ing] at more from the point of view of whether [a certain practice] promotes health and efficiency and less from whether it is traditionally permitted or prohibited" (1966: 56). Importantly, the author differentiates this term from 'modernization', which refers to urbanization, literacy, access to media, economic and political participation (ibid: 53). Moreover, he juxtaposes Westernization with "Sanskritization", a term used to describe a particular form of upward mobility within Indian caste hierarchy. Precisely, this form of social change points to "the process by which a "low" Hindu caste, or tribe or other group, changes its customs, ritual, ideology and way of life in the direction of a high, and frequently, "twice-born" caste" (ibid: 6). These emulations of higher caste practices consist for instance in adopting food habits, kinship roles, political action or dressing styles. Sanskritization constitutes a positional change of the actors, which remains within the hierarchical caste order. Such mobility is not to be confused with a structural change, as the actors do not aim to change the system of inequality itself.

The independence in 1947 again promoted the establishment of a set of modern values alongside the founding of an Indian nation state under Prime Minister Jawaharlal Nehru. In the Constitution of the 1950s, his Congress party pursued ideals such as socialism and secularism in order to preserve communal peace and uplift disadvantaged castes for the purpose of promoting democracy, equality and liberty. The proclamation of those values throughout the entire country suggests an Indian "oneness" (Heidemann 2013: 2) and a contrast to the former Indian civilization, which, following Gucharan Das, appears as a "virtually static society of the previous thousand years" (2000: 333).

---

3 The anthropological discipline has approached Indian modernization within two traditions: firstly, the Anthropology of India that has been defined by Heidemann as "the national discourse on Indian society and culture" and secondly, the Indian Anthropology constituting "the academic practice of anthropologists working in Indian research institutions and universities" (Heidemann 2013: 9).

Indian anthropology focused on the implementation of integration strategies through five year plans[4] (Oberdiek 1991), including the consequences of the governmental reservation politics (P.G.R. Mathur 1994). Adoption and creative utilization of state schemes, motivated by Western democratic ideals, advanced to the most popular subjects within that discipline. A prominent focus in relevant ethnographic studies lies in the peculiarity of Indians to address and encompass external influences, a phenomenon which Oberdiek designates as "inclusivism" (1991: 25). Precisely, the term refers to the ability of incorporating foreign elements and products in such a manner that it corresponds to the principles of the indigenous culture. As an example, the author mentions the digital watch: in India, its primary use lies not in considering the time but in exhibiting it as a status symbol. Further tendencies, discussed in the context of modernization, are idiosyncratic combinations, for example the entanglement of Western technology and rationality together with spirituality and wisdom. According to Das (2000: 342), this combination constitutes the "perfect modernity". Other phenomena, referring to the period of state formation, have been analyzed under the expression "enculturation", which describes the process of learning one's own culture. Some examples include the reinterpretation of Hinduism, "revitalization" to oppose and criticize European influences (Srinivas 1966: 75ff., Jeffery 2005: 22ff.) and "communalism", the organized union of localized communities (Randeria 1996; P. Jeffery 2005: 38).

While throughout the abovementioned periods 'modernity' was largely defined by Europe, industrialization, nation state, social democracy, national bureaucracy and the beginnings of a mainstream society, contemporary studies focus on the interplay between the "local" and the "global" (Assayag & Fuller, 2005: 1), in other words "national sites" and "transnational cultural processes" (Breckenridge 1996: 4). The central historical impetus for this research interest has been attributed to the liberalization in 1991, followed by far-reaching transformations in Indian society due to the opening of the national economy to the world market (Varma 1999). One of the principal problems contemporary anthropology faces when examining the effects of globalization is the terminological definition of 'locality'. Respecting cultural diversification through migration flows or the digitalization of communities, Appadurai rejects a definition in terms of a geographic site or place. Instead, he advocates for conceptualizing locality as "primarily relational and contextual rather than as scalar or spatial" (Appadurai, 2010: 178).

4 Five year plans are accessible on http://planningcommission.nic.in/plans/planrel/fiveyr/welcome.html.

The opening of the Indian economy to the world market has sparked a range of academic studies analyzing the consequences of globalization. Held et al. (1999: 2) divide the scientific community in three perspectives: "hyperglobalists", who define globalization in terms of capitalism alongside the weakening of the nation state, "sceptics" who view the whole process as an exaggerated myth since the economic integration across the world is neither exceptional nor is the significance of nation states decreasing, and finally, the "transformalists", who regard globalization as a "long-term historical process which is inscribed with contradictions and which is significantly shaped by conjunctural factors" (ibid: 7). Other studies have adopted a rather neutral focus and concentrate on the interplay between local and global levels across several research fields. They range from the shift from private relationships to those in the public sphere (Kumar 2007: 18; Appadurai & Breckenridge 1996) and the discussion of national and transnational spaces (Gupta & Sharma, 2006).[5] Henceforth, spheres of local and global are conceptualized as "mutually constituted vis-a-vis each other through social relationships and cultural patterns" (Assayag & Fuller 2005: 2).

The historical sketch has shown that the rise and influence of 'modernity' have been analyzed and evaluated in relation to a respective time period. A closer look further reveals a positive connotation toward introduced values during the colonial period and independence, based on the principles of European Enlightenment. However, social transformations that have emerged as part of economic liberalization are considered an alarming sign of Western ideological dominance. Moreover, the debate highlights a persisting opposition between two layers which correspond to the initial pair of the 'modern' and 'ritual sphere': 'British' versus 'Indian' throughout the colonial period, 'Nation state' versus 'Indian society' after independence and 'global' versus 'local' in times of economic liberalization. Those categories suggest a continuous presence of two domains which continue to comprise a rewarding field in ethnographical research. Conflicting effects shall be presented using the example of the educated Indian middle class, which finds itself 'in between' those strata.

5 Current studies argue for an understanding of India's modernity as a "global experience" (Appadurai & Breckenridge 1996: 1) since "most societies today possess the means for the local production of modernity".

1.2 "In between"? Locating the educated middle class

Historical epochs not only enhanced a controversial discussion about modernity, but gave rise to diverse perspectives on the Indian middle class, defined by Patricia Uberoi as "the social stratum that is regarded as the vanguard of consumerism, innovation and modernity" (2011 b: 273). As a social base for economic growth and democratic stability, this section of the population contributed to the articulation of a modern Indian nation (Jodhka & Prakash 2011: 45, 59). Thus, the colonial period incited a range of Indian academics attached to British administration to adopt propagated European values of secularism and equality. A second section of the middle class emerged within the public service of a post-colonial Indian government. During the first two decades after independence, its bureaucratic system produced a cluster of functionaries whose power stemmed from the autonomy of a self-regulating public sector. Finally, the liberalization in the early 1990s enhanced new forms of lifestyle for an aspiring middle class. The increasing influence of a large-scale market poses new challenges to the Indian population since it introduces new, globalized standards that transcend principles formulated at the state level. Excessive demands and status symbols caused new forms of social inequality and damaged the image of the Indian middle class, bringing it into disrepute more so than was the case of permanent employees or higher professionals during colonial and post-colonial periods (Jodhka & Prakash, 2011: 49).

Until the mid-21st century, South Asian middle classes have been comparatively neglected among Indian and Western scholars alike, whose interests centered on caste inequalities, tribal culture and folklore in line with the research tradition of an 'Indian Anthropology'. An emerging focus on the effects of and practices associated with modernization processes in India, however, has brought the subject group of the middle class back to the fore of attention. One statement by Dickey might explain this new orientation: "class is one of the most salient idioms of identity in contemporary India, especially in urban areas, and wealth and education provide two of the most direct means to social and political power" (2010: 194). Class identification seems crucial for gaining status in Indian society, where a secure income, assets, educational background and lifestyle are becoming more decisive resources than indications of caste. In recent decades therefore, the Indian middle class is examined in relation to consumption patterns and social changes induced by a market-oriented and capitalist economy (Brosius 2010; Varma 1999).

Unlike case studies of customs and practices within an ethnic group, the assessment of middle class phenomena has become a far more complex endeavor due to the impracticality of defining a bounded social category – a difficulty which evoked a range of classifications according to income, profession or consumption. [6] Leela Fernandes and Patrick Heller propose one such classification and distinguish between three social categories: (1) an upper middle class, advanced through highly qualified credentials like senior professionals and higher bureaucrats; (2) a middle class, which constitutes the petit bourgeoisie including merchants, rich farmers, small business owners and; (3) an aspiring middle class with a considerable educational background but low economic capital, a section of the middle class which continues to occupy positions at the bottom layer of bureaucratic hierarchies (Fernandes & Heller: 2006).

Emphasizing socio-cultural inequalities, the authors point to a second analytical problem, namely the diverse backgrounds within the middle class, the internal subsections of which diverge in caste, religion, gender and origin. In fact, caste background complicates the categorization of an Indian middle class. Jodhka and Prakash (2011: 53f.) indicate that a wide range of professional sectors remain dominated by a caste-related and religious identity. Dickey (2012: 569) highlights the way caste groups and associations become a supportive source in professional and financial fields. Moreover, belonging to a caste proves to be a decisive determinant for consuming strategies of middle class members who invest their acquired goods in accordance to their community background.

A third difficulty consists in the multiple and divergent views on class belonging, which the actors themselves express. It is therefore important to consider indigenous criteria of class characteristics and attached desires, interests and concerns. Dickey, who has focused on "self-ascription" using the example of the middle class in Madurai, finds that "few, if any, objective features of income, occupation, education, consumer goods, housing, or leisure practices [...] can be used to define the middle class in Madurai" (ibid: 561f.), an observation which led her to conclude that "this 'middle class' is even more heterogeneous than the Indian 'middle class' that others have described as fragmented and divided" (ibid). Moreover, the middle class continuously becomes redefined and needs to be affirmed by distinctive codes, assuming that perceived boundaries in the Madurai population "are neither arbitrary nor highly elastic" (ibid: 575). Beyond relatively evident factors such as salary, assets or profession, the author identifies several indicators that constitute class consciousness in Madurai,

6 For an elaborated overview see C.J. Fuller and Haripriya Narasimhan (2007: 122).

including education, work skills, sophistication, modern sensibility and social connections (2010: 198).

Dickey's focus turns away from former understandings of 'class' as a category or empirical condition towards a research field which Mark Liechty designates as a "cultural project" (2003: 20). This term stands for an analytical scope that circumvents the complex and heterogeneous facets of conceptualizing the middle class as a social stratum. Liechty distinguishes two different ways of approaching the term 'class'. The first one assumes class as factual, in his words "a taken for granted, natural, universal category or concept that speaks for itself" (ibid: 8). Here, the middle class represents a feature of an economic and productive process. A second attempt conceptualizes this social category in an *empirical* manner, notably by grasping its application and behavior in everyday life. Instead of determining a class by properties or power, the author explores how "economic dominance is always culturally mediated in patterns of socialization, lifestyles and discourses of honor and prestige" (ibid: 14). Citing the example of practices attached to the contemporary urban middle class lifestyle in Nepal, he defines class consumption not in terms of possession, but rather of being and belonging (ibid: 10). This approach has shaped most current ethnographies on South Asian middle classes. One related study in India has been carried out by Christiane Brosius, who observed the "cultural sphere" of the middle class in urban spaces, religious-leisure sites, as well as the wedding and beauty industry. This multi-sited fieldwork illustrates how consumption patterns and mobility, which certainly do not take place in a social vacuum, are always connected to forms and values, defined by a "cultural reinterpretation of respectability" (Brosius 2010: 20). The cultural sphere of the urban middle class is marked by a distinct aspiration toward a performative prestige accumulation. Her argument draws on the theory of Arjun Appadurai (2004), who regards the "capacity to aspire" as a competence which is reserved for a particular class. She points out that status manifestation takes place in the form of conspicuous consumption, distinct lifestyle and new pretensions, notably by "culturedness, taste and adequate strategy of display" (2010: 20). In Tamil Nadu, insights into the realm of experience of high-profile sections of the population are provided by Christopher John Fuller and Haripriya Narasimhan (2007). Their ethnography among professional employees in the information technology (IT) sector illustrates that mechanisms of distinction function alongside their particular job conditions, characterized by "staff work in modern, open-plan offices and team members, [involving] interactions between young men and women" (ibid: 126).

The distinctive lifestyle and attitude of the Indian middle class has caused severe concerns and negatively afflicted stereotypes in public discourse and academic accounts alike. Alarming consequences have been highlighted by Pavan Varma (1999), who perceives an increasing "social insensitiveness", particularly among the new-rich middle class members. This formulation points to a remarkable indifference vis-a-vis the poorer groups in the population. Such ignorance emerged as a result of unrestrained consumption caused by market liberalization, an external economic system which dismissed established ideals of modesty (ibid: 170ff.). Throughout all parts of India, the skeptic view of middle class members is directed toward an alleged disregard for conventions based on caste, kinship and gender relations or local hierarchies and forms of respect. IT employees face similar stereotypes in the abovementioned study of Fuller and Narasimhan (2007), considered to be "overpaid, greedy, materialistic and obsessed by dreams of migrating to the West" (ibid: 133). Moreover, their survey participants considered them "overworked, which drives some of them into depression or even suicide, although many of them allegedly lead wild lives in bars at night and have lots of illicit affairs as well" (ibid). Exploring local attitudes toward consumerism in Baroda, van Wessel (2004) reveals how middle class members are associated with a wasteful attitude and a hard-edged orientation towards material desires. From the perspective of her survey participants, such characteristics serve as a root cause for their "moral depravation" and a "loss of humaneness" as well as their disregard for local customs involving a lack of family intimacy, solicitude and loyalty (ibid: 103).

Qualitative approaches have made attempts to deconstruct such undifferentiated images. Ethnographies on self-definitions have shown that the reality proves more complex, as middle class members do not build their identity primarily upon a consumption-oriented lifestyle and they may even distance themselves from wasteful attitudes. Moreover, several in-depth studies uncovered alternative explanations about the distinctive features of 'middle classness'. Indeed, Fuller and Narasimhan (2007: 136,147) recognized that high salaries and transmigration constitute competitive elements among employees at IT companies in Chennai. Nevertheless, detailed interviews revealed that such features do not define the "primary currency" for status acquirement. Most survey participants neglected the importance of fashionable clothing and adhered to traditional dress. Furthermore, they expressed concerns about leaving the country and their anxiety that such a move would prevent them from performing their familial commitments. In Baroda, van Wessel dismisses the common notion of consumerism as a mere class dilemma forming people to "cultural dupes, hapless victims of capitalism" (2004: 111). Far from representing a conjunctive element, shared by a social section which defines itself as middle-class, consumption constitutes an unbiased tool for social mobility or, expressed in the words of the author, a "form of status that can be achieved by anyone regardless of character, and in relative anonymity" (ibid: 112). Rather than presenting a unique and uncontestedly desirable goal, consumption here is individually reflected upon according to one's particular socio-economic disposition. Related to this modest attitude, the author takes the stance that the terms "simple" or "backward" by no means contain a derogatory connotation toward low-class members. Instead, they imply a nostalgic view of an idyllic setting, characterized by close, functioning social networks (ibid: 99). Van Wessel finds that expressions like "non-modern" or "backward" appear to be qualified as "good", particularly regarding the association of new-rich people with "wasteful" practices. Correspondingly, Dickey observed that middle class members in Madurai seek their distinctive niche precisely by consuming "with moderation and deliberation" (2012: 574): Thereby, they position themselves 'in between' a pleasure-driven upper class and an economically weak section of the population that lacks any capacity to participate in consumption. Regarding such divergent perceptions, contemporary studies have stressed the pressure and uncomfortable situation for middle class members as a concomitant of their economic resources, access and ambitions. The possession of refrigerators, brand-name clothes or a car has become not only a sign of privileged status but involves requirements through demands and unspoken expectations by socio-economic peers (van Wessel 2004: 97).

Similar sentiments were also expressed during my own fieldwork when conversation partners complained about a latent compulsion to wear expensive sunglasses, to possess a new smart phone or to dine out in foreign restaurants. Vijay, a graduate at Madurai Kamaraj University who acquired a well paid position, complained about the pressure to wear a fashionable outfit, have a suitable hairstyle and socialize in specific localities: "When I do not go regularly to an expensive restaurant or drive a costly car, people will say: look, he is stingy. He finished his MBA degree, now he works in a finance consulting agency but still doesn't know where to eat properly. He is behaving *piṉtaṅkiya* (backward)". Apart from materials and physical appearance, students felt constrained to act and perform in accordance with an imagined personhood. Hence, they were expected to control emotions, speak with a soft voice and to avoid colloquial language (see chapter 4.1). Similarly, Dickey finds middle class members in Madurai subject to a strict imperative of respecting existent moral standards: "The 'middle people' however must do everything just right. They cannot drink in public, they must wear clean clothing, and they must marry within their caste, because otherwise 'everyone will talk about them'" (2012: 588).

This dichotomy between the demands of the liberalized market economy and local requirements is what Dickey subsumes in her abstract under a "precariousness and potential instability of middle-class life" (2012). The inner strife seems to affect middle class sections across South Asia, such that several ethnographic case studies reveal an alienation from an ascribed materialistic lifestyle and progressive attitude. In Tamil Nadu, Fuller and Narasimhan describe that distinct self-perception of the middle class when they conclude that "at least in their own eyes, they are not selfish materialists with a secessionist understanding of India, but modern professionals whose well-paid work in a new global industry enables them to lead better lives with their own families according to their own traditions in their own country" (2007: 148). As a response to an externally imposed lifestyle, they redefine their particular status in their own terms: in Madurai, middle class people justify their positioning in society by a "decent" demeanor (Dickey 2012: 577). From this perspective, "middle class" is not determined by extravagant affectations or a 'progressive' mindset but by principles such as "plainness, ordinariness, decency, and cleanliness-tied by nodes of order, self-presentation, and modernity" (ibid). Similar attitudes have been found in other South Asian regions. In Kathmandu, Liechty (2003) makes a parallel observation and argues that the challenge of mediating between two edges – upper and lower classes – is negotiated by a commitment to "suitability", a self imposed behavioral code. Between "too much" and "too little", they attach a "suitable" behavior and a "suitably" fashioned body for their own class. Classes below and above them are situated along a continuum from "unsuitable" and "antipatriotic" to "vulgar" and "immoral" (ibid: 73). The author positions his studied group in a new space of cultural "betweenness" of high and low, global and local, new and old, tradition and modernity (ibid: 25). Among the high economic classes in India's megacities, Brosius (2010: 19) finds that middle class members mutually expose an excessive lifestyle by rejecting ascriptions such as "pretentious", "dishonest" and "unfair" at the same time. Her respondents continuously negotiate between 'local' values on the one hand and the orientation towards a globalized India on the other. The author finds that they not only aim to join the ranks of a world class, but to stay entrenched within an Indian Nation. Thus, they find themselves amid the commitment to market-oriented development and democratic ideals, proclaiming the promise of fair participation.

Despite geographical and economic variations, the outcome of all accounts suggests a common struggle within two contrasting layers of identification. In the words of Wilson (2013: 35), "the middle classes are both culturally and socioeconomically located *in between* what they perceive to be extreme upper-

and lower-class lifestyles". This balancing act causes a permanent state of instability. Likewise, empirical data in the subsequent parts will reveal that the actors of the study, university students and graduates, find themselves entangled in two opposing systems: one which values equality, acted out within educational institutions and against a second, rigid caste, kinship and gender structure that characterizes South Tamil society.

2. Research question: Peer groups among Tamil graduate students

In this chapter, the above reflections on modernization, local values and middle class identity in India become more concrete with the example of university students and graduates in the Tamil town of Madurai. This research inquires into the significance of peer groups among young academics in relation to a hierarchically structured Indian society. In Tamil Nadu, status, caste and hierarchy have remained permanent issues of discussion in Indian ethnographic literature. Primary objects of investigation include mechanisms of maintenance, circumvention or rejection of established social configurations. Particularly in times of urbanization, governmental development plans and new possibilities of political participation, recent accounts have concentrated on the relationship between the local caste system and an increasingly paramount class society (Alex & Heidemann 2013: 263). Vis-a-vis these transformational processes, most accounts circulate around the following question: Does hierarchy remain a central value, or do we find principles of an egalitarian society?

That inquiry splits scholars into two main camps. The first group posits a deterministic hierarchical principle, building upon the approach o Louis Dumont. The French anthropologist considers the Indian caste system not only in an empirical, but ideological sense. Beyond its concrete configuration as "a successive inclusion of groups of diverse orders or levels", the Indian caste order presents a product of underlying principles, a "state of mind" (1980: 34). In his view, it reveals a pan-Indian institution, notably "a system of ideas and values, a formal, comprehensible, rational system, a system in the intellectual sense of the term" (ibid: 35). The principle of hierarchy constitutes a central value, in which status ranks are determined by their degree of purity or impurity. His classic account *Homo Hierarchicus* illuminates how this mindset is not confined to the caste system, but encompasses complete aspects of Indian society such as marriage arrangements, judiciary or food practices. The hierarchical imperative remains the central element to which all further interactions in Indian society are to be reduced (Dumont 1980). Today, its significance is evidenced, among other manifestations, by a persisting stratification of communities or status affirmation through established codes of conduct – particularly visible in asymmetrical constellations such as between elder and younger people or between men and women (Osella & Osella 1998). This approach has been frequently applied in the southern Indian and Tamil regions: assuming that caste membership affects all fields of social interactions, Washbrook, for instance, argues that even material interests are negotiated in terms of social concerns, especially caste differences, but also religious or political movements (1989: 209).

In contrast to proponents of this holistic approach, a second set of scholars insists that alternative social systems indeed exist, which remain untouched by a comprehensive hierarchical order. The Osellas described such systems as "islands of anti-hierarchy within a wider hierarchical system" (1998: 189). In his study on youngsters of the Newar caste in Nepal, Steven Parish (1993) explicitly opposes Dumont's theory; illustrating how his conversation partners discursively distance themselves from the hierarchical status ranking by critical and ironic comments, he concludes that "people might exist in hierarchical society without being homo hierarchicus" (ibid: 65). In a more generalized argument, Renato Rosaldo criticizes Dumont's rationalization of social patterns merely with rigid rules; rather he suggests thinking about common practices as spontaneous reactions. In his view, "fixed cultural expectations and social norms do not suffice as a guide to behavior" (Rosaldo 1993: 92). With this contention, he challenges the underlying assumption of classic ethnographies, namely that "social life appears to be regulated by clear-cut, uniformly shared programs for behavior" and suggests alternative models which are not integrated into a superior social structure.

Dumont's idea of Indian society as an accumulation of humans in which each member contributes to a comprehensive order (1980: 9) is further opposed by Mattison Mines, who highlights the role of individuality, which "lies at the crux of Tamil sense of self [and] plays a vital role in civic life" (1994: 2). His research on leadership patterns in Georgetown, the nucleus of Tamil Nadu's capital Chennai, reveals that public and private expressions of individuality indeed exist. Based on personal narratives, observations and anthropological interpretation, he developed a concept of a South Indian individuality, which he differentiates from its understanding in the Western sense: through public displays of behavior, individuality is defined by recognition of status, demeanor and occupation. On a private level however, it is expressed through a sense and reflection of the self. A crucial finding is the notion of an individual's responsibility for her or his own behavior within Tamil society. Based on those insights, Mines refutes the common assumption of individuality as reserved to Western societies and argues for a shift in attention toward local perceptions of personal uniqueness in the Tamil context.

Though the debate about status and anti-hierarchy dates back to more than half a century, its relevance prevails until today; recent processes like modernization, urbanization and the reservation politics of Indian government have led to a new understanding of status ranks. Especially within the urban context, traditional barriers have gradually faded; instead, established principles appear in a modified way. For instance, an emerging class consciousness has triggered new forms of distinctions, marked by economic rather than caste-based differences (Béteille 1996). Recent standards, trends and desires opened space for social constellations, which are not primarily determined by established social restrictions such as caste. Peer groups of young university students and academics present a revealing example. Their situation is characterized by remaining unmarried for a long time, an exposure to a public educational institution and common aspirations and uncertainties at the beginning of their vocational career or family planning. Due to similar challenges, the significance of networks among young people has considerably increased (Osella and Osella 1998). Such a development calls for a reexamination of whether culture-specific boundaries persist within these circles or whether they become replaced by other categories.

The following study therefore explores the ways in which the principles of Indian caste hierarchy are upheld, denied or reaffirmed by the young generation of Tamil Nadu. Formations between university and college students offer a rewarding case study because they have arisen only recently. Most low caste members among them constitute the first generation of degree holders who benefit from the national education regime (see following chapter). Characteristic for the situation of students and graduates is their exposure to two realms of experience: within the campus, they are confronted on the one hand with educational imperatives, including the value of equality and simultaneously, they face the requirements of a local caste, kin and gender order, maintained through the rules of an arranged marriage. The central question is therefore: do networks of young university graduates organize themselves in a manner independent of Indian hierarchical society or are they determined by traditional exclusive mechanisms? My inquiry contributes to the above discussion about whether all social interactions can be reduced to a hierarchical principle as a central value of Indian society or if anti-hierarchical constellations exist beyond a few exceptions and shape the interactions of contemporary Indian society.

2.1 EDUCATION, MODERNITY AND "COLLEGE CULTURE"

"Educational institutions have become vehicles through which to promote modernity, equality of opportunity and a caste-less society." These words of Patricia Jeffery (2005: 23) suggest that public education in India represents one of the primary displays of a 'modern sphere'. It aims to promote the value of equality beyond established social barriers – a contrast to a hierarchically organized Indian society, characterized by mechanisms of exclusion, traditional belief systems and a strict gender division. Schools, colleges and universities therefore created a history-charged dichotomy that corresponds to the above-mentioned divide between the modern sphere and local order. Already in the mid-19th century, South Asian students found themselves confronted with two parallel educational systems, one within and one outside the class room (Kumar 2007: 13).

As a "historical facilitator", education has been paramount in implementing "the nature of modernity in South Asia" (ibid: 20): In the pre- and early colonial period, religious foundations or caste and trader's associations still mainly ran its institutions while the curriculum was adjusted to local hierarchies based on community, religion and gender relations. During colonial times, Western discourses of foreign rulers shaped the educational sphere. British established schools, colleges and universities grew at the beginning of the 20th century, rising from 186 in 1911 with 36,284 students up to 385 in 1939 with 144,904 students (Jodhka & Prakash 2011: 47). After independence, education constituted an essential instrument for the attainment of Nehruvian goals of state socialism, equality and secularism (Jeffery 2005: 13). More than promising employment opportunities, the primary interest in education lay in its function within the nation building process. Training centers played a major role in defining values of a modernized, independent Indian state. Introducing the English language, teaching modern values and conveying skills to children, public educational institutions appeared as part of a pan-Indian system.

In the early 1990s, liberalization of the Indian economy overtook state responsibility in the educational sector and augmented the commoditization of the educational landscape by introducing new challenges and objectives. The establishment of private institutions and programs with an international orientation not only created new inequalities within the educational system, but caused several transformations of its role and significance. Rather than participating in a pan-Indian modernization project, the mushrooming of sundry colleges offered a range of options for individual advancement, self-optimization and the realization of one's own possibilities (Jeffery 2005: 16ff.). Exploring trends and effects of privatized education, Henrike Donner highlights the increasing shift to the individual level, as it "encompasses [...] hopes for upward mobility and the desire for personal refinement" (2008: 125). Since the end of last century, the discourse on education revolves around the right choice, responsibility and commitment, a development involving considerable pressure and overextension, particularly for the middle class (ibid: 181). *Videlicet*, a defined parental duty, is to provide the right education, suitable to the personal profile of the child who embodies a "latent potentiality which must be seized" (ibid: 154). Liberalization henceforth set educational provision into a broader context, as a cornerstone of development policy with the primary aims of literacy, skills, civilization, human capital and gender equality.

Achievements of public education become evident by a range of efforts, including the construction of schools and colleges or the provision of materials for disadvantaged pupils and students (Alex 2009: 142f.). Pursuing an equalized access to education, the Indian government has implemented several schemes including the quota system in the 5-year plans.[1] For the young generation, education offers a promising platform for career opportunities including government jobs, access to the most attractive industrial sectors and to influential political positions. Thus, degree holders acquire the chance to compete on a separate level of the labor market, independent of parameters assigned by caste background or place of origin. Glossy papers such as the career journal 'Make your own destiny' (M.Y.O.D.) reflect professional aspirations and challenges of present youth in contemporary urban India. Readers not only find advice or possibilities of exchanging experiences and common challenges regarding their prospects, but also a platform for reflecting on intangibles. Under the title "Changing Tracks", the edition in December 2011, for instance, published a cover story of young professionals who left their career to pursue "personal fulfillment" (Tyagi 2011: 9ff.).

However, those success stories should not suggest that inequalities have been eradicated. Aside from the fact that a large section of the Indian population has been denied the advantage of schooling (Kumar 2007: 21), micro-level studies indicate that ongoing discrimination circumvents the envisaged equality between pupils and students throughout different educational institutions. Among primary school children in rural Tamil Nadu, Gabriele Alex described the gap between official principles propagated in class rooms or school books, and the actual everyday interaction within pupils, students and their social environment (Alex

1 At the state level, this program prescribes a proportional share in educational institutions for all registered castes and tribes (see chapter 2.3.2).

2009: 160). Furthermore, education appears as a contradictory resource that interacts with local and individual characteristics to visibly frame and affect outcomes. Graduation and further prospects partly depend on caste background and familial situation.[2] While lower castes hope for a platform for social mobility (Osella & Osella 2000), high caste members rely on education as a vehicle to obtain a good job, as the quota system increased the barrier for them to obtain positions in government (Fuller & Narasimhan 2014).

Other aspects of education and its impacts on everyday life practices have been subject to a range of research in other ethnographic contexts beyond India. The anthology *The cultural production of the educated person* (2006), edited by Bradley Levinson et al. elucidates the multifaceted significance of education in different parts of the world. The common focus of all contributions lies in a holistic concept of the educated person, perceived through the lense of each person's own culture and society. In that sense, education cannot be understood without considering the manifold and often contradicting perspectives that contribute to reshaping this term. Images, clichés and expectations attached to the idea of an educated person remain continuously challenged and contested, so that Levinson and Holland suggest that "all cultures and formations develop models of how one becomes a fully 'knowledgeable' person" (ibid: 21). Moreover, the multifaceted understanding of education and educated people requires an anthropological treatment for studying the critical implications of education as a root cause of social gaps. Unlike sociological approaches in the mid 70's that merely evaluated its outcomes, contemporary accounts regard educational institutions not as a neutral site but as a potential strengthener and reinforce of local inequalities. Aspects such as the stigma of an uneducated person featuring alienation, condemnation and refusals remained neglected for a long time, but advanced to central issues of investigation (Levinson and Holland 1996: 4, 24).

In general, the authors regard education as decisive for the social and cultural shaping of a new generation and as one of the most constitutive elements for contemporary social change (Levinson and Holland 1996: 1). In a Nepalese Hill community, Debra Skinner and Dorothy Holland, for instance, demonstrate that school texts promote ideas considered "progressive" (1996: 280) by rejecting caste and gender differences. Students composed songs for a festival about the destiny of remaining "uneducated" or the unequal access to education between boys and girls. Describing political discussions and events, the authors identify education as an instrument for political action and influence (ibid: 288). Using

2 For a detailed description on how education is implemented according to caste, see Alex (2009: 147ff.).

the discourse of equality through campus events, public discussions or songs, students express grievances in the political, social and economic system such as corruption, deprivation among the rural population or oppression by wealthy land owners. Such practices incite the authors to regard Nepalese schools as "sites for the opposition of systems of gender and caste privilege" (ibid: 290).[3]

A further relevant issue associated with exploring the consequences of education lies in its implication for the self-image of the individual and its role within the social environment. Elsewhere, Liechty argued that education and socialization in schools provide spaces in which people are encouraged to perceive themselves in terms of economic class (2003: 212). Accordingly, Levinson examines strategies of Mexican students to transform skills which they acquired in school to a vehicle for guaranteeing social recognition and protection (1996: 217). Typical examples of such tools include math competencies, which are applied to manage financial issues, or language skills for better presentation in job interviews. Together with Holland, Levinson points out how education itself produces "distinct societies" (1996: 2). Such a distinction is reflected in certain competencies, tastes, or cultural products, languages, clothing style or consumption that enables a person to obtain a higher legitimacy in society. Those resources are identified as the *cultural capital*, a term which has been introduced by Pierre Bourdieu and outlined by Jeffrey as a "range of goods, titles and forms of social behavior that provide distinction in social situations" (2010: 19).

In the Indian context, most anthropological studies on education explored its effects in relation to social mobility, political engagement and mechanisms of inclusion and exclusion. In line with the considerations outlined above, the formation of an 'educated' class has produced a sense of a distinctive identity and stereotypes that have been found in every part of India, reaching back to the colonial period. Reviewing the situation as early as in 19th century Bengal, Dipesh Chakrabarty points to a constructed division between the "educated Bengali middle class man" and the "peasant", the latter of which represents "...all the seemingly non-modern, rural, non-secular relationships and life practices" (2000: 4). Such associations have persisted until today such that Kumar (2007) perceives a continuing distinction between "the Indian intelligentsia, as lodged in South Asian metropolises, produced by colonial and national education [...] and the provincial and rural in South Asia that produces other histories and modernities to those of the colonialist and nationalist

3 In fact, the transformative character of schooling is highlighted within discourses on human development that stress its high potential in the "creation of people with a 'modern' orientation towards the world" (Jeffery 2005: 15).

intelligentsia" (ibid: 3). In contemporary North India, Jeffrey (2010) observes strategies of young male degree holders in rural Uttar Pradesh to transform their uncertain job situation into communicating and reinforcing class privileges. Most of them belong to the dominant *Jat* community who lack the means to achieve their vocational aspirations, due to a poor economic background. Beyond financial and social capital, education buttresses further privileges and related skills, including how to invest or save money or maintain useful connections for vocational success. The author finds that such competencies enhance local inequalities, since those who acquire expertise and commitments in one particular scope retain the capacity to invest their skills in other domains as well. Special contacts to the government, for instance, are attached to local values and remain reserved for those with an educated background (ibid: 19f.). In a preceding study together with Roger and Patricia Jeffery, the author accompanied young unemployed men of different social communities in rural northern India on the search for career, respect and "cultural distinction" (Jeffrey et al. 2005: 1, 2008). The research team finds that investment strategies are related to social background, such as caste or religion: while young Jats engage in prestigious agricultural work, *Dalit* members take up political duties and those with a poor economic background lack the resources to build their identity through the alternative path of education. Muslims, in contrast, reinforce their masculinity by recourse to their original activity as artisans and by promoting the significance of handicrafts. Other unintended impacts and trends become apparent through a revitalization of localized structures, customs and belief systems as well as a strengthening of caste and regional identities (Jeffery 2005: 23). Those insights into multiple impacts of education reject the idea that it produces a category of a consistent globally-orientated middle class.

In Tamil Nadu, ethnographies have shown that educational institutions provide pupils and students with a distinctive identity of "progressiveness, modernity and economic success" (Alex 2009: 162). Already in primary schools in rural Tanjavur region, Alex observed that school children contradict the rules of the local caste order by intimate gestures, such as exchanging blouses or food. The classroom, "a model for modern society", unites children from different social backgrounds and transfers principles, symbols and values of a progressive Indian nation (ibid: 134). Thus, the first page of school books proclaims equality and condemns untouchability as a "crime" and a "sin" which "should not be an issue articulated in school" (ibid: 159). Similar tendencies have been found in the Madurai region: Yasumasa Sekine explores the changing status of those low caste members who acquired education. He argues that a degree exceeds economic privileges and establishes its own hierarchy (Sekine 2002: 222ff.).

This phenomenon becomes visible in schools and colleges through new forms of discrimination, not in terms of caste, but against those who lack the opportunity of acculturation (ibid: 232).

The above chapter emphasized the importance of acknowledging the gap between formulated goals, everyday realities and cultural reinterpretations of the educational sphere in India and elsewhere. In the words of Patricia Jeffery (2005: 25), we should not underestimate "different voices, numerous interest groups and a cacophony of opinions about educational priorities and what education should aim to achieve and how". With regard to the various and often unintended consequences of higher education, I examine how the multi-faceted construction of the educated person finds itself continuously reformulated vis-a-vis existing hierarchies in South Tamil Nadu. Such an examination focuses on the question: what is understood as 'being educated' in a particular society and which processes participate in constructing the notion of an 'educated person'? The contrasting social experiences of young graduate students within academic, domestic and ritual contexts compose a rewarding field for understanding the contact zones between local boundaries and the 'modern' sphere, exemplified through the value of equality. The chapter further explains why higher education and new professional prospects do not necessarily cause a social transformation.

The campus of Madurai Kamaraj University presents the point of departure for my research. The state institution constitutes a setting for social constellations and interactions, disconnected from local caste barriers. Consequently, student life forms a basis for friendships between young people of different castes and places of origin. Maintenance, behavioral patterns and limits among those constellations is what the Osellas captured with the expression "college culture" (1998: 191). A range of scholars have assessed this phenomenon and examined its further implications beyond the campus context. With reference to the abovementioned academic discussion which frames my research project, the central focus lies in investigating whether such egalitarian constellations compose a part of or a counter model to the South Tamil status ranks.

Drawing on the hierarchical imperative formulated by Louis Dumont (1980), respective studies have conceptualized the divide between the educational sphere and local structures in line with an encompassing principle. The Osellas (1998, 2000: 228ff.) argue, that local caste segregations ultimately determine peer groups of young students, which, on the surface, appear to be organized by an egalitarian structure. Examining how young men in rural Kerala subvert ritual ranks in everyday life, the authors suggest that on the surface, relationships between youngsters seem to be based on equality, pleasure and freedom from any social restrictions. Their disregard for hierarchy as well as 'private' property or accumulation, however, is recognized as a sign of not having reached full maturity, including respect for social status, as required among adults. Such relations therefore remain bounded to a particular context and do not affect the wider social organization in India. Thus, the authors (2000: 230f.) recount the awkward sequence that they witnessed between two friends in their home village, one belonging to the high caste *Nayar* and one to *Izhava*. By joint consumption, road trips and regular exchanges of gifts, they overtly neglected caste restrictions. One day, the Nayar ran out of gasoline near the house of his friend. The Izhava proposed for him to take gasoline from the motor scooter of his older brother by siphoning it off through a tube. A salient turning point of their relation occurred when he offered his high caste friend to rinse his mouth with lemon water inside of his house to get rid of the petrol taste. The Nayar, though, refused to enter his home and even hesitated to take the tumbler of lime water which his low caste friend offered him afterwards. The situation ended with the uncomfortable departure of the Nayar; it became apparent for both – as well as for the authors – that their long-term friendship is restricted by caste differences at least within the domestic context.

In his study at the campus of Madras University, Martyn Rogers (2008) goes even a step further: analyzing the social dynamics of young peer groups of scheduled caste (SC) students, he points out that a caste-specific hierarchy prevails not only *within*, but also *between* different college groups. One consequence is the exclusion of low caste students, particularly visible in the separation of leisure activities. While the SC groups primarily gathered on beaches and watched Tamil action movies, higher caste students spent their free time inside shopping malls, coffee shops and multiplex cinema where they watched foreign blockbusters (ibid: 82).

In sum, those approaches highlight the persisting principle of hierarchy among friendships between peers of pupils, students and graduates, although they are created within a non-ritual context. This continuing entanglement of caste-based characteristics supports the argument that such egalitarian constellations are not opposed to but included within a comprehensive hierarchical order. Following that view, an egalitarian structure among students constitutes a phenomenon that resists ritual ranks, but does so in a temporary and locally limited sense. Despite undermining existing hierarchies, members of egalitarian constellations remain aware of their restrictions. Hence, campus relations represent a temporary outbreak in line with a contesting college culture that external structures eventually overcome. Ultimately, spheres of the home and family remain uncontested and the prevalence of a hierarchical principle unchallenged. I close the discussion with the words of Osella and Osella (1998) who, rather than a parental compulsion, assume a 'self-adjusting' process when finally

"in the interests of familial and personal reputation and social mobility, the 'normal' rules of hierarchy common in mainstream society are reasserted: family above person, elder people above younger, but also [...] one's own community above others, and other communities above one's own, making exogamy practically unthinkable." (ibid: 201)

2.2 THE CONCEPT OF CONVIVIALITY

Asserting a prevalent hierarchical principle in Indian society, the question has been raised: through which mechanisms, practices and ideologies are egalitarian constellations maintained? In an attempt to combine the divergent accounts of status ranking and anti-hierarchy, the concept of "conviviality"[4] provides an analytical framework for examining egalitarian forms of interaction within Indian society. That recent approach has been primarily elaborated on by Christian Strümpell in his monography, published in 2006 under the title *Wir arbeiten zusammen, wir essen zusammen. Konvivium und soziale Peripherie in einer indischen Werkssiedlung* ("We work together, we eat together. Conviviality and social periphery in an Indian company settlement"). Since his investigation follows a similar theoretical focus as the present one, this thesis will draw upon and reexamine his insights throughout the following pages.

Essentially, Strümpell pursues the question of whether industrialization leads to the creation of a uniform social structure, a discussion which diverges in two directions. The first direction is related to the Manchester School, which postulates the urban sphere as a consistent realm in the sense that urbanization follows one prescribed trajectory and city spaces can be subsumed under one umbrella across the world. This conceptualization, defined as the "universalistic approach", assumes a separated coexistence of two different entities: the urban and the village sphere, which remain juxtaposed as two exclusive compartments (Strümpell 2006: 16f.).

4 This term is not to be confused with the mainstream meaning in English corresponding to sociability. Throughout this thesis, I employ conviviality as a translation from the German term "Konvivialität" which corresponds to the Latin term (Konvivium).

In the Indian context, Strümpell rejects the idea that urban patterns of interaction compose a coherent sociological phenomenon. Opposed to the concept of the universalistic approach, Strümpell adheres to the "cultural-specific" view that conceives of the urban sphere as part of a particular culture. Adherents to that approach suggest that in each culture respective ideas of values exist, which constitute a unique mentality and rationalize the behavior of the group member. Recalling the pure-impure divide as a fundamental value of Indian society, Strümpell regards this dichotomy as continuous in urban, rural and village spaces alike. Social patterns in contemporary urban India therefore can be classified according to the same value system since they are determined by a hierarchical principle that encompasses the entire Indian society (ibid).

His research took place among male migrant workers in a public-sector power plant in Chatamput, South Orissa, a locality which he designates as a "modern compartment" (ibid: 33). This term represents institutions, settings or activities where modern values prevail and consequently enable social configurations opposed to the ritual structure of Indian caste society. Typical examples are associations, urban neighborhoods, schools, colleges, unions but also activities like farewell parties and excursions among colleagues (ibid: 75 ff). Moreover, such patterns are cultivated on the occasion of joint celebrations, for example the completion of a degree or contract as well as feasts where ritual status differences remain irrelevant.

For the most part, migrant workers comprise young bachelors from different castes, backgrounds and origins. Since they are acquainted as colleagues, their relationships are determined by business structures within the factory while caste segregations cannot be upheld. During his 17 months of fieldwork, the author observed how a specific egalitarian social relation is practiced among his study participants. Taking part in everyday interactions, he discovered anti-hierarchical patterns that found their expression in commensality, conflicts carried out on a level playing field, common joking, a mutually respectful address and physical contact. For the author, such constellations nevertheless do not oppose the Indian hierarchical society, but occur within it, in the form of "convivial" equality (ibid: 74) – a *temporary* constellation which is acted out within social, geographic and time-bounded preconditions and most importantly requires a secluded sphere. Typical domains are modern compartments but also remote areas or activities which exceed the ritual everyday life in India, for example trips, sports events or rallies. Such realms stand in contrast to the domestic sphere of villages and private homes, which are determined by an encompassing hierarchical order. Neglecting ritual activities, "convives" (ibid: 77) – those actors who engage in a convivial relationship – share common private or professional interests that constitute a distinct basis for their interaction. Typically for students, academic interests, anxieties concerning vocational perspectives, romantic feelings or the common excitement of visiting bars and clubs intensify such a contact. In the case of professional workers, in contrast, the common ground poses a higher (political) aim to improve working conditions.

In a second step, Strümpell inquires into the way in which those relationships are maintained outside the scenery of the industrial terrain. In the first instance, workers negated the significance of caste restrictions and adhered to acquired egalitarian forms of interaction. This attitude proved relevant particularly for bachelors in the initial stages of their employment. So far, it can be concluded that anti-hierarchical configurations remain tolerated as long as they are attached to a modern compartment and take place within a distinctive professional sphere that represents the transition to a new time and space. In that stage, convives did not pose a danger to the ritual order.

However, the author encounters limits of conviviality, precisely marked by the entry into a realm determined by the ritual context. Life-cycle events, the formation of families or the relocation of the workers' wives and children to the settlement serve as typical breaks in the practices of conviviality. Strümpell's observations suggest that within that ritual sphere, anti-hierarchical patterns suddenly become perceived as polluting behaviors (ibid: 218). As soon as convives reunited with their families, they started to pay attention with whom they ate and usually did not invite their colleagues to ritual ceremonies. Before returning to their home or place of origin, the men took baths – a purifying act usually executed after contaminating events, such as death ceremonies (ibid: 259). When workers occasionally encountered each other during functions, they symbolically undermined the low status of their constellation by activities which are considered as impure. As an institutionalized act, convives frequent separate places for consuming alcohol, beef and cigarettes. Interestingly, though, alcohol presents a taboo in Indian society, collective drinking among men is accepted within convivial relationships. Such activities, however, never occur in the presence of women who are considered representatives of the ritual order and a barrier to convivial patterns. Correspondingly, in classical scriptures, the Indian wife is associated with the Lakshmi goddess and linked to fertility, fortune and prosperity of the family (ibid: 80).[5]

5 In the milieu of IT sector, Fuller and Narasimhan describe how young male professionals drink regularly while their women usually do not join those sessions (2007: 133). For further accounts on the position of Indian wives as a guard of morality see Susan Wadley's anthology "The Powers of Tamil Women" (1991).

In contrast to *commensality*, the horizontal relationship of members within the ritual sphere, conviviality is based on a *secular* order. Importantly, both forms of equality are classified within one system of values, categories, social patterns and ideologies. While commensality presents a constellation of the highest purity, conviviality is classified as impure and therefore accompanied by polluting activities (ibid: 74ff.). Conceptualizing commensality and conviviality within one system, the author therefore argues that conviviality is not detached but *ranked* inside the hierarchical order, so that it remains within a culture-specific Indian context. In conclusion, he finds that workers, engaging in an anti-hierarchical constellation, "do break with the rules of caste order, but not with the ideological base and concepts of Indian society" (ibid: 255).[6]

Following Strümpell, an overriding principle that the author defines as a "pan-Indian, ideologically purely intellectual system" (ibid: 24) encompasses convivial patterns. This form of anti-hierarchy contradicts the Western ideal of equality in a categorical sense. Instead of questioning the hierarchical principle, the actors are aware of the impure status of their egalitarian constellations. Adhering to the culture-specific approach, Strümpell therefore argues that cross-caste configurations as part of the industrialization process remain related to a particular culture (ibid: 22ff.). Hence, conviviality cannot be considered a 'counter model' to Indian society but rather an integral component of it.

Illustration 1: Convivial and Western equality

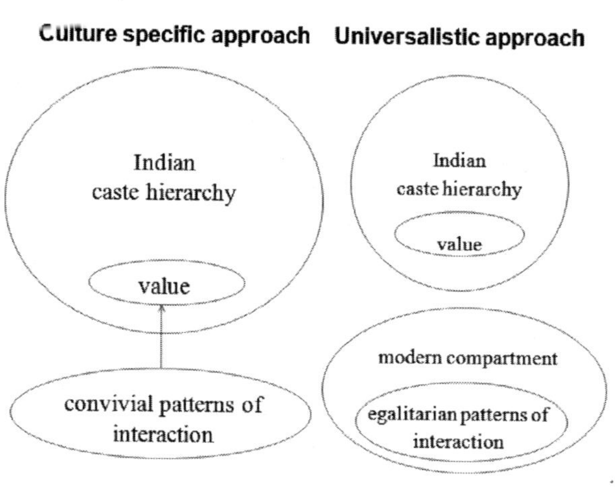

Source: Author

6 Translated from German.

The model of conviviality shall be applied and scrutinized throughout this thesis, particularly since Strümpell explicitly assumed student life as a rewarding base for acquiring convivial identity. Anti-hierarchical interactions are further enhanced by a common notion of "being educated" which establishes a separate identity irrespective of the Indian social structure (ibid: 75, 210). In fact, chapter 3 defines the university campus as a 'modern compartment' which constitutes a typical framework for relationships and practices opposing the ritual caste and gender structure. Before turning to the setting itself however, I introduce the region, scope and implementation of my research project.

2.3 REGION AND DESIGN

> Maturaiya cuttiṉa kaḻutai veḷiya pōkātu!
> "A donkey once in Madurai will never leave!"
> TAMIL SAYING

This famous proverb repeatedly cited by South Tamils suggests the outstanding flair of the city, often referred to as the "Athens of the East" (Arya et al.: 2) and the 'birthplace' of Tamil culture. With more than 1,000,000 inhabitants[7], Madurai town is the third largest city in the state of Tamil Nadu. The cooperation consists of an area of 148 square kilometers and is situated 450 km southwest of Chennai and 250 km North of Cape Comorin, the tip of Tamil Nadu. Bordering the banks of the Vaigai River, the center is surrounded by a range of small villages that have partly been incorporated into the city.

Madurai's history reaches back more than 2000 years, which highlights its great significance in South India. Ruled by diverse kingdoms, the town constituted a pivotal scene for historical milestones in Tamil Nadu's transition from centralized to decentralized feudalism. The sovereignty of the first Pandya Empire dates back to the pre-Christian era until the 6th century. By that time, the city played a prominent role in Tamil poetry and literature as it gathered many *sangams* – academies, who are said to have flourished at the beginning of that

7 At the time of my research, Madurai had a total population of 3.038.252 with 1.526.475 males and 1.511.777 females according to the official Census 2011. This reveals a sex ratio of 990 women to 1000 men. The data refer to the entire district, of which the urban population constitutes 60,78 per cent with a number of 1.846.801 and a rural population of 39,22 per cent areas which count 1.191.451 people (Directorate of Census Operations, Tamil Nadu: 2011).

century. The second Pandya kingdom in the 13th century superseded the dynasty of Chola and led until the conquest of the sultanate of Delhi ended its rule at the beginning of the 14th century. In 1372, the Hindu Vijayanagar kingdom became one of the most powerful empires in South India and defeated the Islamic rulers. Its military governors, *nayaks*, assumed power after the fall of the Vijayanagar in 1565 and contributed to the extension of its landmark, the *Meenakshi temple*. After the 16th century, Lord Nayaka established a regional dynasty, which was superseded in the 18th century by the Nawabs from Arcot after an internal conflict between Madurai and Tanjavur. In 1801, the city eventually came under British control, which constructed the industrial new town, situated in the north of the Vaigai (Bate 2009: xi ff., Fuller 2003: 152f.).

Map 1: Location of the field

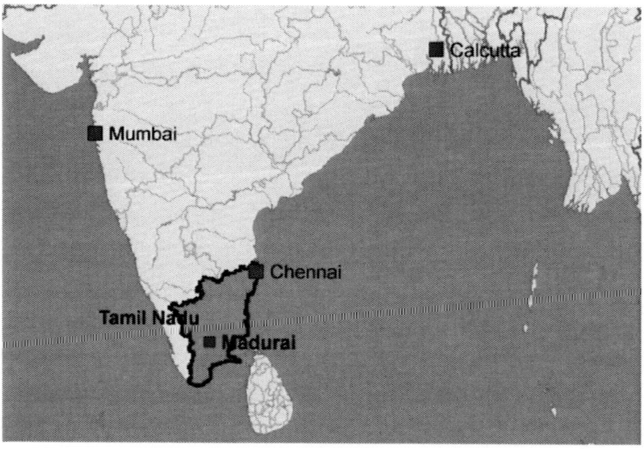

Source. stepmap.de

Today, a glance at the city map not only reveals the city's historical significance, but unfolds a salient entanglement of ancient and contemporary influences. The Vaigai river divides the city into two distinctive parts (Sekine 2002: 1ff.). Bordering the south bank, the old town is dominated by the twelve towers of the Meenakshi temple. Around the holy place, more than six hectares surround the temple's architecture. As an extension of the inner temple configurations, adjacent streets branch off in concentric circles until they reach the main roads that mark the boundaries of the historical district. With a scenery of traders, markets stalls, bullock carts and around 10 000 pilgrims every day, the heart of the city emits a pulsating vitality of busyness and religiosity. Touristic sights bear witness to the outstanding relevance of the region until today. One of the most famous testimonials of its past is the king's palace, erected by the Nayaka dynasty. Segments of this building have been preserved until today and attract visitors every evening to experience parts of the *Tale of the anklet*, animated by a vivacious 'light and sound show': The 6th century epic and key legend of the town tells about the legendary Tamil woman Kannaki who, furious about the execution of her husband Kovalan, caused the destruction of the city and its apotheosis.

While this district is associated with a religious and traditional character, the new section in the north houses many industrial institutions, including Kothandaram cotton, Fenner Belts or Madura Coats and emerging enterprises and foundations, as T.V.S. Motor company and Apollo Eye Hospital. Beyond the industrial and migrant quarters, sprawling granite hills mark the horizon. Following Bate (2009: xiii), this border bestows the city with an "embodiment of antiquity, a sacred center, and an icon of the centrality of religion in Tamil", guarded by Madurai's queen, the goddess Meenakshi.

Picture 1: Chithirai festival at Meenkashi's temple[8]

Outwardly, Madurai appears to be a counterpole to the internationally oriented state capital, Chennai. Having attracted a range of local and multinational companies in recent decades, the coastal city has become the economic and cultural center of South India and has moreover advanced to the most significant scene for the South Indian film industry. While the industrial metropolis represents progress and cosmopolitanism, Madurai upholds its reputation as the 'cultural capital' of South India – an ambivalent image which accentuates its

8 All photos in this book were taken by the author.

charm of originality but also decries the place as reactionary. The dichotomy between a 'modern', 'civic' Chennai and a 'primitive' South has been extensively addressed in celebrated blockbusters. In his article *Tamil Cinema: The cultural politics of India's other film industry,* Rajan Krishnan (2008) explores how South Tamil Nadu consistently pays for a milieu of castism and forms a contrast to Chennai, a suitable locality for a prospering "urban modern middle-upper class life" (ibid: 152). The film *Kathal* ("love") directed by Balaji Sakthivel offers a vivid example of these contradictions. The story tells about the hopeless love between Murugan, a scooter mechanic, and the rich student Aishwarya in Madurai. This infatuation reaches a dangerous level when both escape from familial constraints to Chennai to unite in marriage. However, the romance takes a turn when Aishwarya's family tracks the couple to the capital and persuades them to come back to Madurai where they bludgeon Murugan almost to death. Throughout the plot, the cinematography depicts Chennai as a modern city that enhances egalitarian social relations and transgresses barriers of social limitations while Madurai remains determined by a backward attitude and savage, 'uncivilized' characters. With regard to the audiovisual reinforcement of such stereotypes, Krishnan warns against assuming the social structure in megacities to be a normative model and argues for a "different coding of nativity and modernity" (ibid). In his article on ideological guidelines framing Madurai as a film setting, the journalist Karthikeyan (2011) expresses a similar concern. With reference to Sivaji's film *Pattikada Pattanama* ("village versus city"), released in 1972, he notices that "Madurai is always chosen as epitomic representation of *pattikadu* [villagers]. Though a pre-modern sphere, but the one which protects the glorious ancient Tamil culture, the city is shown as a space concomitant to all evils of society." Moreover, Karthikeyan notes that a range of Tamil movies deployed protagonists from the dominant *Tēvar* castes to elevate castes and caste-based characteristics which in fact evokes a distorted image of the local population.

Notwithstanding the concerns presented above, my own experiences revealed that such stereotypes of a backward, caste-oriented and reactionary South is accompanied by an invigorating aspect: videlicet endows Madurai's population with a 'genuine' Tamil identity. Far from feeling inferior or less modern, Madurai's inhabitants persistently accentuate the unique flair which characterizes their place of origin, populated by the 'pure' Tamil people – a formulation that ascribes responsibility, honesty and consciousness of tradition to its inhabitants. Well aware of the historical and religious significance, citizens of Madurai welcome visitors with the promising and confident sentence: "If you did not see Madurai you do not know anything about South India".

2.3.1 Earlier accounts in Madurai

Academically, Madurai has attracted a wide range of scholars to work on representative social configurations in Tamil Nadu. Several studies have enriched the ethnographic debate on caste, kinship, political movements or gender relations throughout the last century. Dumont's pioneering study on the dominant *Piramalai kaḷḷar,* first published in 1957 under the title *A South Indian Subcaste: Social Organization and Religion of the Pramalai Kallar,* provides a fundamental collection of data on information pertaining to different life aspects of this community and continues to inspire the work of anthropologists even today. Yasumasa Sekine, for instance, rejects Dumont's concept of a rigid and discriminatory caste system by disconnecting 'impurity' from 'pollution'. In *Anthropology of untouchability: 'impurity' and 'pollution' in a South Indian society*, published in 2002, he indicates that *Harijans*, former untouchables, continuously strive towards an improvement of their living situation. Analyzing rituals, daily routines and hierarchies based on caste and further configurations within an adjacent village of Madurai, he identifies polluted phenomena not necessarily as "objects of repression and rejection" (2002: xxi). Instead, the author argues that the marginal nature of pollution enhances space for creativity "where it is possible to radically change one's own sense of order through encounters with others" (ibid).

As a hot spot for party activism, Madurai further provided a rewarding setting for politically oriented studies. Exploring the strategies of the *Dalit Panther Iyakkam* (DPI), also known as the *Liberation Panthers* and the most powerful union of Scheduled Castes in Madurai, Hugo Gorringe (2005) analyzes the correlation between democracy and social movements. Based on a long-term cooperation with leaders and members of the party, he finds that DPI-supporters do not necessarily negate democratic principles. His monograph *Untouchable citizens: Dalit movements and democratization in Tamil Nadu* suggests that Dalit associations take place within established structures of the political landscape in Tamil Nadu. Political strategies had been also explored by Bernard Bate (2002), who approached the field from an ethno-linguistic perspective. In *Tamil Oratory and the Dravidian Aesthetics,* he unmasks the speech-making of Tamil politicians who started using ancient and literary expressions during the second half of the last century. Interpreting political events in Madurai and Chennai, he demonstrates how the deployment of the highly elaborated scriptural centamiḻ serves as an integrative part of today's Tamil political landscape and democracy.

With its numerous holy sites including temples, shrines and caves, myths and spiritual centers, Madurai and its surroundings have been subject to a range of influential studies on religious issues. Particularly the Meenakshi temple constitutes a popular setting for substantial ethnographies. Most noteworthy are Christopher Fuller's long-term observations on the disadvantaged position of temple priests. In his latest monography The renewal of the priesthood: modernity and traditionalism in a South Indian temple, a sequel to earlier publications, the author notes an improvement in their deprived situation. Revisiting the temple, Fuller (2003) analyses essential conditions for their regaining of authority. Beyond the ritual context, he considers the economic potential of priests, the domestic situation and the role of the state. His study detects that their recently acquired fortunes derive from a peculiar entanglement of traditionalism on the one hand and an orientation toward modernist values on the other hand (ibid: 152ff.).

Reputed as a traditional stronghold for Tamil folklore, visual culture and a popular residence for artists and actors, Madurai constitutes the principal setting for Susan Seizers dissertation Stigmas of the Tamil stage: an ethnography of special drama artists in South India. The purpose of her study is to explain the skeptical view that Tamil society expresses toward actors in special drama for their participation in a form of art they consider neglectful of Tamil culture and social norms. Taking a feminist perspective, she finds that the disavowal particularly affects female actresses since their behavior on stage contradicts the upheld ideal of the virtual Tamil woman.

Despite this outstanding concentration on an established social and political landscape, Madurai has become a focal point of social transformations in the face of urbanization, migration and the increasing presence of an aspiring Tamil middle class. Working on class identities in urban South India, Sara Dickey (2012) explores formation, stigma and self-perception of Madurai's high income section of the population as well as the newly arising power relations and social hierarchies in domestic services (Dickey 2000). Finally, recent ethnographic material on today's changes of marriage practices is provided in Isabelle Clark-Decès' The right spouse: preferential marriages in Tamil Nadu (2014), a study which will be referenced throughout part III of this thesis.

The aforementioned range of sources should suffice to accentuate the multi-faceted significance of the region for studying established social configuration as well as its social, political and economic implications. With its persisting caste system, kinship order and rigid gender division, Madurai offers a rewarding analytical framework for my research purpose. Because I inquire into the formation and maintenance of egalitarian peer groups in relation to local status ranks, the regional jāṭi constellations need to be elaborated upon in detail.

2.3.2 Caste constellations in the field

> Tamilnadu is more cultural than North, we are following the traditional caste society and we are lining like one for one. In North India it is diluted.
>
> NAVANEETHAN, *KŌNĀR*, RESIDENT OF AYYAR-BUNGALOW, NEW TOWN MADURAI

The term *caste*, derived from the Portuguese word casta ("decent", "race") designates a bounded group of people within a society, defined by particular religious, economic or legal duties. In India, the caste system is grounded in Hindu thought and structured by the eternal principle of *dharma*: That concept comprises comprehensive 'order' and 'assigned' obligations. The most common expression for caste in India is the word *jāti*. It includes membership by birth, *endogamy* (marrying within one's own caste), *commensality* (eating with each other), assigned occupation and specific rituals and deities. The more than 3000 jāti in India are subsumed under the four *varna*, a category which literally means "color" (Böck & Rao 1995). Varna, as overarching categories, are ranked in a hierarchical order:

1. Brahmins (priests, experts of Holy Scriptures)
2. Kshatriya (kings, rulers, aristocrats, warriors)
3. Vaishya (merchants, traders, money lenders)
4. Shudra (agriculturalists, farmers, potters, weavers)

A fifth category below this varna complex consists of the *Harijan*, today mostly designated by the common term *Dalit*. The question of whether they belong to the caste system remains contentious and their occupations include cobbling, tanning, fishing and washing. Due to their contact with 'impure' substances, they were designated as "Untouchables" and exposed to widespread exclusion and discrimination.[9] After independence, the Indian government abolished the caste system by law in 1949. In an attempt to elevate disadvantaged groups, it listed the numerous jāti under political categories, which in Tamil Nadu consist of Forward Castes (FC), Backward Class (BC), Most Backward Class (MBC), Scheduled Castes (SC) and Scheduled Tribes (ST). Beyond a system of inequality, caste in India represents communities of solidarity, identity and

9 For a detailed account on different designations, their present situation and political organization see Martin Fuchs (1999).

security. A complete discussion of the significance of caste and the caste system in different parts of the country, however, exceeds the scope of this thesis[10], so that I limit its treatment to my research area.

In the region of Madurai, classic ethnographies about social cooperation, status differences and everyday interactions suggest a fragmented and localized caste structure (Washbrook 1989, Subramanian 1999, Palanithurai 1994). Solidarity and relationships among different groups are widely explained by endogamous marriage practices, community-specific occupations and family clan deities. Washbrook (1989: 205) regards *jāṭi* in South Tamil Nadu as small units that exert their influence within a limited local context. In his words, the inhabitants of that region "may be best described as a society of small family groups inserted into an economic context of peasant farming, artisanal production and exchange" (1989: 205). By contrast, the identification of Tamils with wider, overarching movements and networks is of only marginal significance. Following Gorringe, who provides a substantial insight into the local caste organization, social mobilization merely played a role in the course of the centralized political economy, implemented by British colonialists (2005: 90).

While members of the upper category (Brahmins) and Shudra are predominant in South Tamil Nadu, the mid-ranked castes of Kshatriya and Vaishya are fewer in number (Washbrook 2005). In the region of Madurai, the dominant *Tēvar* castes are composed of small farmers and agricultural laborers and represent the major land owning caste (Gorringe 2005: 59, Census of India 2001). With reference to their name, derived from the term "God", they are well known for an outstanding caste pride. The approximately one million members of Tēvar[11] constitute the social category of *Mukkulattōr* – a term which signifies "people of the three clans" – and are divided into the following hierarchical categories: *Maṟavar, Akamuṭaiyār* and *Piramalai kaḷḷar* (PK). The former mercenary-community Maṟavar is located at the top of the hierarchy, followed by Akamuṭaiyār, whose position as wards provided access to the inner halls of the king's palace. The third category, Piramalai kaḷḷar (PK), which served as the focus of the aforementioned study by Louis Dumont, deserves a particular description, since their jāti identity has considerably influenced the region as well as my own research.

Until the end of the 19th century, this sub-caste of the Tamil *Kaḷḷar* community controlled large tracts of lands. As local authorities, protectors and

10 For an elaborated overview see Böck and Rao (1995).

11 This is an unverified estimation based on an outdated census in the year of 1931 (Gorringe 2005:58).

watchmen, they safeguarded the wealth of local peasants, large landowners and merchants. This activity not only enabled them to levy a fee, but made them to an unpredictable challenge to other communities in the region of Madurai (Krishnan 2008: 148). The discretion of this community gradually became an administrative problem for the British rulers. In order to make them pay taxes and accept the British government, the colonialists challenged the local dominance of Piramalai kaḷḷar. Attempting to 'discipline' the community and break their power, British rulers designed a strategic rehabilitation program. Henceforth, PKs were forced to attend class regularly to enhance their education. One 63 year-old woman of this jāṭi, living on my street remembered the tales of her ancestors: "If they missed the lesson, the parents had to pay one rupee or they had to stand bowed for 24 hours." To protect the village population from arbitrary attacks, Piramalai kaḷḷar had to leave the village after finishing their duties and register themselves in an adjacent locality where they also slept. Those efforts found a great echo among the rest of the population that suffered to a large extent from their former dominance and united to a collective revolt against this community. For Krishnan (2008) this "anti-Kaḷḷar movement" caused their "anti-modern position [...] from the early days of colonial statecraft" (ibid: 148) and culminated in the declaration of the jāṭi as "criminal tribes", representing "the region of the south as unlawful" (ibid: 149). Political elevation for PKs came at the beginning of the 20th century with the formation of the "All India Forward Bloc" in 1939 of the Bengal politician Subhas Chandra Bose. The aim of the leftwing nationalist party was independence from British rule. From 1952 onwards, Pasumban Muthu Ramalinga Thevar, a political leader from the Maṟavar community near the district of Ramnad in Tamil Nadu took up the position as national deputy chairman of the party. His engagement for the Tēvar castes in South India included the abolition of their precarious situation, which equally rendered them a supportive voting bloc. When the Indian government introduced the quota system after independence, Piramalai kaḷḷar finally came under the political category of *Backward Castes*.

Referring to the significance of their caste name Kaḷḷar, which is translated as 'thief', 'stealer' or 'belier', they willingly emphasize their criminal energy until today. This attitude explains the proud statement of Gokulam, a PK student, when we crossed the prison of Madurai on the way to the university: "This jail is built only for us!" Later on, he expressed his opinion about the image of his jāṭi in society: "Normally we PKs are dominant. On the other hand, they (other castes) like to dominate us. We are trying to make ourselves soft. We want to avoid such situations ... They are scared and they maintain a distance from us." As mentioned above, a range of movies portrayed this community as a physically strong but 'pure' people. One of the most famous examples is *Thevar magan*, which underlines the power of the titular character with a large sword in his hand. This movie deals with a modern, ex-migrant Tēvar, who, confronted with local conflicts, finally becomes an activist for the education of the Kaḷḷar people. In Bharathiraja's movie on female infanticide, *Karuthamma*, PKs are compared to the bushes, dominating the landscape in the west of Madurai. Thorny on the surface, they contain a smooth and milky juice inside. That allegory indicates their genuine soft nature of their hearts. According to Krishnan however, such medial strategies underline jāṭi identity and lead to a resurgence of caste pride (2008: 151).

The region of Madurai is shaped by permanent conflicts between the Tēvar castes – especially the Piramalai kaḷḷar – and Dalit[12], today registered as Scheduled Castes (SC). Increasingly gaining economic and political power, this section of the population, transformed into an organized challenge for higher and dominant castes. Still, Tēvar occupy political, religious and administrative institutions and control the distribution of public resources and finances. In response to the protests of the Dalit, dominant communities carry out social boycotts or engage in acts of violence. Such conflicts contribute to the salient community identification in that region (Gorringe 2009). Riots annually erupt on 30th October, the birthday of Ambedkar and Muthu Ramalinga Thevar. One of the most tragic outcomes of this hostility occurred in 1997 in Melavalavu, a village approximately 20 km away from Madurai town. Murugesan, a member of the Dalit community was elected in the third voting round into the local *panchayat*. The regulation of government schemes enabled this appointment, however, the village high cast members undermined this decision by refusing to cooperate with the village head. Insisting on his position, Murugesan finally went to see the Collector in Madurai to make a complaint and demand official support. On the way back to his home, he and five of his party members were massacred by his opponents with sickles and machetes (Gorringe 2005: 346).

Dalit communities comprise around 19 percent of Tamil Nadu's population. Within this category, three predominant communities exist in the region of Madurai. The most represented within my research were members of the *Paṟaiyar,* who count 1,8 million in the state. While their original duty consisted of the musical performance during ritual activities, today they have largely profited from the quota system and exhibit the highest literacy rate among Dalit, reaching roughly 66 percent. With 2,2 million people, *Paḷḷar* are the most populous Dalit caste in Tamil Nadu. In their homeland, the foot hills of the Western Gaths, they originally worked as agriculturalists and farmers. Within

12 Self-designation of the former Untouchables.

Dalit communities, they find themselves at the top of the hierarchy and are deemed the most resolute in opposing the suppression by Tēvar communities. Representing a third category among the Scheduled Castes, the roughly 777.000 *Cakkiḷiyar* in Tamil Nadu form a cobbler community that carries out its traditional occupation of tanning until today. They occupy the lowest rank with respect to educational levels and the caste hierarchy alike (Gorringe 2005: 58; Census of India 2001). For a further differentiation within the Dalit communities, Gorringe distinguishes between city and village dwellers.[13] While members of the former category have overwhelmingly undergone higher state education and acquired at least an undergraduate degree, Dalit in the rural parts of the country remain in their traditional occupations, which makes their jāti background visible to the rest of the population. Consequently, those groups remain much more vulnerable to sanctions and discrimination by higher or more powerful castes than is the case for urban dwellers, who have the means to hide their ritual status (2005: 129).[14] Additionally, the urban infrastructure enables city dwellers to unite in networks and associations as well as to maintain links with institutions such as business centers or universities. Less exposed to caste prejudices, they aspire to mobility and prestige beyond the ritual order and are often reputed as 'uppity' by their rural counterparts (ibid: 146).

Tēvar and Dalit castes and their conflict-laden relationship shape the social configuration in Madurai to a large extent and play a central role within this paper. Above, I encountered students of trader, merchant and agriculturalist castes out of which I mention the most relevant communities within that region. Belonging to the political category of Backward Castes (BC), the *Kōṉār*, known as *Yātavar* outside of Tamil Nadu, constitute a representative community in Madurai. Originally working as shepherds and milkmen, this group owns a significant amount of land and runs a large number of tea shops in Madurai. Worshipping Lord Krishna, who is said to be born within their community, they

13 Certainly this distinction is not applicable for every caste member, as the mere environment is not decisive for lifestyle and living conditions. Nevertheless, the categorization of 'city' and 'village people' takes on the indigenous perception and presents an important indicator for a visible separation within the group.

14 Originally, Dalit had to express their inferiority to upper cast members through symbolic gestures, for example by removing their tuṇṭu, a traditional towel from their shoulder or in drinking tea from a separate cup. In modern compartments of urban and academic environments those discriminations disappeared, although daily realities reveal new mechanisms of exclusion: Low caste members therefore show their status by dimming their voice or avoiding places frequented by upper caste members (Gorringe 2005: 113 ff.).

developed a strong pride of their jāti. Equally particular about the adherence to their own jāṭi when it comes to marriage are *Nāṭār,* listed as *Other Backward Class* (OBC). Originally, a land-owning community in the South Tamil Nagercoil district, they spread as traders throughout the entire state in order to enhance their business. Their shops and stands where they sell furniture, artifacts and tools, line Madurai's roads for a great distance. *Piḷḷaimār*, a land-owning caste of elite agricultural landlords in Tamil Nadu represents a widespread section of the *Veḷḷāḷar* community in Madurai. Merchants of the *Ceṭṭiyār* Castes settled in the southern area of Meenakshi Temple, where they own the highest proportion of jeweler stores. Brahmins, at the top of the caste hierarchy, are listed as *Forward Castes* (FC). According to their own view, they feel overlooked by the schemes of the Indian government due to their high caste status. Other groups find less consideration within my study. This outline of origin, status and occupation of the most relevant communities in the region of Madurai raises no claim to completeness but rather elucidates the scope of diversification within peer groups of students and graduates.

2.3.3 Methods, access and limitations

My fieldwork[15] took place in three principal settings: the Madurai Kamaraj University (campus context), the native villages of the students and graduates (domestic context) and during life cycle-events, exemplified through marriage practices (ritual context). In a diachronic perspective, my study draws on extended case material, reflecting the situation of the actors in different life stages. Finally, I bring to bear both quantitative and qualitative research methods for the purpose of data collection.

Quantitative methods consist of standardized questionnaires, structured interviews and network analysis, following the guidelines of Judith Schlehe (2003), Martin Sökefeld (2003) and Michael Schnegg (2003). As a first step, I designed structured and half-structured questionnaires for six classes of history, sociology, political science and business administration. Though this procedure might disturb the image of an 'authentic' ethnography, it provided two key advantages. Firstly, I received a clear profile of the respondents, including their place of origin, caste background and socio-economic condition. The questionnaires also inquired into social interactions within and outside the campus as well as their expectations for conjugal life. Second, I succeeded in 'breaking the ice' and gained the trust not only of the students but also from the

15 The research was funded by the Landesgraduiertenförderung Baden-Württemberg and by the German Academic Exchange Service (DAAD).

side of their professors, who turned out to be crucial for continuing my research. Initial doubts concerning the target of my research together with a reluctance to participate in the study without approval of their academic guides hampered the students' willingness to talk openly about personal topics and delicate matters like casteism or gender conflicts. Fixed questions, accepted by the director of their institute, eased the initial research situation and raised curiosity for my project as well as a willingness to engage in further collaboration. Noting their phone numbers, students repeatedly invited me to contact them for further questions or to elaborate on the discussed themes. Out of this data set, I identified representative conversation partners and peer groups with a rather homogenous socio-economic background of the lower middle class stratum. Having established a close rapport, I continued with deeper conversations among four peer groups and carried out approximately 30 in-depth interviews. Network analysis techniques offered principal opportunities to examine friendship activities, several forms of solidarity and causes of conflict. In order to review the validity of my insights, I organized regular 'conferences' in a nearby park or in front of my house for students, graduates, myself and other interested participants.

The main part of my fieldwork relied on qualitative and non-standardized techniques, primarily informal interviews, participant observation and unplanned conversations. Such unforeseen talks occured when I met peer groups at home, on the way to their classes, during lunchtime, or on a spontaneous trip outside the campus, but also through chats via telephone or internet. After establishing a closer rapport, I regularly gathered with student groups in the campus area, joined them at tea stalls or ice-parlors and frequently took part in different leisure activities, such as trips to nearby sights, mountains and temples. To understand persistence and limitations of their peculiar egalitarian constellations, I visited students in three of their native villages and observed how they maintain friendship ties.

The second principal research field relates to peer group' behavior during life cycle events such as marriage practices. Specifically, I focus on the role of public education in influencing views and the conduct of the students and graduates under investigation. For this analysis, I included post graduates who already completed their degree at MKU but maintained friendships with their former classmates and peers. With the help of my host brother David (see below), I accompanied his peers along their challenging search for a spouse, including weeding through profiles, consulting assemblers or astrologers and participating in discussions with potential in-laws. Further, I took part in the organization and preparation of the wedding which gave me the opportunity to talk to relevant key agents including wedding hall owners, card sellers, jewellers, caterers, foto- and videographers as well as priests. In addition, I collected marriage-related media such as profiles, invitation and greeting cards, booklets and flyers.

Picture 2: Discussion conference

A supplemental source for data collection stemmed from my own living situation: I found accommodation with a host family, a 'love married' couple from the Christian Paṟaiyar community in a colony located in the new town of Madurai. Angel, a 36 year-old medical assistant lived together with her husband, a music teacher and their nine year-old daughter. Their house was located one street away from her parental house. Here, her mother and father lived together with Angel's sister Suganth, a 30 year-old PhD candidate and lecturer at an affiliated college of MKU. Due to her academic career, Suganth postponed her own marriage, which started to become a serious concern for her parents during my stay. Due to similarities in age and vocational situation, I and Suganth developed a close friendship. Together, we went to fetch water from the nearby tank, watched movies at the cinema or supported each other in academic issues. In between, the family also had two unmarried brothers: David, 34 years old, who worked as a research assistant, and supported my own fieldwork, and Sam, 31 years old, who was employed as a teacher in Ooty, Nilgiri Hills. David completed his graduation in natural science at MKU four years before the time of my fieldwork. His efforts were particularly helpful at the beginning of my research, since my basic Tamil skills imposed restrictions on elaborating profound details during extended interviews. Moreover, he not only facilitated the link with the conversation partners, but also shared his considerations and interpretations of their explanation patterns with me. Eventually, his close relationships to a variety of former classmates provided useful insights into friendship patterns after graduation. With the exception of Angel, all siblings had completed a higher degree at MKU and were pursuing an academic career.

Moreover, all of them found themselves in search of a spouse. Those circumstances gave me the chance to experience directly several facets and implications of contemporary matchmaking procedures among the educated middle class. Taking care of daily chores or jointly relaxing in the evening, I talked in great length in particular to Suganth about the situation as a spinster and preferences concerning her future husband. Additionally, I got the opportunity to listen to internal family discussions, which helped me to figure out the role of each family member in relation to matchmaking strategies. Grasping different perspectives helped me to complete my understanding of the high significance attached to marriage today. Moreover, I had the chance to take part in several negotiations and meetings, usually inaccessible to external, non-familial participants.

My Tamil knowledge – though limited at the beginning – helped me to create confident relationships and friendships. Beyond the interviews, graduate students involved me in university events, informal celebrations within the campus and external activities. Professors and lecturers at the MKU eagerly helped me progress in my project by contributing their own inputs. Some of them even provided time and space during their class for conducting interviews or group discussions and encouraged their students to participate in my fieldwork. The registrar's office also provided me with unexpected support by issuing an official certificate that facilitated unlimited access to all areas inside MKU.

Despite this successful beginning, I faced unexpected difficulties and limitations. One methodological challenge turned out to be the identification of unified peer groups in unambiguous terms. In contrast to the academic conceptualization of 'peer group', friendship circles were different, inconsistent and pervaded by conflicts and separation. Concerning the interview situation itself, I underestimated the tight time schedule of the students which naturally took priority over my research. After the initial encounters, I realized that their expressed cooperation was restricted by daily pressure and routines. Their limitation was further reinforced by internal hierarchies and commitments towards their lecturers and professors who contacted them constantly outside class. Sudden interruptions and cancellations of our interviews therefore were prevalent. The conversations with male students proved particularly problematic. Since in South Tamil Nadu, student life remains highly gendered, I had limited access to their group activities. The attitude of the conversation partners towards my research presented an unexpected and confusing experience. Their active involvement contradicted the 'a-symmetrical' relation between the anthropologist, as the inquirer, and respondents. Far removed from merely answering questions and narrating their view, research participants stroked me with doubts and openly expressed their judgments about my project. Unexpectedly, I was confronted with an "interpretative community"; a term introduced by Jeffrey (2010: 28), which points to the active participation by the respondents in a research format.

Nevertheless, those barriers offered space for further creative research methodologies. One of the most useful techniques consisted in the adoption of locally preferred communication methods, so that I conducted a range of conversations via mobile or internet platforms. While some of my participants felt uncomfortable answering questions in a formal interview situation, over the phone they were much more relaxed and felt free to speak openly. Reviewing the entire research situation, my study constituted a rewarding experience, enriching my expertise in techniques and behavior in the field. All in all, I was lucky to have gained access in such a straightforward process and to have found myself in a welcoming envoronment.

Part II: Making and maintaining friendship

"We live like a joint family!" These words of Murugesh intend to illustrate the character of friendships among peers on the MKU campus. To specify this generalized statement, the following chapter investigates the mechanisms that help establish, structure and maintain academic friendships within and beyond the educational context.

In order to identify 'university friends' as a separated focus group, chapter 3 begins with an outline of the indigenous understanding of *paṭiccavaṅka*, a term which ascribes a distinctive status within South Tamil caste society to students and degree holders. After an introduction to the campus setting, the focus shifts to the formation and activities of peer groups between students and doctoral candidates. Based on selected case examples, my data find that, far from being arbitrary constellations, those contacts are determined both by conditions on campus and the surrounding social order. For instance, there exist closer ties between classmates from the same subject or hostel residents in contrast to commuters who leave the campus after class. A detailed examination of variations, activities and restrictions within their interaction patterns indicates that peer group constellations are not only pervaded by conditions on campus, but by the social structure of Tamil society. The campus-related rankings and mechanisms of inclusion and exclusion that refer to local kinship terms make these patterns apparent. Moreover, campus-related behavior, attitudes and habits are frequently rationalized by characteristics, attributed to jāti backgrounds. Thus, my observations complicate the understanding of university friendships as a counter model to South Indian caste society, as they cannot be conceptualized independently from an indigenous stratification.

Chapter 4 concentrates on status and function of academic peers within the domestic context. At first, I exemplify differing reactions towards paṭiccavaṅka. On the one hand, they acquire a superior position through investing educational capacities into local affairs; on the other, they face problematic effects, including stereotypes, conflicts and widening gaps with respect to the 'uneducated'. Regarding their distinctive status, I point out in which way peer groups maintain, alter or adjust egalitarian friendships in contempt of familial and social constraints. Indeed, classmates become an important resource and key contacts for future vocational life beyond campus borders.[1] By means of several realms of experience, I explore how university friendships are cultivated and argue that graduate students form functional networks that supersede restrictions of ritual boundaries. Importantly, those 'secular' configurations do not counteract South Tamil caste and gender rules. Rather, they develop in conjunction with established social barriers. In support of this assertion, the last chapter of this section concentrates on the perspective of the actors. Their evaluation of university or college friends compared to 'intimate' interactions among peers in their native place reveals different experiences of friendship. All forms of social relations, however, do not remain static, but are remodeled in line with the respective social environment. Those findings challenge the common assumption that anti-hierarchical constellations are limited to modern compartments and argue that they instead dynamically project themselves into other contexts as well.

1 See also similar findings in other countries, for example Levinson (1996: 218).

3. Exposure and status on campus

> The meaning of education is that it must bring changes among people according to their wishes. This is the definition for the word education. Though education teaches me technical skills, changes have been made in my social atmosphere.
>
> GRADUATE STUDENT OF CHEMISTRY ABOUT PERCEIVED CHANGES DUE TO EDUCATION

The distinctive status of 'educated' people, *paṭiccavaṅka*, indicates more than merely a degree: rather than academic skills and knowledge, degree holders conceive of their educated status as an acquisition, an experience described by the term "exposure" (*nēroḷivāyppu*). This expression defines the attitude of students and graduates towards a system associated with comprehensive state values, a widened horizon through college culture, verbal exchanges about far reaching topics and access to a range of media. Characteristics of paṭiccavaṅka are largely associated with external differences, behavioral patterns and a 'rational' mind-set – criteria that enhance the dichotomy between "educated" and "uneducated", a difference alternatively expressed by *muṉṉēṟiya* (advanced) and *piṉtaṅkiya* (backward).

Visibly, paṭiccavaṅka distinguish themselves by upholding a particular physical appearance. Typically, an educated person wears neat and tidy clothes, well-fitting jeans and a suitable shirt. Moreover, his status requires diligent body hygiene and a smart appearance. For men, this expectation entails a standardized hairstyle and cleanly shaven face. Likewise, women should wear a tailored top or *chudidar*, a South Indian dress, well-groomed hair and subtle make up. Importantly, the style and taste presents the defining feature for an educated demeanor, rather than the quality and cost of material or cosmetics. Extravagant clothes, flashy accessories or eye-catching maquillage evokes the impression of flamboyancy which contradicts a 'decent' appearance – the self-ascribed criteria for middle-class belonging. 'Uneven hairstyle' with oily hair, shirts with 'crazy' patterns and a visible but mostly fake brand name is equated with a 'backward' attitude.[1] Changing social effects of such a particular style is illustrated by a 23 year-old MBA graduate:

> "When I was an undergraduate (UG) I used to roam with pants with 16 pockets and shirts with four pockets. So everyone was attracted to me by my clothes. But nowadays I am used to go fully formal, in full formal shoes, full formal pants. And I feel some changes. When I was in UG, the little children from school and colleges would be attracted to my appearance and come and say that the pants look so good, the T Shirt looks so good, the hairstyle looks so good ... but nowadays, when I am in full formal dress and go to college, everyone – including people over 60 and also those 16 years old come and tell me that I look so decent and they have some gratitude [respect] towards me" (Prasenna).

His achievement of advancing to a mature, authoritative and stable personage becomes apparent through the recognition of others. That particular status is visibly emphasized by a neutral style of clothing, which is associated with a 'decent' attitude and responsibility.

A second declared feature of an educated background consists of a 'controlled', 'mild-tempered' character. This particular behavior is defined by a certain 'language style' and concerns articulation and communication skills such as avoiding filthy words. 'Educated' people are expected to behave obediently and show courtesy as Geetha, a 29 year-old PhD candidate in social sciences expressed: "To aged people, we have to respect them. They also respect us. They say that we are educated." As such, being educated is not only visible by receiving but also *showing* respect. Regarding the significance of respectful behavior, *mariyātai*, and upholding one's own dignity, *mānam*, stands for a social competence and understanding of how to navigate in Indian society. Rajendran, a 21 year-old master's student, characterizes such a capacity the ability to "mov[e] around with all sorts of people".[2] The talent of maintaining contacts among different communities requires communication skills and the ability to distance oneself from prejudice. Further, an educated background is exhibited by a controlled behavior and the absence of hotheadedness and

---

1 Similar attributions have been found in other ethnographic contexts: In Latin America, Levinson (1996: 214) points out that Mexican students utilized external features like language, style, dress for categorizations such as "rurality" and "Indianess".

2 Throughout part II of this thesis, uncommented quotations are extracts from written responses.

emotional displays. Such a personage is represented by Gautham, a prototype of the educated urban middle class in M. Saravanan's film *Engeyum eppothum* ("anywhere, anytime"). Cinematically, his elaborated attitude is particularly highlighted when he travels on an overland bus from Tiruchirapalli to Chennai. During this journey, some troublesome passengers disturb him and ask him to change seats. While this scene presents the remaining bus travelers as emotional and tense, the protagonist remains unaffected by those happenings and proves his superiority by remaining calm and reacting in a composed way.

A third defining feature of paṭiccavaṅka relates to a *rational* outlook. Graduate students described this peculiarity as an "understanding of the seriousness of life", the "ability to capture the situation", and a "sense of time" by "thinking positively and logically" and "working independently". Knowledge regarding how to invest resources in an appropriate way, namely spending money and time with reference to its rational outcome instead of prioritizing superficial prestige goes hand in hand with these capabilities.[3] Geetha contrasts this talent with the behavior of 'uneducated' people who perceive the need to raise their standing by showing off their wealth through luxury goods: "Educated people will save money for a good education for their children and intellectual items. Uneducated people spend money on economic things in order to demonstrate their belonging to a higher class. So they have to buy more jewels and silk saris to attend a party." The ability to solve problems or make the right decisions from an objective point of view locates paṭiccavaṅka in a position of 'experts' as explained by Prasenna, "Educated people have to think and then do. They do not take any actions suddenly and so, others come and ask for advice and show respect."

Those designations reveal not only specific associations with more highly educated people, but also an image of their counterpart, notably 'uneducated' people. Hence, an educated person is characterized by his adherence to an external system associated with 'modernity'. The exposure to a distinct (college) culture, which transcends the ritual caste order, causes a transition from community-based attitudes towards an 'individualistic' lifestyle and the aspiration "to make history with one's own life" (Rajendran). Regarding this widened horizon, the idea of paṭiccavaṅka appears detached from local

3 Accordingly, Jeffrey (2010: 12) illustrates how degree-holders in different cultures shift their understanding of time from classifying seasons towards a Western lineal system by counting in days, weeks and months as well as life stages that are connected to specific duties. The author finds that graduates who remained unemployed after completing their degree perceived this state as 'failure' which evokes a sense of "wasting time".

particularities and oriented towards a pan-Indian level which has been designated in Chapter 2 as the 'modern sphere'.

3.1 ACCESSING MADURAI KAMARAJ UNIVERSITY

In comparison to the rest of India, the educational level in the district of Madurai proves to be fairly high: the government census of 2011 counts a number of 2,273,430 literate people, which amounts to an average rate of 83.45 percent and a rise of 77.82 percent since 2001.[4] At the time of my research, Madurai Kamaraj University offered predominantly graduate programs and the students consisted exclusively of master's or PhD students. Motivations for entering into a higher degree program differed according to a range of variables, including place of origin, caste, gender or familial and economic conditions. Certainly, principal reasons consisted of high career chances and hopes for upward mobility in financial and economic terms. Frequently, students summarized their enthusiasm for a higher degree with comments such as "best university, good reputation, better job, higher position or bigger salary". Detailed conversations, however, revealed that their primary intention is not the prospect of a lucrative career. A commonly formulated motive relates to the acquisition of *exposure*. Most of the respondents expected access to a modern domain that transcends the structure of South Tamil caste society and shapes the abovementioned demeanor of paṭiccavaṅka. Correspondingly, master's and PhD students expressed their aim to "widen their horizon", "develop and improve their lifestyle" and to get "personal satisfaction".

The choice to enter higher education is further family- or community-related. In particular, first generation students see a chance to raise the family status, as Ramesh, a 33 year-old PhD student from Paṟaiyar Community explained. "In our community, people are poor. Most of them are not able to afford college education. At the same time, they send their children to work jobs in order to help support the family. This is the state of our own community." If their parents received a higher education, students generally intend to maintain the particular status of their family. Gheeta, for instance, perceived the way in which village inhabitants address her and her family members as an "interaction

4 Gender wise, male literacy lies at 89.72 percent and female literacy at 77.16 percent. Moreover, the census reveals a divide between the urban population, where the literacy rate constitutes 89.41 percent, and rural areas, where it does not exceed 74.14 percent.

of respect". This explanation clarifies why parents found it more important to invest their fortune in the education of their children instead of spending it on material status symbols. Additionally, families make the decision for continuing education dependent on their jāṭi background. For low castes, a higher degree such as a master's serves to enable them to escape community-based disadvantages. Although he enjoyed secure employment in a butcher store, Ramesh continued his education because "education will open the chances for a better life." These views correspond to the findings of Skinner and Holland (1996: 283f.), who describe education as a tool to overcome social barriers: envisaged professions that exceed community-specific occupations (*kulatoḻil*) are assumed to enable lower castes to overcome local restrictions. Moreover, the possibility of concealing their ritual status by an altered 'educated' appearance and demeanor provides an external opportunity for them to interact and compete in their society. High-caste students, in contrast, aimed to escape their disadvantaged status within the quota system through a graduate school education.

Other motivations expressed by the students and alumni relate to the degree course and gender: while students of business administration and natural sciences selected their subject mainly because of its vocational prospects, graduate students in social sciences expressed a particular interest in the subject itself. Male students in political science stated that they envisaged learning more about Indian politics and global influences. History student Eashwaran explained his choice with the aspiration "to be a good citizen and be useful for society" while his classmate Rajesh intends to "take things from the rich and give it to the poor". Both criticized higher government officials who misuse the system. A widespread goal among women was the delivery of charitable and social services. Apart from such idealistic motives, pragmatic reasons for a degree in social sciences exist that particularly affect Scheduled Castes: the humanities are the most accessible to them within the framework of the quota system. Moreover, a degree in social sciences serves as a necessary precondition to apply for the exams in the government sector, in particular in the Indian Administrative Service (IAS), Indian Police Service (IPS) or Indian Forest Service (IFS).

A salient motivation for entering graduate school relates to marital prospects: education significantly enhances social mobility via marriage, as an academic title raises the chances for a promising match. Male students therefore intended to invest their economic resources in the selection of a spouse for their unmarried sisters. Young women expected better outcomes for their marital life because a degree not only promises them a rewarding match, but improves their negotiating position within their community – or even the possibility to escape the local community setting. Professors further inspire their students to proceed with their educational career, which presents an additional motivating factor. In Madurai, the relationship between a professor and his students is not limited to the academic field. Typically, professors assume the role of a mentor and take charge of the individual career of their protégés. Frequently, university staff members entertain a rapport beyond the educational or vocational domain and constitute an integral part of their students' family functions, including weddings or birthday parties. Individual consultation and support is especially necessary for low caste members or degree holders in the first generation who are not sufficiently informed about their career options.

Those manifold reasons for joining MKU suggest that the decision to enter graduate school exceeds the mere prospect of a degree. It promises access to an external value system, connected with a particular status that in turn is reflected and acted out at the local level.

3.2 THE CAMPUS

Named after the former Chief Minister of Tamil Nadu, Kumaraswami Kamaraj, Madurai Kamaraj University is a statutory institution, established in 1965. Today, it receives its funding from the government of Tamil Nadu and is recognized by the University Grants Commission (UGC). The entire institution counts 2,428 students across the 41 doctoral, 35 masters and 17 diploma courses. Located approximately 18 km to the west of Madurai, the campus is situated on the foothills of the Western Ghats, a mountain range that separates Tamil Nadu from its adjacent state of Kerala. University departments, institutions and attached centers cover an area of 750 acres. The interior hall of the main building contains the administrative apparatus, including offices of the chancellors, registrar and the dean. Other bodies suggest an awareness of prevalent jāti configurations in the surrounding area: as a precautionary measure to impending encroachments and discrimination, respective institutions have been installed, such as the *Scheduled Caste Office* or an *Anti ragging*[5] *committee*. This administration block is surrounded by the library and the departments. The dormitories are situated at the very right and left side of the campus area and are divided by gender, caste and subject, so that there are not only hostels for men and women, but buildings reserved for Scheduled Castes or natural science students. Opposite of the main entrance in the south, several tea stalls, a post

5 Indian expression for harassment in college or school.

office, a branch of the State Bank of India, a gym and sports fields provide the occasion for joint relaxation and diversion. At the edge of the entire complex, wide areas of grasslands and thorny bushes offer an ideal setting for unwatched activities, gatherings and discussions.

Within the rigid South Tamil caste society, the university provided a unique analytical site for studying phenomena of college culture. Regarding the high prevalence of status ranks and social restrictions in the region of Madurai, an excessive campus life has not flourished to a similar degree in comparison with college activities in an internationally oriented metropolis. Vivek, the owner of the trendsetting clothing store 'Body language' in New Town described the situation for youngsters in Madurai as such:

"Chennai and Bangalore are big cities with modern institutions and people from many places, so there are many different influences. Madurai is a smaller town but with some modern institutions. Still the people are very conservative. (…). In Madurai, they won't go out in bars. The control of parents is very strong. They will meet at common places or at a friend's house when he is alone – nowadays it is easier since most students have a bike."

In contrast to other ethnographies on campus life that suggest a cosmopolitan attitude manifested in activities such as watching foreign films or dining out in international hotels (Rogers 2008), MKU students tend to invest their know-how rather in locally relevant issues and informal events. Many of them formed political associations, published journals to counteract prevailing discrimination or engaged in the revitalization of ancient folklore. Ongoing projects have been an exhibition of *Raja Rani*, an ancient painting art by the Cakkiḷiyar caste or the performances of *tappāṭṭam*, a folk dance accompanied by percussion instruments. Other commitments concerned campus-internal grievances. During my research for instance, huge rallies and strikes against the closure of the women's hostels took place in support of disadvantaged class members. Additionally, the Vice Chancellor was absent during my stay, which restricted official university events such as festivals. The main canteen directly in the center of the campus remained closed, so that the students gathered around the buildings, on the road or in the fields. In these places, they had their home-made lunch and space for conversations and learning sessions. Due to the restricted campus life, the unofficial actions especially attracted my interest and constituted the focus of my research.

Map 2: Location of the campus

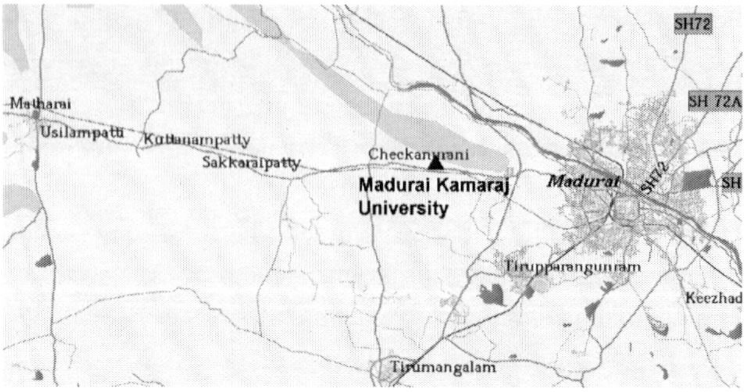

Source. stepmap.de

Map 3: Campus of Madurai Kamaraj University

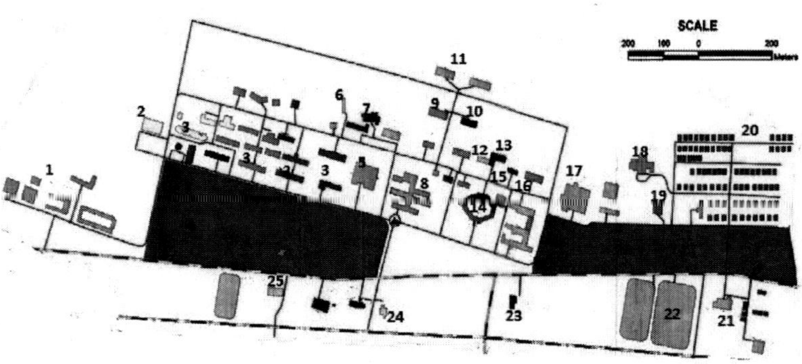

Source: www.mkuniversity.org/ (edited version)

<u>Legend</u>

1. Men's Hostel, 2. Faculty Guest House, 3. Departments of natural sciences, 4.Botanical garden, 5. Library, 6. University Public School, 7. Computer Science, 8. Administrative Block, 9. MBA, 10. Indian languages, 11. Centre for Educational Research, 12. Social Sciences, 13. Historical Sciences, 14. Complex of Tamil Studies and Economics, 15. Political Sciences, 16. School of Religion, Philosophy and Humanist Thought, 17. Women's Hostel, 18. Main Guesthouse, 19. Residence of Vice Chancellor, 20. Staff Quarters, 21. Health Centre, 22. Playground, 23. Post Office, 24. State Bank of India, 25. University Press

3.3 PEER GROUPS

The majority of the participants in my research belonged to locally resident castes. A large proportion studied as the first generation of their families to do so and came from families of farmers in the adjacent agricultural fields. Since the income of their parents revealed a similar economic background, the most significant group can be subsumed under what Jeffrey deems a "rural-urban-middle-class" (2010: 172). This group is characterized by a vivid involvement of its members in the local affairs of their immediate vicinity. Roughly half of them drove to the campus as commuters and the others resided at the hostel for a fee of 10 000 Rs for accommodation, not including additional costs for food.[6] Male and female students from six different subjects and courses comprised the interviewed peer group. Below, I list four peer groups with which I interacted continuously throughout my research. The first two groups consisted of master's students, completing their graduate education, while members of the third group pursued their PhD. I register them as mixed gendered groups, but they regularly split into pure women and male constellations to undertake related activities (see the following section). Additionally, I engaged with one network of former male MKU-graduates that already completed their degree but still remained in contact beyond their studies. Those members to which I gained access via my host brothers particularly attracted my interest, as they present a rewarding field for the purpose of studying the function of academic networks beyond campus life. Their status within the ritual context will be particularly examined in part III. Regarding the clustering of friendships and peer groups below, I am aware that such consistent categories prove artificial; unlike defined unions, assemblies or clubs, a peer group presents an empirical constellation with fluid borders, internal separations and reconfigurations. Nevertheless, with reference to their internal structure and networking, the indicated groups turned out to be exemplary for my analytical purpose.

6 The admission fees vary according to caste and subject.

Table 1: Peer groups

Name	Uma	Pogkani	Rajendran	Eashwaran	Rajesh
Caste	Paṟaiyar	Piramalai kaḷḷar	Akamuṭaiyār	Paṟaiyar	Paṟaiyar
Religion	Hindu	Hindu	Hindu	Hindu	Hindu
Age	22	23	21	24	22
Subject	MA History	MA History	MA History	MA Sociology	MA History
Origin[7]	Pallapatti	Usilampatti	Alagkanallur	Usilampatti	Vadipatti
Marital status	Unmarried	Unmarried	Unmarried	Unmarried	Unmarried

Name	Ajitha	Soundariya	Sinjuta	Suresh	Prasenna
Caste	-	PK	Akamuṭaiyār	Kōṉār	Brahmin
Religion	Muslim	Hindu	Hindu	Hindu	Hindu
Age	21	21	21	22	23
Subject	MBA	MBA	MBA	MBA	MBA
Origin	Madurai Town	Cirumalai (Dindigul)	Madurai Town	Madurai Town	Madurai Town
Marital status	marriage fixed	Unmarried	Unmarried	Unmarried	Unmarried

Name	Gheeta	Anitha	Gokulam	Murugesh	Ramesh
Caste	PK	Paṟaiyar	PK	PK	Paṟaiyar
Religion	Hindu	Christian	Hindu	Hindu	Hindu
Age	29	27	26	29	35
Subject	PhD Sociology	PhD Sociology	PhD Sociology	PhD Sociology	PhD Political science
Origin	Chellam patti	Madurai Town	Chinnavahai Kulam	Vadipatti	Nagamalai Pudukottai
Marital status	Married	Unmarried	Unmarried	Unmarried	Unmarried

7 Unless indicated otherwise, all villages are located within the district of Madurai.

Name	David	Prakash	Nataraj	Sasi
Caste	Paṟaiyar	Veḷḷāḷar	Paṟaiyar	Akamuṭaiyār
Religion	Christian	Christian	Hindu	Hindu
Age	35	38	36	38
Subject	Bsc Physics, MLM	MLM	MBA	MA Economics
Occupation	Research assistant	Marketing	Banker	Finance consultant
Origin	Madurai Town	Tirunelveli	Tirunelveli	Tattalagkottai (Ramnad)
Marital status	Unmarried	Married during my research	Married	Married during my research

Name	Kanni thevar	Mishak	Selva kumar	Charles	Morali
Religion	Hindu	Christian	Hindu	Christian	Hindu
Caste	PK	Paṟaiyar	Ceṭṭiyār	Paṟaiyar	PK
Age	35	33	34	35	29
Subject	MBA, BL (law)	Computer science	Design	Economics	MBA (not completed)
Occupation	Lawyer	Software engineer	Interior designer	Manager (NGO in Delhi)	Machine operator
Origin	Kokkulam	Madurai	Madurai	Madurai	Usilampatti
Marital status	Married	Recently married	Married	Unmarried	Love-married

3.4 (BOY)FRIEND AND (GIRL)FRIEND: GENDERED IDENTITIES ON CAMPUS

Unlike popular and academic images of unfettered gatherings within campus borders of other Indian universities (Osella & Osella 1998, Rao & Rao 1998), relations between MKU graduate students remained restricted by internal rankings, social background and gender. While prevailing hierarchies shall be highlighted in the subsequent section, I first present college-related activities and discuss the wider implications of local notions of manhood and womanhood.

Male friendships[8] present a salient feature of college culture and are strongly shaped by vocational prospects and the campus locality. Typical activities in the university context consist of discussing, jointly studying, laboratory work, consulting media or visiting browsing centers. Interestingly, conversations with academic friends are considered to be of a particular type and often portrayed as "knowledge sharing" rather than chatting. Popular topics present in these conversations include topical challenges for Indian politics, such as pollution, global warming and poverty, education, astronomy, sex, hunger or water facilities in villages. This intellectual approach to socially relevant issues consistently drifts to the articulation of extreme or radical political attitudes. A typical inclination is the glorification of one's own jāti by outlining its superiority. Above, university peers were the first and unique point of reference for career purposes: Ramesh outlined the strong support he experienced from his close friends when he applied for an external scholarship at Jawaharlal Nehru University (JNU) in Delhi:

"Two of my friends connected me to JNU. They helped me a lot. They encouraged me to face the interview. One of the guys is my friend, but also he is like my relative[9] ... Both of them gave me advice for the interview. I lost my confidence because I was not good in English, and I do not know Hindi. They encouraged me to face the interview. They energized me. Then I was ready to face the interview."

---

8 Being a female researcher, access to male groups was restricted. Certainly, as a European woman with a respective research project, I enjoyed an exceptional status. However, it is considered unsuitable to regularly cling to men, particularly because they undertake prescribed activities. Hence, for my data collection on male groups, I additionally relied on unforeseen encounters, interviews and reports by my male research assistant who occasionally joined them in my stead.

9 This expression points to a similar caste background (see follwing section).

Non-academic issues such as family or village affairs are equally discussed among college friends who are expected to offer an objective perspective and give constructive input, as Ramesh explained: "Sometimes I discuss family issues with my friends from the college. For example, if there is a fight between my parents, I will have a discussion about that problem at university and try to solve it in an amicable way; whereas in the village, my local friends would start a fight".[10]

Casual outdoor activities include hanging out, chatting or playing cricket games on the campus, a site that furthermore permits precarious activities like hunting, smoking and drinking. A secret but popular pleasure consists of standing outside the department to admire the female students or even to watch and tease lovers. Outside the campus, students regularly visit 'prestigious' bars[11] or hang around at tea shops, a meaningful activity for the articulation of masculinity. Correspondingly, political anthropologists (Bate 2009: 26, Jeffrey 2010: 99) have stressed the significance of tea stalls as a male-dominated and politically charged locality that enhances heated debates about the events of the day or ongoing grievances including dubious party politics and caste inequalities.

To a large extent, students impart strong intellectual support by practicing their English skills, motivating each other to continue education or jointly drafting applications for jobs. Moreover, they serve as a support for personal concerns, but also function as companions for campus-related leisure activities. In a sort, the contact between peer group members seems to take on an impersonal and task-oriented character. The quotation of Murugesh, a PhD student in sociology expresses the decent and unemotional attitude with which he approaches his college friends: "I talk to them nicely, and address them straight and I don' t mind sitting and discussing academic issues; I have a good relationship with them. Then, if they face some difficulties and some girls [with whom they are having romantic engagements] come and cry, then I say that I told them already and that they chose their own way" (own insertion).

I fostered a far closer rapport within female peer groups that I regularly joined in the women's hostel, in remote areas or outside the campus. Much like their male counterparts, young women undertook university related activities, such as joint readings, studying, exchanging books and collecting materials for research. While for male students, campus life commonly provides a space for 'forbidden' activities, women preferred the safe shelter of their hostel for their

10 Differing ties between 'university' and 'village' friends will be outlined in section 4.3.

11 This expression most likely refers to costly places with foreign offers. Unlike metropolises like Chennai or Bangalore, Madurai does not house official strip clubs.

leisure time or gathered in visible campus sites. For women residing in the hostel, assigned wards, who rigorously supervise the activities of their protégées and the obedience to the curfew at 7 pm, restricted their possibilities for going out.

Likewise for women, the campus offers a unique space to come together without familial or social restrictions. During the day time, female groups leave the buildings and visit shops, restaurants or tourist sites in the adjacent area. Outdoor leisure activities included trekking, excursions to historically significant places or swimming in nearby lakes. While male groups gather in front of tea shops, women find pleasure in enjoying places in town to visit restaurants, especially those serving North Indian or Western food, sweet shops, theaters, canteens and ice-cream parlors. Such a gender-specific orientation is further understood as a female affinity and provides space to escape from male gazes and approaching (Jeffrey 2010: 100).

Their common educational background not only shapes discussions about academic experience and perspectives; frequent talks concerning personal challenges like romantic encounters, family duties or a delayed arranged marriage form a central feature of their friendships. Ajitha defines the emotional support through mutually cheering each other up as the defining aspect for friendships between female students: "We share all our feelings, strengths and weaknesses." Sinjuta, for instance, who suffered a great deal from the authority of her older brother, found the most understandable listener in her university class. Distant to her hometown in a suburb of Madurai, she openly confided in her friend her anxiety about his future plans for a marriage with an unwanted groom. Such intimate circles have a high potential for common energy and strength. One incident exemplifies this joint power: Prasenna and Suresh were strolling nearby and Sinjuta loudly sent them away. While doing so, she declared that she could not talk about her concerns in the presence of male friends. Immediately, she received support from Soundariya, who strongly commanded the men to leave the site with the words: "*Pōṭa*!"- a very direct and colloquial form to send someone off that is often associated with the harsh behavior of 'village people'. Smoothly, she turned to Sinjuta and calmed her down by assuring: "They won't listen, what boys!" She then explained to me: "That's why Soundariya is needed."

Exchange of feelings not only occurs through conversations, but also through watching films, jointly listening to music, singing songs or playing games, as both friends explained, "We just hear music. We listen to songs. We just roam around ... We use every medium: TV, radio, walkman, phone. South Indian girls do not move much." While in urban metropolises like Chennai or Bangalore it is common for college students to visit clubs, bars and discotheques, the region of Madurai lacks that form of party culture. Instead, students create their own space for having fun together by playing and dancing to music. Audiovisual media therefore present a preferred form of social gathering that substitute the diversion of nightlife. Similarly, Alex (2009: 138) argues that playing and enjoying music in groups sets free common emotions and romantic feelings since Tamil film songs mainly celebrate topics of love and desire.

A comparison between male and female groups reveals a range of similarities that are framed by the college context. Topics attached to academic life, vocational perspectives and wide-ranging social concerns unite graduate students irrespective of gender. Besides, the campus disconnects students from the restrictions within Tamil society and provides an environment for certain excesses: for men particularly by conspicuous dissipation, for women by amusement and openly bringing forward feelings, anxiety and desires. At the same time, the above description reveals a gender-related separation among campus activities, a division which originates from Tamil everyday life. While men and women share a common childhood, women become attached to the domestic sphere once they reach puberty whereas young men dissociate from family constraints to compete with peers (Alex 2009: 130, Hubermann 2011: 177f.). Sinjuta rationalized this dichotomy by the fact that as they grow in age, "[they] will have certain kinds of problems and [the men] will have different expectations and chat differently than [the women]." Gender-specific premises prevail within the campus domain where hostels are strictly divided into male and female sections. This regulation limited uncontrolled amusement and the interactions between male and female students as Soundariya stated, "About 20 percent of the girls may roam alone. They won't roam freely with men on bikes. Wherever we go, we remain amongst ourselves and we join with men [in a distant place]" (own insertion).

Although Tamil gender restrictions pervade to some extent, at the same time, the academic context provides a setting to loosen established boundaries. Typically, cross-gendered groups take part in the few university-related programs, including festivals, strikes or presentations. Outside class, they undertake trips to historical sites or join for informal gatherings. A closer observation identifies those supposed classmate cliques as peculiar social constellations and unusual phenomenon in Tamil society: More than merely classmates, male and female students consider themselves as *naṇparkaḷ* (friends)[12]: To enhance and celebrate their amity, hostel residents at the

12 A variety of local expressions to designate and value friendships will be elaborated in the following section.

university cut cake on "friends day", July 30th and call or send messages with warm greetings and compliments to their absent college mates.

This interaction between genders commonly drifts into mutual teasing or even flirting. Once, Suresh explained a controversial term to me, when Soundariya interrupted him. Speaking at the same time, Suresh put her in her place by admonishing her to wait. Soundariya raised her voice even higher and strongly insisted, "You wait!" Then Suresh jokingly pointed to her and said: "See, how she is dominating – I'm asking in a polite manner but she shouts like a rowdy." The discussion ended up in mutual teasing, accompanied by soft expressions and caressing. Casual interaction does not correspond to usual gender norms in Tamil society and is strongly limited within the domestic and ritual sphere as Soundariya explained, "For example I was messaging Prasenna yesterday evening and he called back at 11 o'clock. If I am with my parents or married and someone calls at 11 o'clock, I cannot tend to the call. My family or husband would interrupt. If it is during the day time, they will give permission, but if it continues, no guy will accept."[13]

In some cases, cross-gendered relationships turn into love affairs, as in the case of Gokulam, a 26 year-old Piramalai kaḷḷar and Anitha, a 27 year-old Paṟaiyar. Having studied for several months together, the two PhD students fell in love. At the time of my fieldwork, they had been a couple for six months. Usually, they meet after class and withdraw themselves to distant areas of the campus or outside the university. At the beginning their liaison, they attracted the attention of younger students who followed them to make provocative comments. As an authoritative PhD student however, Gokulam gradually managed to compel respect for his relationship. After a few weeks, their relationship became well known to their classmates and professors. However, this constellation remains within the framework of "college culture", which would not be tolerated within familial context. Gokulam described the situation as such:

> "We both simply sit and talk... about, I don't know. She encourages me and she is my sweetheart. Here, on campus no problem. When we return (from their trips) everyone

13 The severe consequences of unsuitable contacts between male and female colleagues within the domestic context became clear to me when my host sister invited a male co-worker into her home. When her older brother and father found out that nobody else was present at that time, this incident caused an outburst of verbal abuse and a family-internal arguments that prevailed for almost three months. While initially this gesture seemed harmless to me, she not only crossed local gender barriers but damaged the reputation of her family members.

knows and they might gossip. But I don't mind. If we want to have peace, I shout at the others and send them off. But my parents will not allow me to marry Anitha. Caste and age are the problem."

Although on a global level, pre-marital affairs have been recognized as an important aspect of acquiring adulthood (Hart 2007: 352), in South India the cultivation of romantic feelings between young men and women has only recently attracted academic attention. Following related anthropological studies, such relationships proved to be temporary, limited to a certain time and space, so that they do not contest prevailing gender norms. Reiterating two anecdotes from her informants, Clark-Decès (2014) points out that indeed a notion of individual choice and romantically motivated alliances exists. Discourses circulating around extra-marital affairs, particularly cultivated in modern compartments, however, "do more to obscure than illuminate the ways in which Tamil young men love and marry" (ibid: 146). Likewise, Gabriele Alex locates romances within the public sphere, diametrically opposed to arranged marriage as part of the private sphere, which is exclusively organized and practiced among family members (2009: 137). Those findings correspond with my own insights at MKU, as exemplified by the case of Gokulam and Anitha. While on campus, their constellation is not only accepted but strongly defended, both are aware of its limits within the private context. In fact, popular sites for exchanging romantic feelings are touristic places like fords or ruins as well as public parks where young couples gather behind bushes or sitting on benches. Moreover, romantic encounters and love have been adopted by a public discourse as they are overtly performed in movies, film songs and magazines (ibid: 140).

Flirting as a foundation for romantic involvement enhanced a controversial discussion among academics. On campus, Filippo and Caroline Osella define flirting as a tool for subverting social hierarchies since young men from different castes and economic backgrounds engage in equalized constellations, marked by the common activity of teasing female students. Instead of perceiving it as sexual harassment, the authors regard this form of flirting as a special discourse, particularly enabled within the distinctive social framework of college culture. Through glances and commentaries, male and female students create "a line" (1998: 202f.) – moreover, it is the young women who determine the course of the relationship. Rather than merely considering its pressuring effects, they argue for a recognition of mutual teasing as a space for gentleness and affectionateness: "When we consider the links between harassment and flirting, aggression and love, and the difficulties in identifying the differences, these problems do not appear amenable to easy solution (ibid: 193)". In their view, flirting presents a form of "tuning", in which both men and women perform their gender-specific identity, albeit an identity created within and as part of college culture. The Osellas' argument has been strongly attacked by Kevin A. Yelvington, who opposes their view of flirting as a "prototypical 'game'" (1999: 457). Debunking such an assumption, he in turn identifies flirting as an "exercise of power" (ibid) and a performative act of harassment, aggression and apparent hostility. While those studies focused largely on a female perspective, other accounts have located the downside of amorous contacts for young men as well. In South Tamil Nadu, Clark-Decès (2014: 154) describes the tragic experience of a youngster whose loved one played with his feelings and took advantage of him to satisfy her own self-affirmation – a humiliating story which drove him into desperation, self-destruction and alcoholism. Also, Gokulam regularly suffered from the pressure and negative comments in conjunction with his liaison with Anitha: "Other students think that I am close with her because she is rich. They gossip that I am grabbing money from her and I am cheating her. Professors also warned me that I should not hang around with her. But above all, we are very good and close friends."

Thus far, I have highlighted the gender-related aspects which structure campus-internal configurations into male and female groups, cross-gendered cliques and romantic affairs. Indeed, educational background, vocational prospects and exposure to a 'modern' context produce distinct constellations, unrelated to local gender realities. The interaction includes joint excesses, chatting, flirting and engagement in sexual relationships. At the same time, I called attention to gender-specific restrictions, deriving from indigenous notions of manhood and womanhood and established marriage practices. Further impacts of South Tamil caste and kinship segregation shall be elaborated upon in the next section and challenge the idea of a 'uniform' college culture at MKU.

Picture 3: Group of masters students at 'Samy kadai'

Picture 4: Mixed gendered group at lunch on campus

Picture 5: Gatherings and cricket games around MKU

3.5 "LIKE MY RELATIVE": TIES, RANKS AND BOUNDARIES

Rather than reflecting a consistent constellation, relationships between and within college peers are classified and ranked by evaluative terms. One set of categories refers to the degree of intimacy, designated by terms as 'intimate' or 'just' friends. While inner feelings and family problems tend to be shared with 'intimate' friends, the latter category constitutes a group for entertainment and casual talks. Particularly close ties usually exist between students from a similar caste and place of origin.[14] Within this personal category, friends designate each other as *tōḻa* (male)/*tōḻi* (female), *naṇpaṉ*, or *pāvā*, a Telugu expression frequently used among former migrants from Andhra Pradesh and today the Piramalai kaḷḷar community. The terms *boss* for men and *madam* for women represent a common form of addressing rather distant college mates as 'just' friends.

Table 2: Expressions of friendship, used among peers

Term	**Application**
naṇpar/naṇpaṉ (m.) naṇ root word of nalla ("good") paṉ ("he"/ "she", "mate") naṇ+paṉ ("good mate")	General and most frequent term for "friend"
tōstu (m./f.)	Hindu word, used mainly among North Indians, today adopted in Tamil Nadu
ṭēy (m./f.)	Colloquial address, used only among male friends of equal or inferior status. Prefix, to indicate the intimacy to somebody. Example ṭēy naṇpar (intimate friend) Recently, young women adopt this term among themselves

14 A similar tendency has been observed in Mexico where 'peublitos', students from rural villages, unite to preferable cliques, which are characterized by a common background (Levinson 1996: 227).

naṭpu	This term indicates a strong and special relationship. It is frequently used to differentiate the strong bond between close companions within a group
tōḻa/tōḻā/tōḻaṉ (m.)/tōḻi (f.)	(Trustful) companion, buddy/girlfriend. Used in a political context as a frequent form of addressing among party members.
boss (m.)	Formal expression among distant fellows/ colleagues.
madam (f.)	Formal expression, used to address distant and respectable female students/colleagues.
Cross kinship terms (māmaṉ maccāṉ) (examples in table 3.5-2) māmā/māmu/māms (maternal uncle, elder cross cousin, elder sister's husband) maccāṉ/maccā (cross cousins) māpḷa/māps/māppi (orig. term māppiḷḷai = younger sister´s husband) pāvā (telugu word for cross cousins and sister's husband) adopted from Telugu community (Naidus) who invaded during 13th and 14th century. It is particularly used among Piramalai kaḷḷar in the western side of Madurai who had a close relationship with that community.	Intimate friendship among academics Used by younger to older friends. Close friendship, equal constellation. Used by older to younger friends. Applied for friends of an equal status with a Telugu speaking background. If the person is younger or older, this term is not applied in the following situations 1) at home 2) at family functions 3) when other peers of one of the friends are around. In this case, both friends refer each other by name.

nāttaṉār (sister in law) macciṉi (sister in law)	Equal constellation, mostly older to younger Equal constellation, mostly younger to older -> these terms may also point to an affair between one of them and a paṅkāḷi kin of the other
Parallel kinship terms (paṅkāḷi) (examples in table 3.5-3) aṇṇaṉ tampi akkā taṅkaicci	Used for non-ritual but, asymmetric constellations Younger to older Older to younger Younger to older Older to younger

The degree of intimacy and the indigenous understanding of friendship are shaped and articulated in terms of the Tamil caste and kinship system. Such designations among non-kin friends became popular during the last 30 to 40 years. Among the generation of the students' parents, kinship terms were exclusively used within the family and clan. In order to indicate the rank within close friendships, peers utilize parallel or cross-kin expressions.[15] For instance, an asymmetrical relationship is expressed through terms used for parallel kin *(paṅkāḷi)*.[16] In Tamil society, a paṅkāḷi constellation is characterized by a respectful attitude of younger towards older kin. They assume the function of a role model in guiding and looking after the behavior of younger kin. Through daily interactions, the younger relatives express their attention by using respectful designations or hiding disfavored activities such as smoking, drinking or teasing. This form of interaction is transferred into the public context, where the addressing of strangers defines their status and respectability. An older woman, for instance, is referred to as *ammā* (mother), a young tea stall worker as *tampi* (younger brother).

---

15 South Indians distinguish between parallel and cross-relatives, depending on gender in tracing the relationship: ancestry through same sex relatives constitutes a parallel line (paṅkāḷi), and that through brother-sister constitutes the cross line (māmaṉ maccāṉ). For further kinship implications see chapter 5 and Kapadia (1993).

16 This term stems from verb *paṅku* ("share") and refers to male siblings who share property and assets of their ancestors.

On the MKU campus, the interactions between friends who address each other in paṅkāḷi terms are characterized by a *hierarchical* or *distant* relationship. The interaction between senior and junior students presents a typical example of such an a-symmetric relationship: in Indian educational institutions, younger students consider more senior college mates role models. Prasenna, a 23 MBA student explained: "We advise our undergraduates to act in such a way so that they won't get into problems. So we are trying to bring them into a particular line, to have a good character, a good profession and we advise them so that they will get a clear idea how to do that." In turn for their consultations, more junior students are required to provide certain support, such as performing translation, running errands or providing academic assistance. Comparatively, paṅkāḷi designations are applied only occasionally since friendships are supposed to be of equal status.

Illustration 2: Examples for a-symmetrical relations

***aṇṇaṉ* (older brother)** Gokulam, senior, 26, PhD sociology ➔ Mentor, guiding thesis, counselor for academic problems	-	***tampi* (younger brother)** Eashwaran, junior, 24, MA sociology ➔ Small services, i.e. procuring books
***akkā* (older sister)** Gheeta, senior 29, PhD sociology ➔ Women's representative	-	***taṅkaicci* (younger sister)** Uma, junior, 22, MA history ➔ asks for advice in female issues, problems on campus
akkā Gheeta, 29, PhD sociology ➔ Person to be respected, gives guidance	-	**tampi** Ramesh, 22 MA history ➔ Small services, brings tea and coffee

In contrast to distant and unequal constellations, the usage of cross-kin terms (*māmaṉ maccāṉ*) suggests an intimate and symmetrical relationship. Within everyday life, the communication of kinship members from cross lines in Tamil society are characterized by a jolly and playful character; as possible marriage partners, cross cousins usually maintain a jocular relationship by continuous flirting and teasing (Alex 2009: 106ff.). The interaction between cross-members of the same sex has a relaxed and intimate character, intensified by activities like roaming around, jointly eating or sometimes drinking and smoking. Correspondently, friends who refer to each other in cross kin terms, keep an egalitarian alliance by subverting status differences. Eashwaran explained this custom as such: "Maccān, my sister's husband, and I, always have a very good relationship and we show our respect towards each other. In the same way, we call on our friends to replicate the relationship within friendship ... It shows our closeness." This intimate relationship is characterized by a common trust which is cultivated by sharing personal issues, undertaking secret activities and mutually borrowing money or other costly belongings. Recently, such constellations gained increasing attention and have been seized as topics not only in academic but popular discourses and Indian media. The soundtrack of the Tamil movie naṇpaṉ, a popular hit cited in the introduction of this thesis, uses cross-kin expressions to define the egalitarian nature of friendship circles.

Cross kin designations are common among young men and women alike. They not only reflect the harmonious nature existent within friendship circles, but also they are used for indicating cross-gender relationships in a jocularly offensive manner. Thus, the term *nāttaṉār* or *macciṉi* ("sister in law") could imply different meanings: a young woman who calls her friends in that way gives a hint that she finds her brother attractive or that she suspects her of having an affair with her own brother. Another provoking expression is *cakkaḷātti*, a designation used for women who entertain sexual contact with their own husband. Kinship terms further indicate affairs and romantic relationships. If, for example, one male friend is referred to as aṇṇaṉ, his girlfriend may be called *aṇṇi* ("older brother's wife"). Couples address the siblings of their beloved as *māpḷa,* a short form of *māppiḷḷai* ("brother in law, groom").

More than simply serving as slang among youngsters, these designations structure friendship relations and provide peers with a defined status within the group. The example of Ramesh and Rajendran who normally call each other maccāṉ illustrates the impact of using such terminology. Once, after finishing afternoon class, they took a trip into the city. Having passed the exit, they saw Vijaya, a younger fellow student, who Rajendran had fancied for a long time. Ramesh, aware of his companion's passionate feelings, turned to him and remarked, "See, your beloved one, *aṇṇaṉ*, how beautiful she looks today." When I asked him afterwards why he suddenly referred to his friend in a patrilineal form he explained, "We use the form of māmaṉ maccāṉ because we are equal, but when we see this girl we cannot refer like this. If I call him as my cross cousin, Vijaya becomes my sister. But I find her attractive, too." That instance and Ramesh's explanation demonstrate that those different expressions in fact contain a meaning, related to a wider social context.

Illustration 3: Examples of symmetrical relationships

maccāṉ **(brother in law, cross cousin)** -	***maccāṉ***
Suresh, 22, MBA	Prasenna, 23, MBA

➔ sharing academic and private concerns, mutual help, common activities on campus and beyond

nāttaṉār **(sister in law)** -	***macciṉi*** **(sister in law)**
Soundariya, 21, MBA	Sinjuta, 21, MBA
➔ teases Sinjuta to marry her brother	➔ expresses her feelings for her brother
māpḷa **(brother in law, cross cousin)** -	***māpḷa***
Gokulam	Ramesh
➔ boyfriend of Anitha	➔ younger brother of Anitha
aṇṇi **(older brother's wife)** -	***tampi*** **(younger brother, brother in law)**
Anitha, 27, PhD Sociology	Eashwaran
➔ girlfriend of Gokulam	➔ junior student of Gokulam

Importantly, this system of address is exclusively practiced *within* college culture and not expanded to wider family networks. Friends who refer to each other as cross-kin do not designate their actual family members in such terms. If Suresh visits Prasenna, who he addresses as maccāṉ, at his house, he is not entitled to call his father *māmā* (mothers' brother). Further, he is not eligible to marry his friend's sister. Thus far, the usage of terms has demonstrated that far from abstract constellations, peer groups reveal a variety of friendships whose category and status are indicated in terms of the Tamil kinship system. Next to internal ranks, which stem from factors such as age, grade or educational success, friendship interactions are shaped by a common notion of caste identity. Regarding the prevalence of local jāti segregations, I draw attention to the way in which academic social configurations are reconstructed by an encompassing hierarchical Tamil society.

First, it must be noted that far from presenting a 'neutral' domain, the academic context constitutes a distinctive sphere for caste-related activities such as political associations, revitalization projects or the organized celebrations of popular personalities.[17] Classrooms, assembly halls or the courtyard provide frequent sites for jāti-based profiling. Those events risk ending in wider conflicts and outburst of violence. Jeffery (2005: 30) points out that school-internal activities like theater, rallies or sports events do not merely present unbiased settings; rather, they serve to revitalize social inequalities in the sense that they are frequently used for acting out caste and class behavior. Other jāti-motivated activities within campus are outlined by Martyn Rogers (2008), who examines the way in which the status gap between students from Scheduled Castes and Backward Classes is manifested through university-related activities. Following his findings, inter-caste and class conflicts are enhanced via an aggravated gender relation: Through Eve teasing or sexual harassment of higher caste women, SC students contest their subordinated status. In pressuring female students, they appear hyper virile, which, according to the author "should be seen as a source of anxiety as much as a structure of power and security" (ibid: 80). Confronting higher caste fellow students, SC members aim to regain power by demonstrating the "inability [of the higher caste members to] adequately [...] 'protect' the women of their own 'community' from being assaulted" (ibid 88).

While South Indian caste differentiation strongly influences rural colleges in the district of Madurai, students and graduates at MKU discursively detach themselves from community-related events and conflicts. Within the academic sphere, casteism constitutes a taboo, as it stands for a 'backward' attitude (*piṉtaṅkiya*). In contrast, tolerance and a neutral interaction with other *jāti* members are considered a reflection of an advanced mind-set (Alex 2009: 162). This notion explains the reserved reaction to my inquiries regarding the significance of jāti differences or the occurrence of discrimination and groupism within the campus. Most of the conversation partners vehemently insisted that "caste is not important" and immediately count the varieties of communities within their friendship circles. The dissociation from jāti identity is further enhanced by the possibility to conceal the ritual rank by a decent demeanor, style and casual clothing that corresponds to the status of 'educated' (Strümpell 2006: 116).

Against the background of this expressed alienation, I turn to the question of whether one can regard the university campus as an external domain, where ritual caste and gender constellations remain subverted or even eliminated. Closer observations reveal that campus relations indeed circulate around local *jāti* membership. However, caste differentiation is not performed in terms of a ritual rank, based on physical avoidance or discrimination. While among

17 I am grateful to Professor Thamburan Dharmaraj for drawing my attention to prevalent caste conflicts within the campus.

industrial workers, Strümpell examined the prevalence of a pure-impure ideology by institutionalized practices – the joint smoking of chillum pipes, mutual assistance or addressing each other with forms of respect – such criteria remain less relevant within my setting. Instead, the articulation of caste boundaries occurs in a more subtle way, notably by its *transformation* into the academic context. Hence, jāti differences serve as a popular and acceptable justification for explicating failures within the educational field. Community conflicts quickly serve to explain university-related frictions or unsuccessful projects. Gokulam, for instance, rationalized an organizational failure to properly prepare a workshop with caste-related peculiarities: "If there is a conference on PK issues or conducted by a PK professor, other caste members won't support us. We have to work on our own."

Moreover, caste differences are reformulated within everyday casual and academic discussions and as such, they function as a structuring element of daily interaction; while ambiguous answers are considered characteristic of the Brahmin caste, dominant or rude gestures are associated with Piramalai kaḷḷar. Unsolicited interference or unqualified advices in turn characterize Paṟaiyar. On one of the rare occasions in which I was able to join a male group in their leisure time, I witnessed such a drift when I sat with Suresh, Prasenna and Ganesh, a junior *Piḷḷaimār* in front of a shrine. Suresh declared that he would enter the temple in order to conduct a *puja* for an interview at a human resource center that would take place the next day. Immediately, Ganesh and Prasenna complained that he did not involve them in his plans: "Why did you not tell us about this opportunity? We would have helped you to prepare the interview!" Suresh, pointing to Ganesh replied, "You know, these Piḷḷaimār will complicate the situation." Then he cited a local slogan, "One Piḷḷaimār is enough to split one village". Annoyed, Prasenna interrupted him by emphasizing, "Don't bring caste into this!"

Although students relate to each other as paṭiccavaṅka, a status disconnected from the ritual rank, they bring up caste characteristics to evaluate achievements or failures of their university colleagues. Other ethnographies have noted similar observations. Among urban intellectuals in contemporary India, André Béteille (1996) finds that status differences based on education, profession and income are associated with jāti background, even though they are not directly related to the actual community. One business partner, exerting a superior position in professional terms, might be designated as a 'typical Brahman' (Fuller 1996: 17), a contrasting figure to the inferior and submissive attitude of a 'typical Harijan' (ibid). In his study about changing caste relations within a village context, M.L. Reiniche (1996) identifies a similar phenomenon among different jāti members of Tiruchengodu: faced with new professional opportunities, inhabitants of that village justify their degree of success as well as their chosen business strategies with caste characteristics, leading to the author's conclusion that, "what people state about themselves and others largely complies with a sort of traditional image, a kind of natural identity" (ibid: 142). Studies that assess these observed phenomena and address the contemporary significance of caste largely rely on Louis Dumont's understanding of *substantialization*. This concept assumes a transition from the religiously-grounded caste system towards a social structure consisting of units who compete on a secondary, socio-economic level. Everyday interactions between members of different castes within modern compartments do not comply with the ritual hierarchy. Instead, they are based on characteristics attached to local communities. Substance in this sense supersedes structure (Fuller 1996: 10ff.). However, emerging constellations within this substantialized system remain incorporated into an overriding caste order and allocated to the ritual rank. Eventually, the modern sphere remains encompassed by a religious sphere. Adherents to this approach therefore reject the idea of a fundamental transformation of a culture-specific system (ibid).

3.6 CONCLUSION

The first subchapter of this section highlighted the implications associated with education and the manifold motivations for pursuing a higher degree at MKU. Through exposure to a secular sphere, students become modern citizens and attain the status of a paṭiccavaṅka. Consequently, the campus has been defined as a 'modern' compartment where elements of the ritual order are temporarily subverted by the practices of a locally-cultivated college culture. My observation of constellations, activities and interactions of selected peer groups demonstrates that graduate students engage in relationships that counteract local restrictions. As paṭiccavaṅka, they distinguish themselves from caste barriers by forming anti-hierarchical constellations, particularly cross-caste and cross-gender friendships and romances. The neutral setting of the campus promotes the types of interactions observed, which transcend the established hierarchies of the South Indian caste society. Common activities and detailed conversations suggest that the majority of the graduate students define their friendships in terms of common educational experiences and vocational perspectives. A detailed analysis of their relationship patterns, however, indicates that egalitarian peer groups do not present a distinctive counter-model to, but rather remain bounded by South Tamil caste, kinship and gender norms. Activities and interactions within and between graduate students vividly reflect Tamil ideals of femininity and masculinity and the way in which friendships are ranked and classified in terms of Tamil kinship relations. Behavioral patterns and conflicts taking place on an academic level are rearticulated by ascribed caste characteristics. Thus far, I contend that friendships made in the educational context do present a peculiar constellation, yet, they cannot be perceived independently from broader forms of social organization.

The campus offered a site for leisure activities so that university hostel residents and commuters regularly spent their weekend within the university. Occasionally, they returned to their place of origin, where I seized the opportunity to accompany them. The next chapter turns to the domestic sphere and examines whether anti-hierarchical peer constellations present an exclusive feature of college culture or prevail beyond the academic context. I therefore turn to the status and behavior of peer groups and the maintenance of their friendships within the framework of familial and social restrictions in their native villages.

4. Beyond the campus: Among friends in the domestic sphere

The following insights are gathered from regular field trips, mostly during weekends or university holidays to (1) *Vadipatti*, a panchayat town of roughly 22 000 inhabitants, 26 km north of MKU, where I spent several weekends with Murugesh and Rajesh; (2) *Usilampatti*, the hometown of Pogkani and Eashwaran. The principle settlement of Piramalai kaḷḷar, 25 km west of the university, is not only captured in scientific and popular accounts of South Indian caste relations, but presents a famous setting for Tamil movies to depict the lifestyle of its inhabitants; and (3) *Ayyarbungalow*, an urban outskirt of my own neighborhood in the city of Madurai and the home of Sinjuta, Suresh and Prasenna.

Map 4: Location of the hometowns visited

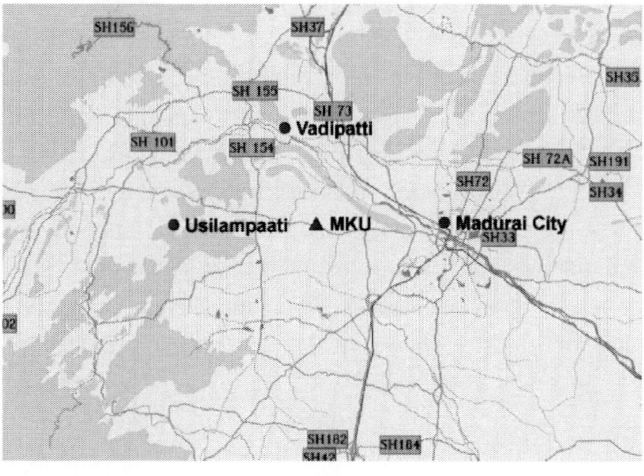

stepmap.de

Living together with their families, I experienced the situation of the graduate students beyond campus borders. Certainly the background of students varies in income, family constellation and village structure. Notwithstanding distinct settings, my case studies entirely concentrate on the functioning of friendship networks. The data are complemented by observations among my host family and narratives from other peer group members.

4.1 *PAṭICCAVAṅKA*, AN AMBIVALENT IMAGE

"In my village, I get respect. There are some graduates from the upper caste people. But I am the one in my caste and the only PhD student in my village. In my own caste, when I go to my village, I have a superior feeling. They all appreciate me. They often speak amongst themselves about my struggles to reach this level in my education." Rajesh

According to his statement, the 22 year-old history student from the Paṟaiyar caste experienced increased influence throughout all social sections in Vadipatti, his hometown. With his educational background, he acquired a superior position by "clarifying others' doubts", "being good for all" or "giving motivation to others by suggestions and advice". He aids family members and same-aged neighbors in translating letters, evaluating jobs or completing application forms. He teaches English to older village members, conveys negotiation skills for contracts and instructs them on how to use cooking recipes from the internet. Particular responsibility and authority has been acquired by offering evening lessons or preparatory classes for young children before entering school. Assuming the position of a mentor, he evaluates and signs transfer certificates from primary to secondary school. Further, he corresponds with teachers regarding the pupils' progress in class. Additionally, he motivates adolescents to continue higher education or discusses with them different college options. Irrespective of his academic background in humanities, he is considered a qualified expert for social issues not necessarily related to his education. Within family circles, he is occasionally consulted for his opinion about financial matters, land holdings and marriage partners (see chapter 7).

Among most of graduate students, receiving such particular attention within their hometown evokes increased "self esteem, confidence, pride and rightfulness", a condition which allows them to "walk tall". Eashwaran noticed an increasingly respectful attitude from the side of his neighbors and relatives: "Now, everyone is calling me by using the polite form and expression 'Sir' instead of 'ṭēy'". The PhD candidates Gokulam and Murugesh ascertained that village youngsters, well known for their cheeky comments hide 'bad' habits like drinking or smoking in front of them. Their colleague Geetha felt taken more seriously in public institutions and described her experience in the primary health center when her two year-old daughter felt sick:

"When we used to go there earlier they simply said, 'Your child has loose motion'. But when they found out that I am working and doing my PhD, they explained, 'There is an indigestion problem with your daughter'. Then, they give an explanation about the cause, progress and risks of taking medicine. They do not speak like that with uneducated people – there is a differentiation."

The status of paṭiccavaṅka and its impact at the village level affect men and women in a different way. Young men mainly gain influence on a political level. Beyond the visible skills of speaking and writing well, it is especially their decency and serious demeanor, a widened horizon and their capability of a neutral sagacity that renders them eligible to attend to social concerns. Murugesh therefore continuously emphasizes his talent for "becoming active against discrimination" or "solving problems without violence" as one of the most important outcomes of education. Other studies in rural surroundings of Madurai find that educated people are characterized by the ability to speak in public places and address offices and functionaries in an adequate manner (Sekine 2002: 227). Among educated Jats in Uttar Pradesh, Jeffrey (2010) even demonstrates the connection between educational background and a specific know-how for tackling social inequalities due to an elaborated writing and speaking style (ibid: 127). The author regards the salient political activism among young, educated men in India as a consequence of a "relatively purposeless youth timepass" (ibid: 4). In his view, boredom and desultoriness evoke new abilities, and creative engagement in local political affairs. This commitment features different forms of profiling, in such a way that his informants act as "brokers between urban poor and government officials" (ibid: 16).

While young men widely acquired an authoritative position via education, their female counterparts adopted new forms of femininity. Due to better career opportunities and exposure, they perceived an increasing strength and assertiveness. Even a delayed marriage, a critical consequence of higher education, now often becomes rearticulated as evidence for an intellectual and bold personality, characteristic of a person who gives priority to a vocational career and self realization instead of simply following parental desires. This attitude corresponds to other ethnographies that illustrate how educated women deliberately separate themselves from their peers who "married young" (Levinson 1996: 222). Importantly, higher education does not seem to be in conflict with conjugal ideals, but equips women with an additional capacity to enforce their priorities within familial life. Notably, female students do not apprehend their acquired background as contradictory to established virtues and ideals of an Indian woman, neither as a daughter nor as a perspective wife or mother. Rather, they regard their educational experience as conducive to cultivating female qualities. "Being more understandable" and "having developed a high esteem", Gheeta felt well equipped to perform as a good *cumaṅkali*, a strong wife and mother who is able to take care of her husband and child. Education enabled her to become a 'dignified' woman, an expression which describes a person who knows how to confront hurdles in everyday life, including difficulties in raising children or coping with awkward habits of her husband. Pogkani described the position of cumaṅkali as a 'backbone' for the family:

"In many families, women fight. But with an educated background, a wife knows how to conceal. So she never blames her husband but she will act like a psychiatrist. She can balance her life and she never has problems. Men are cowards, they run away when they feel guilty but we can confront the problems. If we would run away, the problem follows us and we feel guilty also."[1]

Cited experiences thus far largely suggest status elevation through education. Both men and women acquire increasing responsibility, authority and influence in several social realms – qualities which are indeed compatible with local gender constellations. At the same time, they perceived the downside of their educational improvement and encountered opposition, condemnation and mistrust: One of the most severe difficulties constituted financial distress. Economic pressure particularly affects students from a poor economic background or those studying in the first generation. Engaged in traditional jāti activity and agricultural labor, South Indian families increasingly invest their income and savings in their children's education as a strategy for social mobility (Osella & Osella 2000: 9ff.). Negative outcomes for the students related to pursuing a graduate degree include continuous concerns and feelings of guilt for neglecting familial duties. In a pan-Indian, interview-based enquiry about the subjective experience of higher education among Dalit from a poor economic

1 This perspective resists negative stereotypes of a 'demanding' attitude among highly educated brides (see section 6.2).

background, Jules Naudet (2008) demonstrates how the moral imperative to 'pay something back to society' determines their upward mobility in class and status. Beyond material concerns, a permanent source of pressure consists in social control, exaggerated expectations and clichés.[2] In all three villages visited, appraisals and stereotypes towards paṭiccavaṅka affect young men and women alike, albeit in different ways. In contrast to their less-educated peers in their hometowns, young men experience an intensified requirement to avoid disfavored habits like consuming alcohol, using strong words or postponing duties. Frequently, such constraints result in compulsory health maintenance, sleeping and waking up early, keeping the house clean, and staying abreast of current affairs as well as the events of the day. Murugesh reflected how he has adjusted his attitude according to this pressure: "Whatever you see, you eat – you become fat – whatever you see, you read, you will become a higher person." Such a self-conscious way of life is expected and appreciated, but equally causes mistrust and condemnation. One situation Murugesh faced serves as an exemplary anecdote. Inhabitants of his home village accused him of pretension and conceit. In fact, he gradually complained about the "dirty" streets or expressed his reluctance to mingle with *piṉ taṅkiyanilai* ('backward' people). Such comments made him appear arrogant, an image which caused a divide between him and his close kin. Henceforth, Murugesh perceived a strong uncertainty among his own family in everyday life: "Here, cross cousins tease each other, but after obtaining education and doing a PhD, this intimacy is over. They (cross cousins) approach me in a different way – with respect and suspicion."

Another irritating effect of higher education turns out to be exaggerated and disproportional demands by family and village members, an attitude that Prasenna described with amusement and outrage alike: "People cannot differentiate: they think, only because I am educated, I know everything." Not surprisingly, he found himself in a confusing state when his father approached him for advice about purchasing a new car:

"I was the first person to make the decision about getting the car: which car to buy, to get, to go for ... My father has the impression of me that I can manage every situation and I

2 Blunt and sometimes relentless judgments about those aspiring social mobility via education and other economic achievements have been found by Sarah Dickey among middle class members in Madurai. Her subjects of investigation presented education as "insufficient as a means of entering a higher class [since] a degree must be accompanied by other symbolic attributes that make one a proper member of a higher class" (2010: 203).

have experience in all kinds of fields. So he asked me whether to get this car or that car. Then he asked about technical data, what the major difference is in mileage and so on ... Even though I am doing my master's in Business Administration, he asks my opinion also about such questions."

If graduate students are not capable of satisfying such exorbitant requests, they face disappointments, accusations and attacks. As a consequence of their 'poor performance' and 'incompetence', they are quickly designated as a *veḷaṅkātavaṉ*, an expression which describes a person who attracts bad luck. I experienced such an argument in my own host family. Ilakiya, an older cousin's sister, and her husband intended to buy several hectares of land near Theni, in the west of Madurai. For competent advice, she consulted Ram, her younger brother, because he completed his Masters in agricultural science. Ram checked and approved the quality of the croplands. The process ended up in litigation when it turned out that the official owner of the lands did not hold all necessary property rights. Disappointed by this failure, Ilakiya's son and husband accused Ram of hiding crucial details. The agricultural expert defended himself by stating that his duty consisted in evaluating the state of the cultivation area but neither its legal position, nor tenure or titles – a task which has to be consigned to lawyers. Instead of differentiating assignments attached to such a process, his family members referred to the cumulative failure and considered Rama veḷaṅkātavaṉ as Ilakiya explicated, "I cannot tell the exact reason. It is just that in whatever he does, things will end in a bad way."

While male graduate students find themselves mainly confronted by suspicion or restraint, young women find themselves exposed to more severe stereotypes. Regularly, they suffer from discouraging comments concerning their education. Gheeta, who received a salary for her PhD and her position as women's representative, lamented that her neighbors accused her family of enriching themselves on her income.[3] Even though a secure employment is considered desirable for women, a degree higher than a Bachelor's evokes negative statements and the prejudice of neglecting familial duties. Since master's students usually postpone their marriage until completing their degree, women are suspected of entertaining an inappropriate rapport with their classmates. Such stereotypes are reinforced by widespread prejudices about 'college culture', which is associated with roaming about until late at night, engaging in illegal affairs and excessive consumption. Eventually, those allegations fuel parental concerns that an outgoing attitude of their daughter could damage the reputation and her prospects for a suitable match.

3 Several stereotypes have been found in other parts of India (Seymour 1999: 200f.).

Soundariya's father expressed his worries to me: "I don't mind if she is speaking to boys in the evening or morning. We don't restrict her from talking to the people who study with her. We restrict guys from talking to her after ten or eleven o'clock, dropping her at home, meeting her late at night. This will give a bad image of our family." The above examples elucidate a distinctive position of more highly educated people, which leads to a higher status and alienation alike. Regarding such ambivalent consequences, the question arises how egalitarian constellations among students can be upheld within the scenery of the domestic context.

4.2 PEERS AS SUPPORT, SPONSORS AND PATRONS

> Schools and colleges are another crucial arena for the production of class futures. In addition to producing a great deal of cultural capital, they can also be significant sources of social capital. Classmates become the social networks that may secure a job, and teachers can provide assistance or pose obstacles in career searches.
>
> DICKEY 2012: 590

As the quote above suggests, academic friends serve as an essential resource regarding vocational perspectives. A closer analysis of occupational advancement reveals that peer groups of university students create veritable networks to inform and support each other outside campus as well. Principle inputs are exchanged by news about career opportunities, fairs and other useful connections. Graduates who acquired well-paid employment inform their former classmates about and prepare them for interviews in order to help them obtain a similar position or they might even recommend them to their bosses or influential colleagues. If they established their own company, they frequently consider their peers as employees. An exemplification of respective cases reveals an elaborated system of mutual favors, but also consistent hierarchies and dependencies. Rajendran, for instance, opted for a job in a human resource center in Delhi. He received the job advertisement from Rajesh, who worked there as an intern at the time. Together with his peers, Rajendran designed the application and borrowed money from them for travel expenses. In Delhi, he found accommodated at Rajesh's house where he prepared himself for the interview.

Also after graduation, peers prove to be useful connections. This phenomenon became evident through the example of my two host brothers. Temporarily employed as a private teacher, David draws on his former classmates in various situations. Kannithevar, a lawyer working at the Tamil Police office, serves as an essential contact person for litigation and legal requests or conflicts. Economically well-situated peers act as sponsors and regularly offer prestigious gifts such as costly jeans or cell phones to less privileged friends. When the entire group undertook a joint alumni trip to Dubai for New Years Eve, Nataraj who was employed in a lucrative position at that time, paid the tickets for all of his classmates.

Such gestures express mutual respect and trust. Additionally, they reveal a functional structure: superior mates become role models or patrons and the supposedly egalitarian friendship turns into an asymmetrical constellation. Correspondingly, influential friends in economic sectors acquire the status of a mentor. David's friend Charles, for instance, owned an international Christian NGO and continuously presented him with job opportunities within the country and abroad. Charles' support does not represent a neutral gesture, but reveals a purposeful engagement. Thus, he repeatedly insisted on David progressing with his graduate degree since it would make him eligible to take up a higher position. This encouragement resulted in regular calls to remind him of exams, a commitment which finally involved David's family members. Charles kept in contact with David's mother and deliberated with her about further steps for her son. The family regarded his efforts not as intrusive, but as a friendly gesture. In turn, David carried out errands to offices for Charles or established links to potential business partners. Moreover, he served as an alibi when Charles met his girlfriend.

While mutual support in professional aspects presents an explicit connecting element among academic peers, space for cultivating anti-hierarchical constellations is not merely restricted to the educational realm, but an important component of everyday life. Their joint investment of acquired skills into social engagement provides a common ground for university friendship: together, they organize social services, including rallies, evening classes or excursions for younger village members. Other forms of cooperative engagement consist in revitalizing folklore and art. Eashwaran teaches *tappāṭṭam*, the abovementioned folk dance to school kids in evening lessons. With members of the folklore department at MKU, he created a tappāṭṭam team and organizes public performances on central squares and halls in the surrounding villages. Commenting on his motivation to invest his time in this way, he emphasized,

"This folk form of dance might be explored and performed only among my own community, but now I am able to bring it into the world."

Furthermore, friends become important resources in delicate but serious familial issues. Typical examples include affairs, health issues, or, in later stages, family planning. Such topics are unlikely to be discussed among family members, so that most consider an intimate friend. For instance, Sasi, whose family suffered from the fact that he and his wife remained childless, entrusted this issue to David, who consulted a doctor and brought him to a specialist. This step took place secretly without divulging it to parents or other kin. Later on, David explained to me that Sasi's parents are reluctant to disclose such family-internal problems. He referred to Prakash, another friend with similar problems whose family has a 'modern' background. In this case, Prakash's sister called him via cell phone to ask him for help. Both examples suggest friends serve as a crucial contact for delicate, but necessary interventions.

Another essential function of peers consists in personal support, enabled and intensified by modern communication technologies as Rajendran emphasized, "Nowadays, communication has developed a lot. It is very easy to have intimate connections with friends. We have mobiles, Skype, messengers and so on. So it is easier to be in contact with many friends." Virtual platforms like alumni and student pages, Facebook or, recently, Whatsapp not only present tools for social networking, but enable the articulation of an individual profile by a particular style, musical taste or political orientation. Young women use their phone as a medium to mock male relatives; male peers send jokes or pictures of their beloved. Unlimited conversations and conference calls facilitate the contacts beyond social, spatial or time-related barriers. Sinjuta, who suffered from the dominance of her older brother, not only expresses her sorrow to her female peers; she also maintains a strong emotional relationship to Prasenna. Conversations on the phone are socially accepted, but at times attached with excessive behavior. For Ajitha, the habit of speaking continuously on her phone sparked a heated argument between herself, her parents and older male cousins who finally confiscated her sim card. Familial authorities condemn such relentless conversing in public as inappropriate since this activity evokes the impression of being engaged in dubious relationships or even an affair.

Whether in the professional, social, or private domain, the above descriptions suggests a continuity of university and college relationships beyond campus borders. Insights into the functioning of peer groups beg the question: How are those constellations valued in relation to the hierarchical structures that prevail in the domestic context? Respective studies on peer groups across different parts of India agree in their contention that friendships formed within educational institutions are bound to the academic context and hence temporarily limited. The domestic scene represents such a defined border, where egalitarian constellations seem to endanger ritual caste ranks. While Donner (2008: 86) points out that parents prevent their children from forging and maintaining inappropriate friendships in the close neighborhood, the Osellas (2000: 230f.) highlight the reluctance of young men to enter the home of befriended low caste peers. At first sight, such a limited interaction is equally suggested by statements like: "Maintaining the relationship with college friends is not possible. Though we uphold the friendship, it would be for a certain period. It won't last" (Eashwaran).

My own study reveals a rather differentiated picture, since academic friends may appear as a distinctive and therefore neutral category. In other words, the academic background is utilized to overcome social obstacles. Classmates usually assume an exceptional status related to an external level of social interaction that does not affect local hierarchies. Though Murugesh's family reveals strong caste pride, his parents invited his classmates irrespective of their jāti background. As long as his peers are introduced as 'college friends', the ritual status is subverted as he explained to me, "My parents will always be friendlier toward my friends because they know that they are from college. It may be a boy or a girl. They will behave in the same way when they come to the house." Rajesh, a Paṟaiyar, not only visited regularly and became a welcomed guest, but also he was invited for food – an act which principally counteracts the rules of commensality. Interestingly however, the common feast is not regarded as a break of caste rules since the encounter takes place within a frame of the 'modern' sphere.[4] Likewise, Gokulam from the Piramalai kaḷḷar community, reported that even his girlfriend Anitha, a Paṟaiyar, is accepted, though not received in his parental home. He rationalized this tolerance by the educated background of both families: "My mother, brother and sister speak to her on phone ... As I said, the entire family is educated, they do not give importance to caste." Importantly, the students often modify their interactions with peers in the presence of parents. Particularly, mates from different castes avoid addressing each other in forms which symbolize an intimate relationship. Rajendran reported an example when he invited Eashwaran to his home in Alagkanallur. While they used to call each other *māpḷa* or *māps,* a kinship expression for co-brothers, they simply referred to each other by name at Rajendran's home. "This is because we give respect", he explained to me their efforts not to provoke his parents.

4 Such examples cannot be generalized to all peer groups and families.

While caste hierarchies likely become neglected within the framework of academic contacts, mixed-gendered constellations compose an unusual and problematic phenomenon and remain particularly supervised. At the time of my stay near Ayyarbungalow, Soundariya, Sinjuta and Suresh were invited to Prasenna's house to prepare a group discussion. After jointly reading on the terrace, the women approached Prasenna's mother in the kitchen to prepare coffee. Meanwhile, the men went out for a joint trip, together with a male neighbor. Later on, we rejoined to discuss my question about why they did not roam in a mixed constellation:

Suresh:	For roaming we cannot take the girls.
Soundariya:	The reason is if women are going somewhere, the guys will say something. And they will be distracted somehow. Only if they are going to official functions, we come as a group.
Prasenna:	It depends upon the place and the gang (with which) we are going. Some of the boys will smoke; some of the boys will drink. We cannot bring women to such places. Same when we are married: when I am roaming with men around, I cannot take my wife with me. I need to wait for a time where my friends will bring their wives to that party or function, then I can bring her. The place matters.

Those comments suggest that although peer groups present a distinctive constellation, they interact in accordance with local norms. Thus, young men and women refrain from joining each other in public, as such outings would damage the reputation of the person and the family. As an alternative strategy for undertaking common activities in line with local requirements, young men and women depart independently and then reunite in remote locations. Moreover, the domestic context restricts colloquial forms of interaction, particularly if parents or other respected authorities are present. In this case, friends mostly refer to each other by name instead of using kinship terms.

Despite certain restrictions, the above paragraphs have questioned the village and domestic context as a limitation of egalitarian constellations, by outlining the scope for cultivating university-related friendships. Outside the campus, peers transform into useful networks, in which it is possible to acquire status, prestige and mobility beyond social and ritual barriers. Such constellations are based on themes and concerns which cannot be shared within familial circles.

Rather than opposing local caste or gender segregations, my findings suggest that academic peer groups persist in the form of an altered identity that does not counteract, but skillfully circumvent established barriers. Hence, they appear as part of a secular sphere and provide evidence for a university-related cosmopolitanism and progressiveness. The following comparison between 'college' and 'village' friends illuminates the meaning of those configurations.

4.3 'UNIVERSITY' AND 'VILLAGE' FRIENDS

Graduate students designate campus peer groups as *college* or *university friends*, a different social category than friendships in their neighborhood, often referred to as *village friends*. The latter usually remain within the same community, typically with relatives and, for the most part, separated between women and men. Joint activities tend to be similar to those with university related friends, but remain shaped by local segregation and daily requirements within the village.

Male groups commonly work together in agriculture. Popular leisure activities consist of outdoor games like cricket or cabbadi.[5] Frequently, they spend their time in public places such as dams and forests or other localities. "Cutti pārkkalām" was the typical response, when I asked male friends about their undertaking what can best be translated as 'roaming around': For this venture, male groups gather inside cars, drive to remote areas such as abandoned roads, parks or beaches for jointly consuming, chatting and celebrating. Frequently, they enter adjacent villages to tease girls.

Conversations are not restricted to university-related topics, but include gossip, village news and family issues, especially conflicts and the selection of a marriage partner. In these exchanges, friends make comments about the physical appearance or the origin of the girl and also motivate and advise each other. During my visit to Vadipatti, Rajesh and a group of youngsters sat on the village playground and evaluated photos of potential marriage partners for Prabhu, a Dalit living in the same street. At the beginning, Prabhu was reluctant to show pictures to avoid comments like "Hey super figure!" Later on, he circulated several pictures and pointed to a corpulent bride by joking, "If you choose this I will kill you man!" Next to passing time, such encounters offer a getaway from daily constraints.

5 A Tamil game which tests the stamina of the players: One group forms a circle in which one member has to hand over a ball by continuously repeating "cabbadi".

Young women take care of daily chores and come together to shop at the local market or fetch water. In their spare time, they enjoy themselves by singing songs, playing in parks, watching movies or visiting temples or churches. Communication between women primarily centers on personal matters. Some of the most important topics include gossip about happenings in the village or family problems. In contrast to the rather academic discussions within the campus, these personal exchanges primarily function as mutual support and active help. Such female networks have attracted anthropological interest and are regarded by Sudhir Kakar as a resource of strength which builds up feminine identity (2002: 59ff.). Those gender-related tendencies correspond with the findings of community studies[6], pointing out that women's friendships tend to be affectionate and intimate while male friendships are predominantly cultivated through common activities (Brandt 2013: 28).

Picture 6: Cutti pārkkalām:
'Roaming around' to remote areas

Despite their divergent character, university and village friends are equally appreciated as they serve distinctive functions. Eashwaran expressed his view, "Both the friends are like two eyes: Friends from university will inform us about the competitive exams and so on. But with village friends I can discuss private things." In intricate situations, classmates appear to be "broad minded" through a "wider horizon". The exchange with university friends is considered 'elaborated'

6 Interdisciplinary field of anthropology and sociology, originated and developed in North America and Great Britain, in the mid of last century (Brandt 2013: 28).

since a great portion of the shared topics requires an educated background. Graduate students regard their academic contacts as the right conversation partners for 'serious' matters, able to evaluate delicate situations "in an objective way". With reference to the progressive image attached to higher education, I argue that the principle outcome of university friends lies in establishing and maintaining an identity as paṭiccavaṅka. Hence, *paṭiccavaṅka paḻakkavaḻakkam* ("those having relationship with educated") is linked to an advanced mind-set and stands in contrast to *kirāmattu paḻakkavaḻakkam* ("those having relationship with village people"), equated with village habits. The words of Rajendran demonstrate how the exposure to a 'modern' context is performed via friendships:

"There is a saying: 'Tell me about your friend and I will tell you about you'. A friend's character decides our character. So if we have connection with educated friends, I will be developed. (…) Rural friends won't be knowledgeable like college friends. So if we need to march towards the development we must have connection to the friends from college. Village friends will have different issues, social set ups and so on. With them we can discuss simple things only. On the other hand, if we have connections with the educated friends from the urban area, the life style, personality and the issues we discuss with them will be totally different. These discussions will lift us up towards development."

Such an elaborated character contains its downside as well. In contrast to the intimate and relaxed interaction among village friends, academic contacts may turn into a source of pressure. The statement of Suresh illustrates the pragmatic and sometimes relentless attitude of university friendships which stands opposed to the 'pure character' of companions in near neighborhood:

"Home friends and colleagues I know from childhood. So there is nothing behind the relationship. But here at the university, friendships are formed out of reason and keeping them up has a cost associated with it: I need some financial means in order to maintain the rapport. But with my colleagues from home, I can survive without a single paisa.[7] Here (on campus) I cannot survive without my purse (…). If they treat me to coffee, I have to be ready to contribute some snacks. At least the next time you should have money. So some restrictions are there ... but with my colleagues from home, there is no need to do spend money because we grew up together. So there's a difference ... I would say that in the village, I get 100 percent out of the friendship. At university, I would say around 60 or 70 percent. Because more than my friend, he is my competitor."

7 Minor unit of currency: 100 paise are one rupee.

This rational basis for academic friendships may be a cause for latent uncertainty or even suspicion. While expectations and limitations of a friendship are determined by social criteria in the village context, the ties of college friends remain fluid which leads to a feeling of competition and contention. This ambivalent attitude has driven students to characterize these college groups as "smart, very diplomatic, but also cunning", whereas they view village friends as "natural", "very open" and "innocent". Hence, interaction within college culture is always characterized by a sense of cautiousness.

In contrast to purpose-oriented relationships, the content of village friendships has been defined as "enjoyment without expectations". Ajitha experiences the interaction with her female companions in the village as "relaxing" and "genuine": "At home it is entirely different ... we don't talk about studies at all. I did this, I did that, I am doing this. This is all we talk about. They know our family members. So we discuss about family members and personal things." With her statement, she identifies a key criterion for defining village friends: mostly, they are aware of each other's social standing, which makes them capable of interacting in an appropriate way. Typical ways in which they mutually support each other include lending and borrowing money, providing a vehicle or assisting in the case of illness. As most village friends have a similar social background, they usually are much more involved in family internal affairs, as Gokulam points out through an anecdote: "Once my mother borrowed money from her younger sister. She was not able to repay the money. This issue ended up in fight. My *citti* (mother's younger sister) started harassing my mother with filthy words and finally she started beating her. I was not at home. My friends from the village were there and they split them up to save my mother." College friends, in contrast, are largely excluded from the domestic context, an important distinction upon which Suresh elaborates: "I cannot take them to all my relatives. To my brother it is possible. But when I am with my distant relatives, I cannot call them to visit. (…) I can only take them to important functions."

In a direct comparison, village friends are considered 'pure' friends and given a higher priority than college friendships widely perceived as 'task-oriented'. Consequently, students qualify leisure time with village friends as "jolly", "general" or "just enjoyable". Likewise, some respondents evaluated their gatherings as more intimate, personalized and homey. Ramesh summarizes the difference as such: "Friends from university help more and village friends will give moral support and other physical help." Thus far, the cited perceptions suggest that groups of graduate students consolidate to a distinctive category that appears superior to 'non-educated' groups. Concerning the quality of friendships, however, most students attribute an incomparably higher value and emotional content to village friends.

Regarding the articulated differentiation between college and village friends, the question remains whether they represent two independent social phenomena. I propose that, while the idea of friendship has been attached to both constellations, it is primarily the context that determines its nature. A range of similar activities are practiced in both academic and domestic domains. Typical activities undertaken in every constellation include joint picnics at the Vaigai dam, excursions to the nearby caves, outdoor sports and joint relaxation. Interestingly, students nevertheless evaluate their encounters and actions between each other in a different manner. One example is the custom of sharing food from the same plate: in the campus context, sharing a meal presents a common feature of a disconnected experience realm. In the village context, in contrast, commensality indicates an emotional connection. Consumption of alcohol and cigarettes among university friends is associated with modern behavior (Strümpell 2006: 115), but regarded as taboo within the village context. This contradiction might explain why certain excesses within the campus become practiced and spoken out overtly while on a domestic level, groups of friends drive to distant places and gather in remote areas. I conclude that it is the social realm that structures the nature of anti-hierarchical friendships; university peer groups emerge as part of a distinctive college culture. Their activities are framed and evaluated according to principles of modern public education. Central characteristics of these friendship patterns include egalitarian constellations, the interaction between members of different origins and the exposure to a system that exceeds the sphere of South Indian caste order.

4.4 CONCLUSION

By presenting the ambivalent position of academic peer groups at the village level, this chapter has outlined how MKU graduate students navigate between different social environments. In the first subchapter, I highlighted how students engage as 'educated' persons within the familial and village context and in line with local gender norms. Members of their families and communities consult them as experts in educational, political or technical questions. However, conflicting attitudes within their native setting equally lead to obstacles and social rejection. 'Being educated' therefore does not present an abstract concept, but becomes constantly reformulated and contested within a particular context. Secondly, I have shown that social constellations that developed as part of an educational system remain active beyond campus borders. Several examples highlighted the essential function of academic peers who serve as a support system for personal, social and vocational needs. Although these networks present an alternative path for social interaction and mobility beyond ritual status restrictions, they do not transform, but rather oscillate between principles of and *in line* with Indian caste society. Nevertheless, they present a distinctive social phenomenon. Graduate students express their notion about the peculiarity of campus constellations by comparing them to those friends from home. Based on their rationalizations, in the last chapter, I further suggest that it is the respective domain that changes the evaluation of relationships and activities. As part of a 'modern' sphere, 'university friends' assume an esteemed status. However, they exhibit a functional character, in contrast to emotional ties experienced between 'village friends'.

This chapter drew mainly on situational observations, narratives and excerpts from shared experiences outside the campus. Subsequently, the last part of this thesis provides a detailed and profound ethnography to position academic peers within the ritual context. The scenario of Tamil middle class marriage practices, in particular matchmaking strategies and wedding ceremonies, provide the principal field of investigation.

Part III: Just a friend? Ritual implications

When it comes to marriage (…) all of them turn to caste
ANDRÉ BÉTEILLE 1996: 162

Part III concentrates on marriage, the central stage of life that degree holders enter subsequent to graduation. As a "crucial part of a person's and family's life" (Mines & Lamb 2010: 10), anthropologists have located marriage unequivocally within the ritual sphere. Assessing the *Brahmana*, the interpretations of the *Vedic* scripts, Uwe Skoda elucidates the crucial significance of marriage as the "most important *samskara* or lifecycle ritual" (2002: 3, italics by the author): "Every single man is incomplete until he is married, for it is his wife who constitutes his second half and this unity can be achieved only by marriage" (ibid). According to most classic accounts, arranged marriage is strongly linked to endogamy and its rules have been defined as decisive criteria for the maintenance of the Indian caste society (Böck & Rao 1995: 117). Regarding social and demographic changes throughout recent decades, Zeff identifies the main purpose of matchmaking and marriage as a "key of maintaining boundaries of caste and class in Tamil Nadu" (1999: 179). Due to its crucial significance for the ritual status ranking of Tamil society, marriage outlines a designated limit to egalitarian friendships made in secular contexts. Friendships among youngsters are assumed to last only until they complete their education, enter work or a professional career and settle down to family life (Alex 2009: 139). Likewise, among MKU students and graduates, marriage presents the most crucial turning point for non-ritual constellations. Nataraj explained the changing situation after his marriage to me:

"My wife expects me not to come home late at night and I cannot roam with my friends like before. When I was a student, I would stay with my friends until eleven o'clock or midnight. We went on bike trips to far places like Kodaikanal.[1] But she won't allow me to go in such a manner. So I need to change myself, too."

Analyzing limits of *convivium* in relations among men, Strümpell (2006: 259) defines marriage as an event of commensal nature in a sphere opposed to 'modern' compartments. Within conjugal life, women appear synonymous with the end of relationships within the framework of *convivium*. That limit is enhanced by cultural appraisals of the Indian wife, oriented towards the goddess Lakshmi (ibid: 79ff.). The wife of Siva and role model for Indian women is associated with prosperity and the well-being of the family, but at the same time carries with her potential dangers of conflicts and cleavage. Soundariya's explanation supports the female perspective of this boundary:

"Wives restrict their husbands from coming back late at night. Before getting married, men will go here and there for drinking and eating. But if they go alone on their bike, it is not safe. So the wife has to restrict her husband. He has to rest early, he has to sleep and go to work ... Also, she cooks for him and takes care of his health. Hotel food is not good for him. Since she knows everything about this, she prepares food in the right way. So the wife cares a lot for him and for his health."

The above statement highlights the event of marriage as significant to becoming a mature and responsible adult, acting in accordance with organizing principles of Tamil society. The following chapters illustrate crucial stages of middle class marriage practices in the region of Madurai using the example of students and alumni who completed an advanced degree. Taking account of educational influences, I principally focus on their own perspectives and realms of experience in order to pose the question of how acquired 'modern' ideals including values of individuality, equality and emotional attachment persist within the ritual sphere. Related to this question, I inquire into the role of peers and their modes of conduct. Do friendship ideals continue, dissolve or become altered? Alongside ritual happenings, I focus in particular on participation, status and significance of non-kin friends. Their 'hidden' but increasing involvement must be understood as a part of those social transformational processes: recent challenges, including new technologies or shifting status symbols considerably shaped the matchmaking procedure and wedding rituals among the educated population – a development which paved the way for new actors beyond the

1 Hill resort in the Palani Hills, Tamil Nadu.

family circle. With reference to the example of students and former graduates of MKU, I investigate whether non-kin and egalitarian friendships represent an 'external' and excluded category from the rest of South Indian society or whether they acquire an integrative function, formerly reserved to kin members.

To illustrate their peculiar position, chapter 5 begins with a range of related ethnographies in different countries across the world, which places a transforming youth culture in opposition to established conjugal ideals. These studies share a common perception of marriage as a root cause for conflicts, social change and a turning point in domestic life. Based on this theoretical outline, I review principal accounts of marriage practices in South India by elucidating recent changes in their significance and exertion. Focusing on the perspective of Indian middle class youth, I extract four relevant research aspects: (1) the ideal of a *companionate* marriage; (2) a higher participation of the spouses, featuring a declining influence of elder authorities; (3) the emergence of the commercial wedding market in Tamil Nadu, which set up new class standards as well as behavioral norms and (4) the impact of self-chosen and elopement marriages.

These developments constitute the ethnographic framework for the subsequent analysis. Among my focus group, a visible shift has transpired from kin to non-kin marriages, a phenomenon pervasive among the South Indian middle class that has triggered the rising popularity of professional or semi-professional marriage assemblers. Chapter 6 examines present conjugal ideals of students and alumni, taking into account educational influences and 'progressive' worldviews. In line with other sociological accounts, they express an increasing preference for similar degrees, education, professional opportunities, personal compatibility and interests (Béteille 1996: 162ff., Clark-Decès 2014: 144, Fuller 2008: 740, Kapadia 1993: 38ff.). At the same time, their priorities and exclusion criteria for a marriage partner are articulated within the categories of Tamil endogamous marriage principles. Thus, youth expectations reveal a preference for a companionate marriage. This term has been defined by Fuller and Narasimhan as a "system that reproduces both caste and class, specifically 'middle classness' as social practice and discourse" (2008: 752).

A second crucial development relates to the increasing participation of the younger generation during the matchmaking process. Particularly in metropolitan areas, decisions surrounding arranged marriage are no longer exclusively reserved for elder authorities, but became a collective act of senior kin, parents, spouses, siblings and friends (Donner 2008: 71, Fuller and Narasimhan 2008: 751). Tracing the matchmaking process from remedy rituals to initial encounters and the finalization of the match, chapter 7 concentrates on the conceivable scope of action for participants, including familial and non-familial members. Non-kin alliances, new possibilities through digital media and behavioral norms have aggravated the process of finding a spouse to an exhausting and instable situation. While peers remain excluded from institutionalized functions, they indeed take up an important role as 'facilitators' in supporting and advising spouses, family members and in-laws alike.

Third, a challenging aspect of what I subsume under the label of 'middle class weddings' is the strenuous effort to display not only caste and class identity, but also taste, an educated background and exposure to 'modernity'.[2] An emerging wedding market in Tamil Nadu has set up categories that establish status ranks both of the host family and the wedding participants. Exploring the impact of mushrooming wedding halls, catering services or beauty parlors, chapter 8 defines the supportive role of peers in the principal preparations. It further takes account of their significance during ritual activities and their optical representation in paraphernalia such as invitation cards, banners and videos. As a digression, a last and fourth point addresses the crucial role of peers in self-chosen matches and elopement marriages. In light of the delicate implications of such unions, I explore the overt participation of non-familial friends who not only prove essential in the organization and exertion of love marriages, but mediate between individual desires of the couple and requirements of Tamil caste society.

---

2 Among the higher income sections in Delhi and Mumbai, Brosius (2010: 274) observes that "wedding have become the single most visible expression of a person's social standing and wealth, an expression that is both acceptable and expected." (ibid: 16).

5. "Key site of cultural contestation"? Youth, education and marriage

Worlwide, marriage has been perceived as an event where ideas of youth culture converge with 'local', 'superior' structures.[1] A wide range of ethnographies in different countries, therefore, have defined marriage as a "key site of cultural contestation" (Schrauwers 2000: 855) and analyze how institutional representations of marriage are received, resisted or reformulated by the younger generation. Assuming marriage and youth culture as an area of tension, most studies presuppose a clash in terms of overcoming, negotiation or domestication.

In the Nigerian context, Adeline Maquelier presents marriage as the central rite of passage from childhood to an adult. Referring to inter-generational negotiations on wealth, domesticity and sexuality as well as differing conceptions of gender, family and agency, getting married has become "the litany to save the young generation from impending depravity and destruction" (2005: 61). Viewing the generational politics of marriage, the author places young people "on the borderland along which the global meets the local" (ibid: 73). In her study, hedonistic desires of rebellious youngsters have a destructive influence on local marriage traditions. The intergenerational conflict is paramount, as youngsters' inability to overcome material and other obstacles for a suitable marriage "is widely articulated in a language of crisis" (ibid: 76). Annie Bunting and Sally Merry evaluate the emergence of a distinctive Nigerian youth culture as "shaped by transnational ideas and differing significantly from the cultures of parents and grandparents" (2007: 319). In a historical account of action against child marriage in the northern part of the country, the authors explain this generational confrontation with two contrasting socio-economic

1 According to Sophie Roche "marriage practices are best indicators of generational conflicts between social juniors and seniors over social and reproductive rights" (2014: 164).

contexts: an educational realm and an opposing, impoverished background, resulting in traditional practices such as early marriage, which contributes to a geographical divide between an impoverished North and a more educated and enlightened South. Respecting the gendered context in the northeastern part of Nigeria, Daniel Smith (2010) examines changing ideas about sexuality, marriage and gender equality among young Nigerian women. Regarding their extra-marital sexual experience, the author demonstrates how marriage – an institution remaining "socially imperative" (ibid: 150) – serves as the event of transformation from "promiscuous girls to good wives" (ibid: 123). This conversion is visibly reflected in their self-presentation, for instance by an altered style of dress to mark the shift from a single to married woman. Smith's study stresses the 'conflict' between a pre-marital sexual culture on the one hand and marital ideas on the other.

Also in other African countries, ethnographies have highlighted marriage as an occasion for generational clashes. Referring to effects of education, church, and the modern economy beginning in the middle of the last century in Ngeca, a Kikuyu town in Kenya, Carol Worthman and John Whiting (1987) point out how schooling alters mate selection strategies among the Kikuyu community by offering a social context in which boys and girls from different lineages and localities interact. Traditional priorities like the capability of affording bride-wealth and the assets required for men to establish their own home or the carefulness and a charming demeanor necessary for women become replaced by education and a steady salary. Changing preferences enhance a transformational process in Kikuyu society, exemplified by "decreases in brideprice and reversals in direction of transfer" (ibid: 162). Anne M. Jennings (2001) reveals creative strategies of Nubian youth who engage in pre-relationships to oppose traditional arranged marriage. Intergenerational cleavages are further expressed and reinforced in the form of musical performances, as Rasmussen (2000) demonstrates by highlighting the example of the usage of such instruments as the *anzad* (bow lute), *tende* (drum), and guitar during the wedding ceremonies of Tuareg people. The earlier phase of the ritual, including Islamic religious ceremonies and liturgical music at the mosque, emphasizes the role of parents and Islamic authorities, associated with the 'aged'. Secular evening festivals featuring popular musical performances, courtship, and dancing are classified as anti-Islamic and connected with 'youthfulness' and singles. Such presentations are motivated by local images of adolescent conflicts in times of social change. According to the author, the local youth is struggling between ideals of a nomadic Tuareg culture and the central state. Music performances therefore reflect the role of age and conflicting interests between several generations.

In societies practicing arranged marriages, the opposition of youth culture to parental authority has been frequently analyzed as part of a dichotomy between an emerging understanding of 'modernity' and 'progressiveness' opposed to institutions considered 'traditional' and 'backward'. In western, rural Turkey, Kimberly Hart (2007) observes that a self-chosen love-match is linked with 'modernity', while arranged marriages featuring bride wealth and polygamy increasingly carry with them the pejorative connotation of an antiquated practice. Taking account of local transformations in marriage arrangements, the author analyzes how carpet weavers construct their own understanding of modernity and describes ambiguities and creative ways to bridge the gap between personal choice and parental influence by not appearing backward, defined as *geri kafal.*

Wedding as a key site of cultural contestation not only becomes relevant as part of a generational conflict, but also on an institutional level. Albert Schrauwer's observations among the Pamonas in Central Sulawesi, Indonesia, suggest that traditional, civil and church weddings promote the constitution of a new nuclear household, "a natural unit of production and consumption and [...] the natural site of the social reproduction of kin and of gendered identities" (2000: 856). Analyzing the relation between state power and intimacy in China, Sara Friedman (2005) has detected marriage as a "powerful institution in which state regulation and sexual normalization converge to link personal desires with state goals" (ibid: 312). Among Hui people in the southeastern part of the country, she identifies a tension between the control over family planning, enabled by state surveillance on the one hand and new ideals of sexuality and conjugal relationships as a result of market reforms among village youth on the other. The author therefore highlights "an ongoing struggle over the very meaning and consequences of marriage and intimate attachments" (ibid: 323).

In Northern China, Yan (2005) explores the transformation of bride wealth, which the groom nowadays pays not to the parents, but to the bride directly. Asserting an increasingly powerful position of rural Chinese youth in marriage transactions, the author argues that the young generation utilizes Western rhetoric of individualism, introduced by state ideology, to extract marital gifts. This study highlights the interdependence between the state and individual strategies in larger social developments by highlighting the example of evolving marriage practices.

The aspect of marriage as an act of 'cultural contestation' is further documented in the context of migration, where the second generation in particular faces confrontation with conflicting systems. Bic Ngo (2002) illustrates the perspective of Hmong American female students in the Midwest United States on early marriages. With regard to class- and race-based differences as well as conflicts between and within groups, the author finds that this form of marriage is not merely perceived as a tradition of Hmong culture, but a tool to compensate their underprivileged situation within social and educational structures (ibid: 181). Similarly, in his article on Danish Pakistanis, Mikkel Rytter (2012) shows how youngsters struggle between the preferences of several institutions: families, state ideologies and their own ideals. According to the author, marriage not only constitutes a step towards maturity, but "a process where notions of identity and belonging are negotiated within local and transnational families" (ibid: 572). As a central argument, the author contends that changing priorities in spousal selection affect established family relations wherein particularly love marriage represents an act of social transformation.

Independently of the geographical and analytical context, all of the above-mentioned studies on contemporary marriage point to a clash between an emerging youth culture opposing established structures and parental authority, domestic life or state influence. Consequently, the question arises as to what renders marriage such a vivid setting for inter-generational conflicts? This particular conjuncture becomes evident in light of its principal function to acquire maturity or in the words of Sophie Roche as the "primary ritual marking the transition from childhood or youth to adulthood" (2014: 165). Taking into account the social and demographic change of Tadjik society, her analysis reveals a consistent "tension between parents and their children with regard to definitions and behavior of youth and maturity" (ibid: 197). Comparing marriage ceremonies during the Soviet period (1955 to 1991); Civil war period (1992 to 1997) and Postwar period (1998 to 2006), the author traces the way in which marriage is exposed to modernization and considers a wedding as the key event in which youth culture converge with existing authorities (ibid: 196). In the first period, marriage was largely determined by the spouses themselves, while parents maintained only a marginal role as initiators. During the civil war, a time of crisis, marriage functioned as a domestication of the young generation in response to political instability. In the postwar period, marriage rituals served for young men to display their wealth acquired abroad. Here, the author highlights the importance of marriage as an event, in which the process of maturation of the groom becomes a frequent topic for jokes amongst his peers. Roche therefore evaluates weddings as a key site to redefine their resources for gaining maturity:

"The manipulation of life-cycle rituals appears to be the strongest tool available for reshaping the junior-senior relation. Seniority is based on the control of resources and status, which is eventually contested by young people. In other words, juniors today do not need the elders' resources anymore [...] since they have multiple options open to them for manipulating their social status in other ways" (ibid: 197).

Still, long-established images about maturity including the ability to produce children and social status remain reflected in existing marriage patterns. The postwar generation, however, produces its resources for adulthood through professional achievements. Roche therefore portrays a process of youth 'detachment', which finds its expression in marriage as a "core event for negotiating generational tensions" (ibid: 186). Having presented relevant case studies of other ethnographies, I turn to the Tamil context and ask: Do contemporary trends in Indian marriage signify a transformation in its meaning for status acquisition and reaching maturity? Before elucidating the perspective of middle class youth, relevant anthropological accounts of marriage outline its changing significance through time and social context.

5.1 MARRIAGE IN SOUTH INDIA

Classical anthropological accounts of South Indian marriage have been principally dominated by two main directions [2]: the *structural* and the *transactional* approach (de Munck, 1996: 698). The former examines marriage with respect to prescribed rules as a key to understanding Indian social structure. W.H.R. Rivers (1914) has defined marriage alliances as a central implication of Indian kinship organization. Analyzing the Tamil language repertoire of kinship terms, the author relates Dravidian cross-kin alliances to the usage of local kinship classifications. The term *māmaṉ,* for instance, presents a designation used for "mother's brother" and "father in law" alike. Therefore, the author disconnects such "classificatory" terminologies from natural, descriptive kinship terminologies, based on biological consanguinity (Zeff 1999: 31).

2 Other approaches have investigated marriage in various ways: The "Indological approach", explicates ideals and practices of conjugal relations from scriptural traditions. "Feminist theorists" point to the asymmetry of conjugal relations within patriarchal family structures (Uberoi 2001: ix). Religious studies focus on mystic aspects and analyze the union with the divine sphere (Skoda 2002: 6).

Dumont makes marriage and its corresponding relationships a "focal point" for the interpretation of kinship studies in India, which he deems a "real, self-defining system whose boundary is objectively given" (1961: 76). His comparative ethnographies on North and South Indian marriage practices reveal a divergent tendency: while in the North, hierarchy seems to represent the dominant principle, in the South it is the alliance or *affinity* that appears to be primary. As outlined in chapter 3.5, the terminology of Dravidian kinship separates relatives into two categories depending on gender: parallel (through brother-brother) and cross relatives (through brother-sister) (ibid: 87). Unlike the North Indian vertical kinship system, Tamil cross-kin alliance presents a horizontal constellation and social proximity between both wife-givers and wife-takers. This complementary relationship of female and male elements has been demonstrated in terms of indigenous perceptions of blood purity, which forms the smallest entity of equivalence. In Tamil consanguinity, Fruzzetti et al. (1982: 27) distinguish two aspects:

- "utampu" (body) represents a physical and material element. It is considered a male aspect and is changeable and transferrable to the woman.

- "uyir" (spirit, movement) represents a female aspect, but remains fixed and non transferable.

The cross-kin marriage systems exhibit the combination which guarantees an equal degree of purity and has the potential to transfer the female element of spirit to descendants, so that "South Indians marry precisely those persons of equivalent purity with whom they share the least" (ibid: 14). In contrast to hypergamic[3] North Indian patterns (Dumont 1964: 92), the southern alliance is characterized by "fissiparous tendencies" and "proliferation of relatively small endogamous units" (ibid: 79). Kinship hierarchy becomes less evident in relation to marriage than is the case in comparable North Indian examples.[4] Dumont's structural interpretation reflects the analytical distinction between parallel and cross relationships and takes account of differentiations within other groups and connections, such as between consanguineous and affinal relatives, castes, sub-castes and lineages. Pointing to regular inter-group alliances in Indian society, he contends that "endogamy is to a large extent not the ultimate principle, but an

3 Hypergamy "refers to wife-giving as contributing indirectly to the status of a group perpetuating itself through males" (ibid: 98).

4 In analyzing wedding ceremonies among the Marwada Meghwal in Gujarat, Skoda finds both hierarchy and affinity as enduring principles of marriage circles.

entailment of the all-pervading status distinction" (1964: 84). In other words, Dumont argues that the status of alliances is not exclusively defined by endogamy, but rather other categories, such as legitimate and illegitimate conjugal unions. The distinction between primary and secondary marriage supports this claim.[5] While 'primary marriage' is marked by isogamy, an alliance within equal status groups, the 'secondary marriage' features an inferior rank of the wife. Among men, in turn, he draws a classification between principal marriage, secondary marriage and concubinage (1964: 82). Regarding status differentiations between those unions, he concludes: "On the whole we can posit that all castes in Hindu India recognize a type of perfect marriage, marriage par excellence, generally more strictly regulated, more solemn, more costly, representing the maximum of prestige in the given group" (ibid: 83). Endogamy, therefore, results from the pure-impure divide rather than constituting a primary principle of marriage customs.

While the structural approach rejects the reduction of complementary elements in kinship structure to decency and inheritance, transactional accounts particularly examine in which way marriage alliances are determined by socio-economic rules. Analyzing the relationship between several villages in Central Ceylon, Stanley Tambiah identifies a connection between land inheritance and kinship grouping and finds an "absence of an agnatic clustering, among the landless" (1958: 36). With a particular focus on uncle-niece marriage, William Mc Cormack (1958) presents a range of marriage statistics and findings on behavior and heritage. Kathleen Gough (1956) offers a comparison between alliances among Brahmans and lower castes. Her article considers status differences, notably between wife-givers and wife-takers as well as terminological consequences within the kinship system. Concentrating on the asymmetrical relationships between fathers and sons as well as husbands and wives and their linkage to religious values and joint land ownership, the author finds a higher position among woman within lower castes.[6] The orientation of both accounts has been described by de Munck, who contends that "structural models presume that a prescriptive rule for cross-cousin marriage is encoded in Dravidian kinship terminology, whereas transactionalists presume that the preference for cross-cousin marriage is based on local socio-economic interests" (1996: 698).

5 The primary marriage refers to the first and legitimate marriage of a woman, while the secondary marriage, the new alliance after death of the husband, involves less prestige, rituals and costs.

6 For an elaborated critique see Dumont (1964: 83ff.).

An essential aspect left out by classic theories is what Zeff (1999: 33) coined "disorder", i.e. "strategy, intention, emotion and affect" – themes that have dominated recent ethnographies on marriage. De Munck (1996: 701) critically remarks that the structural as well as the transactional approach not only presume a normative system, but reduce marriage to a purely cultural phenomenon, separated from love as a psychological experience. Consequently, love remained incompatible with social mechanisms of cohesion and isolated from academic discussions about marriage. Reviewing Tamil preferential marriages in the region of Madurai, Clark-Decès has expounded the misapprehension of classic kinship studies in "focus[ing] on more formal terminology or on its structural expression" (2014: 163), neglecting local dynamics and kinship patterns. Her analysis, which examines three cross kin alliances – male ego with the daughter of the mother's brother, of the older sister and of the father's sister – reveals that each constellation "comes with its own cosmology, sociology and psychology" (ibid: 165). Further, the author points to a widely neglected aspect of consanguineous marriages, notably the differentiation *among* relatives. Within the Kaḷḷar community, priorities of certain kin through hereditary aspects or specific relationships pose the question of marrying "the right spouse" (2014). Such explanation patterns suggest that relatives, compatible for marriage, are not defined merely by blood, but also their equal status. Therefore, the author finds that "consanguinity has less social and emotional force than conjugality" (ibid: 168). The religious context buttresses her assertion: observing festive events in the region of Madurai, such as the wedding between Meenakshi and Lord Sundareswarar or the journey of Meenakshi's brother Alagar, Clark-Decès posits that in those rituals, consanguinity is not necessarily attributed a symbolic value and therefore plays a minor role.

With an increasing awareness for deviations, academics from various disciplines explored the connection between privacy, emotion, sexuality, economic change, state regulations and ideologies (Hart 2007: 345). A range of studies focuses on the question of whether the rise of individualism serves as a space for romantic love and whether such developments overcome prescribed social boundaries. The "sociological theories of modernization" (Uberoi 2011 a: ix) comprise one such outcome from this debate and presume a conversion from arranged marriage to love-matches. Adherents to this line of argumentation classify arranged marriage as a cornerstone of tradition and love marriage as a modern innovation (Zeff 1999: 33). One of the main advocates is Anthony Giddens (1992) who argues that familial ethos has been replaced by an individualistic notion. In "The transformation of intimacy", the author regards changes in conjugal relationships as a manifestation of the global phenomenon in which marriage is transforming into a pure relationship for the sake of its own. Within this context, emotional intimacy and fundamental changes in conjugal life appear as symbols of modernity, marked by individualism and ideology of choice. Romantic love, smaller households and nuclear families therefore present features of a counter-model to collectivist norms and practices.

Empirical evidence has failed to support the classification of individualism together with love-marriage und the concept of modernity on the one hand opposed to a family orientation and arranged-marriage subsumed under the idea of backwardness on the other. Pointing to Tamil epics and poems reaching back to the time before the Arian invasion, Zeff shows that in that period, romantic love played a far more significant role than in contemporary alliances (1999: 34). Drawing a historical overview of marriage patterns in the middle ages and Enlightenment in Europe, which never experienced a transition from traditional to modern forms of conjugal relationships, Clark-Decès states that "the grand historical modernization narrative turned out to be a myth" (2014: 171). Presenting contrasting attitudes among Brahmins towards child marriages that were restraint by the Sarda Act in 1929[7], Fuller and Narasimhan (2008) find that their respondents even attribute a higher emotional content to those previous unions. In fact, they expressed a "greater affection and intimacy, because in the years between the wedding and consummation, partners saw each other only intermittently, so that their desire to be together grew" (ibid: 738). The significance of self-chosen and elopement marriage in India today has received wide attention in academic circles and will be discussed in a closing digression (section 8.5).

Despite overcoming sociological theories of modernization, a challenging task in the anthropological discipline remains the examination of the way in which global and modern processes influence and shape ideals and practices of marriage. In an historical overview Rochona Majumdar (2009) identifies contemporary marriage forms as a "process of change in the history of a practice that drew on past and contemporary resources in order to be a functioning element of Indian modernity" (ibid: 4).[8] Correspondingly, Clark Decès has

7 This regulation fixed the minimum age for marriage at 14 years of age for girls and 18 for boys.

8 The principal factors which have enhanced current developments in Indian marriage in the last century include: "urban life, western education, print media (the publishing of matrimonial advertisements seeking brides and grooms), monetization of relationships (the escalation in the practice of dowry), cultivation of distinction and

shown how the essential linkage between marriage and status finds its expression in the modern context among the Kaḷḷar community in South India: ceremonial gift exchanges replace banking systems, kinship rights are treated in modern courtrooms and established ranks are negotiated with the demands of dowry. The author, therefore, finds that "it is no wonder that the standard opposition between the "traditional" and the "modern" [...] is foreign to my consultants' real experience and worldview" (2014: 171). Other studies on social transformations in the marriage context concentrate on education and employment (Kapadia 1993), the shortage of desirable grooms, competition between brides (Zeff 1999: 34), daughter deficits and state regulations such as the Sarda Act or the significance of ancestral status and family background (Fuller 2008: 743).

Studies among the urbanized and educated population pursued a particular focus on how contemporary marriage practices enhance the construction of a middle-class identity. Scholars who elaborate worldviews formulated in the course of alliance-making among members of this social category anticipate a valuable insight "into how modern socioeconomic class identities are created and performed within a segment of Indian society that is projected to become three-quarters of India's urban population by 2025" (Wilson 2013: 47). Leading studies have been carried out under aspects of social mobility (Osella & Osella 2000), consumption (Brosius 2010), or the definition and realization of the 'modern self' (Donner 2008). A series of phenomena challenge traditional Tamil marriages, including: a higher level of female education, delayed marriage, the abandonment of labor, particularly in the agriculture sector in favor of industrialization, the proliferation of dowry and an increase in internal family conflicts (Clark-Decès 2014: 159). These key points present important aspects of the principal focus of this paper, namely the perspective of the younger generation with respect to matchmaking practices today. The next section therefore explores how present marriage practices are experienced among young academics and their families in prospecting a suitable alliance.

cultural capital (debates of what constitutes a tasteful wedding), and law (certain legal reforms to do with property and ideas of rights and personhood)" (ibid: 2).

5.2 KIN OR NON-KIN MARRIAGE: CONFLICTING STATUS ASPIRATIONS IN TAMIL NADU

Notwithstanding various and often contradictory intentions, the forging of alliances in Tamil culture circulates around one central principle: the maintenance of *family status,* which is defined by the concept of *māṉam*. Translated primarily as "dignity", *māṉam* also connotes the notion of "honor" or "modesty". While Western Enlightenment philosophers formulated dignity as an abstract notion, in the Tamil context, it is related to daily characteristics and practices. It presents an aspired virtue that must be continuously maintained by correct behavior toward others, by keeping promises, providing help or telling the truth. A dignified person receives *mariyātai*, a concept similar to "respect".[9] Mariyātai is expressed by the respectful address of *Sir* or *ammā*, polite requests to leave and enter a space (*pōṅka/vāṅka*), and considerate behavior, for example through the invitation to functions.

In secular contexts, māṉam is reformulated in terms of employment, propriety, schooling, or professional competence and acquired by a combination of style, consumption, computer skills and an acceptance of civil, moral and even conservative conduct (Clark-Decès 2014: 149). Within educational institutions, it is practiced and reinforced by respectful behavior toward teachers and degree holders (Jeffery 2005: 30). Rajendran, who assisted his professor with translations, explained to me, "If I commit to something and I don't do it by the agreed time, I lose my māṉam. I recently had to correct a paper for my college, but I couldn't finish the work on time. This is equal to an insult for me!" Moreover, 'bad' habits like drinking or smoking might ruin the māṉam. Importantly, it is not the misbehavior itself, but the performance of such practices in an inappropriate context. In fact, the consumption of alcohol or cigarettes might even be tolerated if acted out in a decent and in a 'suitable' way. Excessive drinking often resulting in drunken staggering, swearing or even harassing people, severely damages one's māṉam. A similar observation can be found in North India in the example of *ijjat*, the equivalent concept of prestige. Next to several components like landownership, wealth, education and employment, Marguerite Roulet defines ijjat as "not static but [...] directly emergent from people's actions" (Roulet, 1996: 94).

In Tamil everyday life, māṉam does not refer to the individual, but is extended to the social environment, including family, kin, caste, religious

---

9   Literally translated as "limit" or "boundary", *mariyātai* has acquired the more general meaning of "propriety", "respect", "deference", "honor" (Appadurai 1976: 197).

community or village. Poor conduct by a single person might result in severe consequences for his or her relatives. Gokulam, whose older sister had eloped with a drunkard, explained to me, "Because of her, we lost our māṉam. When she misbehaves or does something inacceptable within our society or our social construction, this is like an insult. By eloping, she has spoiled our māṉam, our family māṉam." Family status basically signifies a *collective* form of māṉam, notably the "reputation of the family with its immediate vicinity, [which contains a] sense of a strong, interdependent relationship between the individual and the social" (Zeff 1995: 64). Rather than being economically well-off or educated, families should uphold their status through polite and respectable behavior towards their neighbors, a helpful attitude and active participation in public affairs. In a concrete sense, māṉam depends largely on the behavior of women. A 'good' family status is secured by the observation of female ideals, particularly patience, chastity, gentle speech, modesty, obedience, the performance of her domestic duties and hospitality toward guests. Extra-marital affairs, on the other hand, might ruin the reputation of her husband and other members. Māṉam attached to male behavior, in contrast, is acquired and limited to men: the husband upholds his māṉam by accomplishing his duties as a provider. Nevertheless, a woman's failure equally affects the dignity of her relatives, as Jacobson observed, "Guided by traditional concepts of proper feminine behavior and aware that their actions are inextricably linked to family honor, prestige, and ultimately material, women typically carry out their roles as chaste daughters and dutiful wives" (1977: 8). In fact, deeper conversations with my female study participants revealed that women perceive themselves as safeguards of the family's māṉam, a responsibility, restriction and source of pressure alike.

During the matchmaking process, family status presents a decisive criterion since it affects not only other kin, but also the image of the in-law family. Personal qualities of a bride or groom are less defined by his or her actual behavior and more so by external standards linked to the family's reputation. Correspondingly, Zeff contends that "the idea of individual character depended largely on how others perceived the individual" (1999: 66). To a large extent, 'being good' describes a person whose family adheres to local conventions of giving respect and maintaining one's dignity. To find out about family's reputation, most families avoid direct face-to-face interactions and instead request the opinions of others in the social vicinity (see chapter 7). Therefore, it is not surprising when Wilson (2013: 59) observes that "middleclass people with unmarried children often spoke about the need to control household members' public behavior in order to create an image that would be salutary when marriages were arranged."

While in consanguineous marriages, both wife-givers and takers determine family reputation, the maintenance of this image grows complicated against the background of a trend towards *non-kin marriages*. In a nostalgic way, respondents described the matchmaking procedure as an enclosed system within a bounded community, like Navaneethan, one bridal father in my neighborhood:

> "In our time, marriage circles took place within 300 km maximum. We were not supposed to marry in a distance place, when we do not know the other family. The principle is universal brotherhood: we belong to one family, 'your friend is my friend and my friend is your friend'".

He went on describing the change toward consumption-driven marriages, motivated by material desire and aspiration for status and prestige:

> "Those things are gradually getting diluted. As our transportation and communication levels expand – from the hamlet of 30 km radius, we go to one hundred, 200, 500 km, then to all of India, now the whole world. We can have a groom in the US or Germany, we can communicate through the net and you can look for a spouse everywhere. So the world has shrunk. So my daughter goes everywhere within 16 hrs. If I want I can also go."

Especially among educated sections of the population, the preference for a horizontal relationship between cross-kin of common caste, class and religion is declining and becoming replaced by a priority for educational background, profession and financial power (Béteille 1996: 162ff.). That tendency is accompanied by "radical reformulations of marriage and family life in Tamil society" (Clark-Decès 2014: 163), considering the far-reaching relevance of consanguineous arrangements in Tamil everyday life. With a particular focus on childhood, Alex (2009: 106ff.) describes how a jocular relationship among cross cousins at a young age enhances emotions of cohesion and closeness. Ritual implementations through mutual visits between cross kin after initiation ceremonies have been studied by de Munck (1996: 708). Other ethnographies specifically highlighted the gendered aspect of consanguineous marriages, notably the comparatively high status of woman (Wadley 1991, Kolenda 1984). My host mother's sister Victoria, who recently married off her two sons, the first to his second cross cousin and the second to a non-kin spouse, described the social implications of kin alliances in Madurai:

"If we marry among relatives, there will be more affection and love. There will be a good mutual understanding. Positive and negative sides of the bride and groom will be known to each other from childhood. If some issues arise, they can be easily solved. Status between both is equal and relatives of the groom and the bride will be the same people. So the relationship will get stronger."

She further pointed out the intimacy and responsibility within the extended family in cross-kin marriages, which is considered less strong in marriages between unfamiliar families:

"Someday, I will be very old. My daughter-in-law, as a relative, will be helpful for me. This is a great help, whereas brides from an unknown family won't care for me. And if she gives care, it won't be like a relative girl who has more affection and love towards me."

Local explanation patterns about the trends towards non-kin arrangements differed among students. One frequent argument, connected to Western medical discourse about genetic defects, lies in avoiding the risk of developing "physical disabilities" (Zeff 1999: 88). Among the middle class in Madurai, Wilson (2013: 38) identifies "urban cultural associations made between 'sophistication', 'modernity', and 'non-kin marriage'". Exploring matchmaking trends in Kerala, Osella and Osella (2000) come to a similar result and state that Izhava distance themselves from kinship marriages as a form of social mobility. In order to prove their 'educated attitude', this community openly associated kinship marriages with 'backwardness'. Cross cousin marriages are considered a "second rate arrangement" and "uncultured, shameful, backward" (ibid: 90). In contrast they rate alliances with strangers outside the village, ideally with title and money, as prestigious. Apart from preventing physical deformation, students and their families expressed their concern about conflicts within close family circles as a reason to opt for non-kin marriages. Those who had the choice between more than one cross cousin as a marriage partner aimed to avoid competition and jealousy among their family members. Finally, most assumed that, in non-kin alliances, a wife finds herself less pressured by her own family to tolerate any abuse (Fuller & Narasimhan 2008: 742). That view contrasts the findings of Kapadia, who argues that non-kin marriages have led to a devaluation of women's traditionally high status. In Aruloor, a rural Tamil village, women become an economic burden for their parents since they are unable to compensate the dowry that well-educated grooms often demand (1993: 38ff.). Assuming a male perspective, Roger (2008: 84) has observed difficulties for Scheduled Caste men, who feel too educated to marry a girl from their own community, and at the same time lack the necessary cultural capital or caste background to find a companionate wife from a socially higher community.

In Madurai, the priority for non-kin marriages has transformed the forming of an alliance into a considerably exhausting affair. Wilson recognizes among her guest family that "due to this change in marriage preference, matchmaking has surfaced as an intricate and time-consuming cultural practice" (2013: 38). In fact, the trend to choose partners outside their own family caused permanent uncertainty because of the higher risk of falsified information about the in-laws. Repeated checks and visits become more and more difficult, particularly when the in-law family lives in a distant place. Navaneethan, who married his daughter off to a migrant worker, expressed his concerns to me: "I am unsure of her security. In the new place the groom will be far away on the other side of the globe. So I ask myself all the time: is the security good? Will my daughter be safe in the hands of those people? Do I have any control over the situation if there is something wrong?" The increasing suspicion toward unfamiliar families might explain the need for detailed inquiries, hasty cancellation and severe conflicts regarding financial transactions. Victoria explained this ambiguous feeling by pointing to the differences between kin and non-kin marriage:

> "In the case of Stephen (first son), there are no big formalities because we are relatives ... but for John (second son), everything went according to the custom. The first time, my husband Bobby and I visited the bride's family, then we took John there, then they came here to our house. I invited all my brothers and both the families had a talk, it was seven or eight visits, we both made before the marriage."

Formalities and the importance of the correct exertion of marriage ceremonies seem to have a stabilizing effect on the perceived uncertainty towards a marriage arrangement with non-relatives. Another feature is the emergence of additional ritual events, for instance, the recently established *poṉṉu āḷaikka pōratu*, the departure of the bride, accompanied by "ritual weepings" (Kolenda 1984: 111). Originally practiced in Northern parts of India, this performative act has been increasingly adopted in the South. Instead of staying nearby their natal kin, brides find themselves confronted by an unknown family and residing in a distant place. Sinjuta's sister, whose family chose a groom for her, expressed her sadness to leave the house permanently: "They are not well known to me ... This is why I am crying".

All in all, recent trends have complicated the maintenance of māṉam, as class mobility induced most families to marry according to 'modern' customs and to engage in uncertain non-kin alliances. In the words of Filippo and

Caroline Osella, contemporary matchmaking becomes a delicate affair, "a public performance which can enhance a family's social status but which might also damage their reputation" (2000: 73). Limitations in the ability to verify economic achievements and the maintenance of local status obligations comprise a principal challenge for young spouses. The search for a groom for the youngest sister, Suganth, within my own host family presented a vivid example of this challenge because her high degree (MPhil) made it very difficult to find a suitable groom among her own kin. Due to her prolonged education, she had already crossed the age of 30 and thus was in a delayed state in the marriage-seeking process. Additionally, her position as an administrative employee at a private institution only offered her a limited contract, which made her working situation unstable. This balancing act equally affects men with an academic background, whose lifestyle is characterized by an extension of youth. Clark-Decès delineates the severe pressure for male academics in their late 1920s who still do not have a steady job. Higher degrees, employment and social standing become principal obstacles to getting married (ibid: 146ff.). This fate is shared by their counterparts in the North: Jeffrey points out that highly educated Jats are considered overqualified for manual labor (2010: 81ff.). Due to their prolonged state of unemployment, they are rejected on the marriage market, as parents of the bride look for a groom with a secure income. In Kerala, this perpetual limbo presents a particularly awkward situation, since marriage and parenthood signify "requirements of adult status" (Osella & Osella 2000: 81).[10]

Turning to the perspective of my respondents, the following section elucidates the position of students and their explanation patterns of significant changes, notably priorities and processes of spouse selection, wedding ceremonies and the articulation of romantic feelings. My observations demonstrate that alterations in marriage practices are not comparable to those in other countries. Therefore, I close this outline by mentioning the statement by Clark-Decès in advance, notably that "Tamil youth neither grow up, nor marry like their peers in other cultural and social contexts, whether in the West or anywhere else" (2014: 151).

10 Marriage as a major event for status change has been indicated in other ethnographical contexts: Roche (2014: 172) sketches this new social position with a description of the transformation for young men after marriage in Tadjik society: "the wedding allows a man to have legitimate sexual intercourse, start a separate family and thereafter a separate household, gain full membership in the local community, and eventually obtain access to land and to other resources."

6. Reflections on compatibility: The students' perspective

"Some expect a spouse from a local town. Some expect the spouse to work in the same place. Some want fair girls. All these things make our business difficult. If everything goes well, then there is a horoscope matching... If a groom is educated up to a graduate degree, then he expects at least an undergraduate girl. Skin texture also plays a role. Some grooms say that the bride is too fat when they are thin. A groom's family that is in the field of business never looks for a government bride and vice versa ... If both families are in business, then they will look for equal financial status. If the parents of a bride or groom are doctors, then they expect their spouse's parents to be doctors or engineers."
(Balamurugan, marriage assembler, Meenakshi temple)

In conjunction with the trend toward non-kin marriages, conflicting priorities for equal status, physical appearance and economic achievements arose. For the present generation of the educated middle class in Madurai, this development turned the search for a partner into a strenuous endeavor. The present chapter, therefore, attends to the postulated need "to organize the complicated socioeconomic and social position of middle-class Tamils via world views and lifestyles expressed during matchmaking events" (Wilson 2013: 47). A central feature relates to the emerging involvement of marriage assemblers. Far from merely presenting a facilitator to find a groom or bride today, those actors monitor the procedure by imposing new criteria on what constitutes a good match, as well as categories and models of explanation for a promising alliance. With the help of profiles, platforms and match booklets, I detect new vocabulary and usage of words formulating a proper match. Based on the argumentation and justifications expressed by students, families, assemblers and astrologers for their respective selections, I outline current aspirations in contemporary alliance-making among the students. Notwithstanding deviations and developments, the chapter highlights the impact of exposure and new models of explanation for evaluating the compatibility between spouses.

Typically, the matchmaking procedure takes an average of forty days to five months. In most cases, it starts by handing the profile to a trustworthy mediator or a professional marriage assembler. In Madurai, such brokers are organized in ranked categories and acquire the corresponding set of clients. Most assembler offices contain a range of different profiles, labeled according to caste, gender, religion and educational status. Consulting an assembler requires a certain 'code of conduct'. Families carefully select the right people and social constellations for the visit in order to demonstrate their integrity and to avoid misunderstandings. A groom who looks for profiles together with a male friend, for instance, might create the impression of a dubious character who merely enjoys looking at pictures of young, single women. Assemblers welcome interested customers by presenting their conditions, procedure and special offers. With the exception of voluntary assemblers, most charge a registration fee, according to the educational status of the customer and the success of the arrangement. Rates start from approximately 30 Rs for simply looking at profiles and can reach 500 Rs for registering a person's own data together with a photograph. Those costs cover copies of pictures, digitalizing profiles, the salary for assistants and other staff members, gas for courier services, postal fees and financial loss. Usually, brokers demand an additional charge after a successful confirmation of the marriage.

Table 3: Types of marriage assemblers

Voluntary assemblers	Voluntary assemblers carry out their activity free of charge and usually address members of their own community or religion. Such brokers typically consist of businessmen who accumulated considerable wealth and contain a collection of profiles from their customers. Mostly, they keep the folders in a room or building adjacent to their office. Motivated by the idea of strengthening their own community or religious group, their orientation stands in contrast to the rather 'money minded' match-makers.
Temple/church based assemblers	As a structured section of voluntary assemblers, most operate their offices near frequented religious institutions. In Madurai, the Church of South India (C.S.I.) Cathedral represents one such famous address and promotes significant networks amongst its members and influential personalities. Recognized as a reputable and trustworthy

	agency, its staff workers provide a well-researched database about Christian brides and grooms in Madurai and South India. Although their engagement is understood as a voluntary service, the institution entertains an effective system of profile distribution: every Saturday, Church members run several tables in the inner building and assist marriage aspirants in registration, selection and contacting potential in-law families. Each profile is marked by a number. If a client is interested in one profile, church assemblers send a 'letter of inquiry' to the chosen family by enclosing a short form with principal details of the aspirant. They charge a handling fee, which covers expenses for papers, envelopes and postal charges.
Professional assemblers	Full-time assemblers, who acquire and offer profiles as a profitable business, represent the professionalized counterpart of voluntary brokers. Those agents are mostly organized in wider networks. The area in Annanagar, in Madurai New Town, for instance, is covered by 'Sri Rajeswari Matrimonials'. Its owner Ganesh started his business in 1999. His office contains around 50,000 profiles. For effective profile mediation, Ganesh cooperates with so called 'sub-brokers', local assemblers working in a particular area, neighborhood or community. This joint work is based on supplemental foci: while professionalized brokers have access to a wider range of profiles, small scale assemblers entertain a personal and closer contact to the immediate vicinity. Due to their diversified business structure, they cover the widest range of clients throughout all castes, classes and religions.
State-wide agencies	The next level is composed of assemblers who operate in an entire district, state or even across the country. In the region of Madurai, approximately 300 such assemblers can be found, while their total number in the state is estimated at 1,500. Throughout India, they are united by a nationwide association. Similar to a union, this platform endows its members with a vocational identity that guarantees several advantages, including access to a bank loan or financial support in case of an emergency or bankruptcy. Further, the association facilitates the

	cooperation and profile exchange. With their trans-regional focus, they mainly attract sections of the middle class.
Virtual platforms	Websites like barathmatrimony.com or sadi.com are mostly consulted by the upper middle class or migrants who have internet access. While such pages are accessible across different states, most agencies additionally set up local branches in a certain state or region. One example is the Tamil section of matrimony.com. These offices are usually located in commercial buildings or shopping complexes. A lack of transparency in regards to those profiles renders their usage a perilous affair and constitutes the downside of this virtual service. Most of my study participants, therefore, preferred local assemblers who were considered more reliable and personally accountable.

For an appealing design of profiles, assemblers disclose proven 'gimmicks' to marriage aspirants. Such advice includes the design of the picture, application of magniloquent terms for their profession, regulating imbalances and perilous elements of the horoscope or even altering the age. Above all, assemblers assist their clients in evaluating potential partners. Based on their experience and memory, they perform a professional assessment of the match. This consultancy may be particularly helpful in delicate situations, as for example in the case of a second and inter-caste alliance or inauspicious horoscopes. In the case of successful arrangement, both families ceremonially express their gratitude and honor with *dhotis*, garlands and money for the broker. Regarding the growing uncertainty with respect to unfamiliar in-law families, assemblers assume the function of increasing the reliability of the information received, as my 62 year-old host father explained:

"In those days [when he got married], we never had these kinds of marriage assemblers. It was through word of mouth among the relatives. But now, the radius has been extended and these marriage assemblers are used. In our time, it was 300 kilometers – now it is even extended to a 2000 kilometer radius. Actually, we were not supposed to marry in a distance place when we do not know the other family. Now we do. We will enquire about her and her family. So we ensure ourselves ... we carefully go through all those details and see whether she fits for our boy."

This popularity evokes negative resentments, too, and gives the assembler an ambivalent image. Apart from disagreements concerning rates, dubious business strategies can raise suspicions of fraudulent intent. Their modification of profiles and the interference in the matchmaking process can take on the character of persuasion in favor of a particular spouse. In Kerala, the Osellas even experienced that their respondents designated and insulted assemblers as "pimps" (2000: 166). Complains are not one-sided, but expressed also in the opposite direction, due to the fact that a great number of assemblers perceive their own efforts as utterly underestimated. In problematic cases like incomplete profiles, prolonged searches for a match or unsuccessful alliances, brokers feel misused as scapegoats. Frequently, they accuse their customers of stubbornness and obstinacy. Allegedly nasty customers waste their time due to wrong details, continuous demands and complaints or negotiations about the payment. Such difficulties urge brokers to adopt precautions, such as withholding concrete details (picture of the bride, address and number) and handing out the originals after payment. In order to inspire confidence in their reliability, some brokers would contact the potential in-law family in front of the aspirants to verify the indicated data.

Notwithstanding their controversial image, the significance of assemblers and their strategies shape and reflect current preferences in spouse selection. The profile form of 'Sri Rajeswari Matrimonials' provides a vivid point of orientation among my conversation partners. This document lists the principal data required for evaluating a poruttam (match), which I divide into four categories: social, professional, physical and astrological compatibility – this categorization shall structure the wide-ranging criteria for choosing a spouse and serve as a foundation of discussion with my respondents.

The following data highlight students' expectations and preferences, shaped by exposure (*nēroḷivāyppu*) and class-related standards. The opportunity to witness the matchmaking strategies of three middle class families provided me with profound insights into the matchmaking process: my host parents and the families of Suresh and Prasenna. Those observations turned out to be illuminating case studies for examining differing views on spouse selection. Notably, students apply ongoing discourse located within the 'modern sphere' to the matchmaking process by emphasizing the importance of personal desires or equal power constellations within conjugal life. At the same time, I turn to divergent opinions and struggles, partly determined by caste and gendered background. In sum, I intend to illustrate the peculiar way by which Tamil youth reconcile individual aspirations acquired in the educational context with existing social boundaries.

Table 4: List of profile data (Example: Sri Rajeswari Matrimonials)

Sri Rajeswari marriage information center
(Sri Rajeswari marriage assemblers union)

Name	caste	date
Lineage	age	
Education	skin color	height
Place of work	job profile	
Institution's name	monthly income	
Father (alive)	job	
Mother (alive)	job	
Siblings: male, female, married		
Origine or native	Present residence	
Bride groom or bride's wealth		
Expectations:		
skin color	height	education
job profiles	area or location	jewels
Details of the tāli (Sovereigns[1] offered)		
Naṭcattiram	rāci	lakṉam
Place of birth	Time of birth	
Day	Date of birth	
Planet constellation		
Irāci	navāmsam	
Contact details	address	e-mail

1 The Sovereign is the face value of a British coin with a total weight of approximately eight grams.

6.1 "NO SIBLINGS PLEASE" – SOCIAL AND FAMILIAL CONCERNS

Nearly all students expressed their preference for a spouse from a similar place of origin; if the family's reputation (*mā<u>n</u>am*) is acknowledged within one particular area, the alliance stabilizes the local status in political and economic terms. Usually, the young couple possesses lands or titles. Above, a similar geographic background secures a harmonious conjugal life; in the event of domestic conflicts, it is likely to call on a relative or neighbor to act as a mediator and reconcile the conflict. In contrast, spouses from distant places provoke suspicion and critique, which endangers family reputation and social life.

Importantly, the place of origin not only plays a major role in evaluating the perspective of the alliance, but defines the character of the in-law family (Zeff 1999: 66). The question, "*enta ūr*"? ("Which place are you from"?), initiates almost every conversation between two strangers and signifies more than mere verbiage. It locates the conversation partner within a network of friends and relatives by inquiring about family background, kinship constellations, customs and finally their reputation in society (Gorringe 2005: 172). Literally translated as "origin", the term *ūr* has a distinctive meaning in the Tamil context: it designates a "person-centrically" defined location (Daniel 1984: 68), notably a unity of *substances*[2] that are instantaneously linked to the physical substances of its residents (ibid: 77).[3] If one of its members leaves the locality and remains away for a long time, the person risks a permanent rupture with locally-established alliances (ibid: 102).[4] For male respondents, the region of Madurai as a place of origin is associated with the prospect of a particularly promising match, since the expression '*Madurai po<u>nn</u>u*' stands for a woman adhering to female virtues.

A facile conjugal life is further guaranteed by caste endogamy, which ensures a family's prestige in their community as well as personal satisfaction.

2 Valentine assumes "substances" as cultural units on a "suprapersonal and infrapersonal level", inherent to every entity (1984: 2).

3 Correspondingly, Kallars from Usilampatty for instance do not marry Kallars from distant places like Melur, Easanattu or Tanjavoor.

4 The term kirāmam stands in contrast to this phenomenon; although equally translated with "origin", it signifies "bounded, standard, universally accepted and constant spatial units" (ibid: 68).

Hema, Prakash's sister from the Piḷḷaimār community, justified her priority for a husband of the same jāṭi with a sense of autonomy:

"We always preferred to have the same community because the habits and beliefs are the same. So the girl wouldn't find it hard to live in a different family. Suppose, if I married into a Ceṭṭiyār community: even though they are very good friends of ours, they have different customs and different beliefs so everybody has to adapt to these beliefs. And mostly Ceṭṭiyār women live in a joint family. They still share everything and even though conflicts are there, they try to compromise within the same house. So it is our sense of individuality that is the problem. They cannot adapt to other ways and culture."

Particularly within the academic and urban context, however, Indian sociologists have highlighted the diminishing role of endogamy in favor of preferences for degree, profession and salary. Indications of jāti become increasingly permeable, especially through abandoning traditional occupations (Fuller 1996). In North India, Prem Chowdhry (2009) remarks that "on the one hand, caste solidarities are crystallizing and on the other education, reservation, and opening up of the economy are eroding solidarities, by changing the material base of different caste groups" (ibid: 296). Donner (2008: 63) reveals a declared subversion of caste endogamy among Bengali students, while in Madurai Wilson (2013: 38) finds that middle class Brahmins regard a high income as more important than caste. At the same time, in-depth studies have shown that jāṭi remains paramount as an indication of identity. Among employees in the IT sector in Chennai, Fuller underlines the increasing importance of caste endogamy: "For the majority of middle-class Indians, arranged endogamous marriage remains the norm, in both preference and practice" (2008: 750).

In which way do changing priorities affect youth attitudes towards caste endogamy? My conversations revealed that evaluations of community background remain context-related. Within campus, where romantic affairs pervade, students expressed their preference for mutual affection, as Soundariya emphasized, "I don't care about which caste he is from. Not his community, skin type, body structure, nothing. I just want his full heart, he has to love me and I have to truly love him." This declared openness and tolerance towards inter-caste marriage can be regarded as an indication of identity for the status of paṭiccavaṅka and his 'modern' attitude (*taṟkālattavar*). Thus, Osella and Osella have shown that inter-caste marriage even presents evidence of social mobility (2000: 115f). Exploring the impact of education on gender roles and partner selection in Bhubaneswar, however, Susan Seymour (1999: 196) points to the gap between public denial of caste and the actual desire of marrying within the same community. Not surprisingly, in Tamil Nadu, endogamy remains paramount within academic circles. Modern facilities and the use of internet and profiles even enhance the selection of a particular jāti. Matrimonial sites and marriage assemblers provide caste-specific records and internet domains. According to Fuller and Narasimhan (2008), this trend is shaped by a "pervasive assumption that they can rely on their now global network to find suitable partners within the subcaste" (ibid: 742). Apart from controversial viewpoints, the importance of endogamy varies according to the particular caste and economic background. Indeed, certain combinations are likely established and accepted. One example is the frequent alliance between Piḷḷaimār and Paṟaiyar castes. The former are considered profit–orientated, which makes them compatible with the comparatively highly educated and economically successful Paṟaiyar. Merchant castes like Nāṭār instead remain amongst themselves as inter-caste relations might affect their internal community business networks.

Students articulate endogamy not primarily in terms of physical distance. Instead, they refer to the mentioned 'ascribed' caste characteristics. An educated Paṟaiyar spouse might be rejected because of her allegedly furious mentality, a groom from the Piramalai kaḷḷar community appears suspicious for his anticipated savagery and a Piḷḷaimār family will be avoided because of their tendency to cause trouble in the locality. Moreover, endogamy is motivated by a sense of responsibility and maturity. For most parents, denial of the importance of jāti is considered as a sign of juvenile behavior. Suresh's mother explained her perspective to me: "They (students) don't know the seriousness of life. Only after some time, when they are in the process of forming an alliance, will they know about the importance of caste and such formalities. Then, caste won't be something backward, but an important factor, which they do not follow only in order to show respect for their parents, but because they know how society works." This statement reiterates the function of marriage as a key event for entering into maturity and becoming socially upright.

While endogamy ensures harmony and a balanced conjugal life, religious considerations play a minor role for most young people in the study. This unbiased attitude partly stems from the fact that in everyday practices, Indians do not always adhere to one bounded religion. Exploring the theistic richness of the divine, Axel Michaels highlights the "oscillating and porous equitheism" (1998: 233) as an essential entity of Hinduism. In that sense, the divine is never ascertainable and therefore not monotheistic. Several gods and goddesses can be worshipped at the same time and the devout may perceive themselves as Hindu and Buddhist alike. Religious adherence is exemplified by the ambiguous answers of Newar people who respond simply with "yes" to the question to which religion they actually belong (ibid). Accordingly, in Madurai, Hindu family branches that converted to Christianity do not abandon Hindu practices, but rather consider themselves "half-half".

Yet, religious institutions present important hubs of power and authority, so that most candidates opt for a partner whose relatives have a good reputation in a church, temple or mosque. Concerning the execution of the wedding, religious background may become salient. Notably, the choice of conducting a Hindu, Muslim or Christian ceremony affects the political status of the couple. Communities registered as Scheduled Castes for instance, must present themselves as a member of the Hindu community in order to claim their advantages from the government. If the in-law family insists on conducting the wedding in a Christian manner, they risk losing those privileges. Preferences for the same religious affinity, therefore, are largely motivated by pragmatic reasons due to its effect on everyday life, as explained by Soundariya: "I cannot imagine getting married to a Muslim man because their ways of living are totally different. They go to a mosque and then they make biryani[5] every day and they are always in a group. I couldn't adapt to that kind of living."

Place of origin, caste and religion present common parameters for evaluating the compatibility of both spouses in terms of social background. Nowadays, marriage aspirants additionally inquire into the family constellation itself. A recent and salient concern for female conversation partners in particular related to the number and marital status of additional family members. In fact, one of the first answers in conversations about their marital desires was simply "no siblings". Traditionally, brothers and sisters-in-law induce additional duties, responsibilities and pressure. Firstly, the marital status of siblings affects the position of the young bride in her new home. Particularly in non-kin marriages, spouses find themselves as strangers, lacking the traditional support from their own siblings.[6] Secondly, doubts toward siblings-in-law not only stem from power constellations within the household, but include economic concerns as well. Throughout all communities of my respondents, siblings get married according to a certain chronological order[7]: Usually, older siblings marry first, but sisters before brothers, if the age difference is not too high. The main reason for parents to prioritize the coupling of their daughters in marriage is the huge financial and social pressure that requires the commitment of all family members. In case the son marries first instead, this familial responsibility affects

5 Mixed rice dish.

6 Typically, sisters help each other in the chores and brothers solved conjugal conflicts.

7 This order varies for reasons like individual priorities, family pressure, job facilities or also unexpected situations like a sudden death.

his married spouse who has to fear for her own dowry and assets that she brought into the conjugal relationship (see also Osella & Osella 2000: 101). Uma summarized her concerns against a *nāttaṉār* (sister–in-law): "If my husband has many siblings, I have to follow many customs. And if I have many (younger) sisters who will get married after me, then my husband has to help them. Also, we need to give costly presents for the children ... so we don't like to marry a spouse who has lots of siblings."

Aspirations concerning the social background of the spouse reveal a strong attention to the family status, which is safeguarded by a common caste, place of origin and religious background. Above, respondents articulate personal priorities by considering daily routines, familial obligations and the character of the spouse, which they link to jāti characteristics, religion and social environment.

6.2 EDUCATION, CAREER AND DOWRY

Next to social conditions of the spouses, economic parameters increasingly gain importance in matchmaking strategies, particularly among the Tamil middle class. Thus, education presents a key factor for defining a match. Suresh, who originally studied hotel management, felt that his parents persuaded him to finish an MBA degree, exclusively to raise his chances on the marriage market: "They want me to do an MBA because when they search for a match for me, they proudly can say that 'my son is doing an MBA'. But I know that the salary I will get here is definitely less than what I earned before. Still, I need some prestige." According to assembler Ganesh, both bride and groom should be educated "to be of the same mind". Indicated in profiles, it is the degree itself which is matched, irrespective of the content and prospect of the study course. For their conjugal life, graduates prefer a similar academic background and income. Education and earnings potential, however, is formulated in conjunction with local gender norms. Importantly, grooms should be slightly more highly qualified than brides. An opposite constellation is regarded as problematic: "Men don't want their wife to have a higher education than they have themselves because they think that the wife will dominate them," Prasenna explained to me. He proceeded, "If the girl is more educated than the boy ... he may develope an inferiority complex. So, somehow this would become a problem in their family life." Moreover, such a constellation likely evokes social pressure, as Rajendran stated, "Our people are stubborn. If a wife is more educated than the husband, society will treat the husband with less respect."

Having recognized the great value of education in the matchmaking scenario, Indian parents give increasing importance to their daughters' academic career (Seymour 1999: 180ff.). Nevertheless, a high degree involves considerable disadvantages as well: on the one hand, highly educated women are eligible to find a husband with a high earnings potential, but on the other hand, they are subjected to stereotypes of 'commercial girls' who are 'money-minded' and place their career above family values and domestic duties. Often, members of their societies suspect them of "moving around with others" or being promiscuous[8]. This image places them in contrast to the role model of a 'traditional' woman, who corresponds to the ideal of a Tamil *cumaṅkali.* Due to their exposure *(nēroḷivāyppu)*, these women are assumed to have a widened horizon, a great deal of experience and exorbitant expectations for the performance of their husbands. Suresh outlined his vision of that conjugal disparity to me by stating, "If I take a traditional girl to a new city, she will see many new things and be very happy and love me even more. If I take a well-educated girl, she knows all these places and perceives it as natural. So any degree is enough."[9] Suresh's concerns corroborate the findings of Wilson (2013) that "the desirability of a middle-class Tamil girl was often assessed according to the balance between her knowledge of 'tradition' and her hopefully limited exposure to the immodest actions of 'Western' women" (ibid: 39). Uncertainties and self-doubts troubling young men in such a constellation is pointedly described by Clark-Decès: "It is not simply that young men expect women to be submissive, for many have to reckon with strong sisters and mothers – women who take orders from no one. But, normative models of masculinity require men to display *āṇmai* ('manliness'), even a kind of machismo and swagger" (2014: 154).

In contrast to their male counterparts, young women do not see a contradiction between exposure (nēroḷivāyppu) and the performance of their duties as strong wives and mothers (cumaṅkali). Their notion of 'educated wives' considerably differed from that of male respondents. For them, an education renders women mature and responsible. Pursuing her education, Sinjuta intended to invest her academic skills and experience in a prospering family life, which conforms to her image of a dignified and caring wife:

8 Although such judgments mainly affect women, there were similar characteristics attributed to men, such as being arrogant, greedy and demanding too much dowry.

9 Certainly, male graduate students admitted the advantage of educated wives who, due to their background and exposure, are likely to cope with an educated lifestyle and adapt to a new social environment.

"Women nowadays are so mature. They want their life to be well settled. So they learn how to bear and handle them (their husbands). Otherwise, they would ask them to get out of the house. Then, questions arise: Where would we go? Should we return to our parents? ... All women will adapt to the husband's situation because they love their husbands and family more than anything. They even tolerate conflicts with their mothers-in-law."

Accordingly, women prefer a more highly educated husband in order to ensure a domestic equilibrium, as suggested by Pogkani: "Our husbands must be more educated than us. Then they will lead us to run the family in a better way." For most women, a husband without an ego problem is supposed to be a quiet and understandable family head. Moreover, some regarded a higher academic status as prestigious, as Ajitha pointed out, "Regarding his education, I expect the groom to be more highly qualified than I am because of status. It is a question of pride for me. When I go somewhere with my husband, I can say that he has a higher degree!" Female graduate students, therefore, do not tend to engage in competition with men; they present themselves as aware of their qualities, prospects and limits and match their aspiration in line with a functioning family life.

Similarly, occupation is carefully matched according to established gender relations. Most students from the lower economic stratum of the middle class suffered from financial hardships due to rural depopulation and rising costs of living. Despite households' increasing need for dual earnings however, respondents frowned upon the idea of a wife holding a higher position than her husband. The aforementioned inferiority complex of the groom also applies to the income situation, as Suresh described, "If my wife is earning 1,5 lakhs[10], I have to earn more than 2,5 lakhs". Because wives, in turn, raise their demands for the employment and salary of their husbands, male respondents expressed a great deal of pressure to obtain a stable job, which results in perpetual insecurity and frustration because such positions are scarce. The prolonged education and high income of their wives challenge them to fulfill the image of the male family head and provider. Ramesh, a 33 year-old PhD student struggling to cover the expenses for his thesis, faced strong condemnation by his future in-laws when he asked his wife for financial support: "They started to abuse me with bad words. They were telling me that I am female not able to earn money, and that I want to feed myself with the money that my wife earns. Everyone in the family was scolding me ... One even offered me a sari, skirt and blouse. He told me to wear it like a woman." Similarly in an industrial context, Geert de Neve (2004) demonstrates how Tamil Society bluntly devalues and ridicules male textile

10 The unit *lakh* in the Indian numbering system corresponds to 100 000.

workers who do not succeed in fulfilling the expected role of the breadwinner. Indeed, consequences of financial, educational and professional demands have aggravated the situations for middle class men to meet established concepts of masculinity (Osella 1998: 191).

Having abandoned their caste-based profession (*kulatoḻil*) to a large extent, degree holders usually opt for an occupation in government or the private sector. Despite a decline in the number of government employees between the years of 1997 and 2007 as a result of a cutback in the influence of state institutions as well as an emerging new and consumption-oriented middle class (Jodhka and Prakash 2011: 51), government jobs remained highly valued among graduates. Those posts offer continuous stability and life-long economic security. Employment in this domain promises permanent contracts, a fixed time schedule, ensured holidays and the possibility of transferring to another place. Moreover, a government job stabilizes a person's position in the wider community, as Uma explained, "A husband, working in the government sector has a lot of time and holidays. All the village people will have a good rapport with him and he will get paddy[11] and so on from the church members." In fact, employment in the public sector assures considerable prestige; such positions are historically associated with the formation of an assiduous middle class at the time of independence, defined by their loyalty to the ideals of the Indian nation state.

A career in the private sector primarily holds a high economic value for Tamil youth due to its attractive income prospects. Aside from financial advantages, men and women alike perceived the flexibility and lack of safety associated with occupations in the private sector as a disadvantage that implies an insecure and unsteady lifestyle. Imploring the stereotype of overcharged 'IT-people', Soundariya expressed her reluctance to marry an employee from the private sector: "Whenever we go to functions in our free time, my husband should come with us. And at the least, he should take leave one day in the week so that he can be with the family. But IT guys don't have that possibility ... even when he is free, he would bring his laptop from the company." Young men and families of young, unwed men expressed an even greater reluctance to find a bride who works in free enterprise. As has been recognized in other ethnographic settings, such a scenario provokes "a source of great anxiety" because the image of this occupational field is tainted by a "suspiciousness about the moral conduct of young, independent women working long and late hours alongside men" (Fuller & Narasimhan 2007: 139).

11 Rice in the husk.

Picture 7: Preparing together for the exams for Indian Administrative Service (IAS) at Madurai Corporation Campus

The above ascriptions are associated with culture-specific notions of 'female' and 'male' jobs. An occupation within the private sector is regarded as inadequate for women, particularly in the area of information technology, marketing or human resource management. Requiring flexibility and mobility, such an occupation presents an unsafe domain that hampers the fulfillment of domestic duties and induces women to entertain dubious relations with other co-workers. Female graduates therefore justified their choice in employment preferences with their responsibility for familial duties, which collides with unregulated working hours and long business trips. For Anitha, suitable and rewarding professions for women include a school teacher, nurse or accountant:

"They can take care of the family and go to work and come back home. The timing is very suitable for them. If they face too many difficulties, they won't take care of the family and the children. Their mind should remain at peace; they need to relax and have to feel free. So they shouldn't take up jobs in big enterprises where they get stressed and become tense. Then they come home and the stress would remain in the home also."

Such assumptions lead to peculiar evaluation patterns and a gender-related categorization of career opportunities. Women are considered patient and able to suppress their own desires, for instance the need to roam around, in favor of fulfilling household or social duties. Once, I was sitting with some peer group members in front of an internet café near the old town in Madurai. Suddenly, I saw an advertisement for a position, pinned on the entrance door of a copy shop and explicitly addressing female applicants. When I asked Anitha about her opinion of this specification in the advertisement, she explained that women have the reputation of being easy to handle. Moreover, they are assumed to be talented in multi-tasking. Suresh's explanation stresses an intrinsic responsibility for the job: "Women are punctual, mind deadlines, supervise the money and assume accounting tasks. Even if it is late, they are responsive to the needs and requests of the owners. They inform them if there is a delay. Men would say: It is lunch time and we have an hour, so we're going to a hotel." Only for critical situations, men designated themselves as able to control their emotional state and display a certain level of authority. Thus, most interview partners regarded men as suitable for front jobs, where the ability of handling uncontrolled customers proves an asset and a necessity. As a typical example, they mentioned accountants in a hotel who balance contradicting and strenuous demands from clients.

The importance of economic considerations brings the focus to the matching of other material resources in the form of land, assets and dowry. Prior to negotiations for Nandhini's marriage, Suresh's older sister provided me with a deeper insight into dowry practices, drawing on the example of the Kōṉār castes. While land and assets are mainly inherited to male descendants, a woman in turn receives cash that she then invests in her conjugal alliance. In cross-kin marriages, however, properties are rarely negotiated. Usually, both family members are aware of financial and material resources. It is rather the intangible support that they negotiate, for example the care for older family members.

This transparency of inter-familial assets underwent a radical change in non-kin alliances where the financial background is unknown and has to be verified in great detail. The principle concern that most families expressed to me relates to the continuous uncertainty and risk of receiving wrong information. This issue is aggravated by the fact that alliances with unfamiliar families presume an inferior position of the bride in economic terms. Since the groom is expected to have a higher degree and income, his family members usually find themselves in a privileged position to make demands. At the same time, they have to fear the daughter-in-laws' attitude: the conscientiousness and care ensured by a close kin background is replaced by the image of a selfish stranger, exclusively pursuing her own aspirations. With the stereotype of 'egocentric IT-people' in mind, highly educated brides are feared to be arrogant, orientated towards relationships outside the home and inclined to neglect their duties toward in-law parents, particularly in old age. One consequence of this uncertainty on both sides is the rise of ritual activities to mutually demonstrate prestige and loyalty with pre-wedding ceremonies.

The growing non-transparency, mistrust and unequal power constellations raise the demand for financial contributions as an assurance of economic stability. This development results in the escalation of dowry practices in Tamil Nadu, notably the specific transfer of money, commodities and household goods from the bridal family to the conjugal union. Usually, the calculation of the dowry complex emanates from the "bride's beauty, education, employment and the status, prestige, wealth and connections of her family and relatives [which] are weighted against similar parameters on the groom's side" (Osella & Osella 2000: 101). In different parts of the country, dowry practices have been explained in terms of property transmission, the strengthening of affinal links or a resource for women to maintain power and control in conjugal life.[12] In her study among several castes in the North Indian villages Benipur and Phulpur, Marguerite Roulet (1996) analyses the association between dowry and social honor. She asserts that the central function of dowry lies in calculating social status, honor and prestige of the two marriage partners and their families. From this contention, the author deduces three principal cultural concepts of dowry, notably "(i) a voluntary gift versus a demanded gift; (ii) dowry as a traditional practice versus dowry as a modern institution; and (iii) dowry as an institution that entailed trust versus one that entailed distrust" (ibid: 96). Similar complex attitudes have been indicated among middle class members in Calcutta who evaluate dowry practices depending on the outcome of the marriage; if the wedding or conjugal life turns out to be successful, gifts are considered a 'contribution' to their household. In case one side is not satisfied, however, it is designated as 'dowry' (Donner 2008: 77).

In Tamil Nadu, respondents distinguish three different connotations associated with offerings. The first is gold, "a 'hard' currency as well as a liquid asset whose value is well-known" (Zeff 1999: 43). Beyond its actual value, measured by the unit 'pound' (8 grams), gold advanced to an indicator of family status and a compliment to the groom and his family. During wedding rituals, parents and other family members decorate the bride with chains, rings and ornaments. In a celebratory manner, they expose their economic potential, which elevates the value of their daughter (ibid). This gesture represents a prestigious wedding ceremony and indicates their respect towards the in-laws.

A second and most wide-spread form of dowry is described by the expression *cīr,* which "refers to goods that the bride brings to the marriage for the establishment of the couple" (ibid: 43). Those items consist of money and

12 For a various explanation patterns on dowry practice see Roulet (1996).

utilities, such as vessels, tumblers, plates, cots and mattresses. Among wealthier sections of the population, such materials become replaced by equipment like TVs, fridges, mixers, grinders or washing machines. Usually, two or three days after the wedding, relatives of the bride carry all the items in a big procession to the groom's house. In most cases a huge feast for the invitees succeeds this event. Cīr is perceived as a gift donated 'out of love', as Suresh's father described, "My daughter is well equipped – she has gold and assets. So in the event of a crisis, they can use it and she can give it to their children." Using such definitions, bridal parents stressed the essential function of cīr for the future position of their daughter in conjugal life. As a compensation for her inferior economic and academic position, cīr presents a (financial) backup for any distress, strengthens her influence in household decisions and amplifies her range of negotiation with respect to her in-laws.[13] Bridal parents therefore justified their contribution of cīr with a sense of a responsibility to provide material and financial security for their daughter. The significance of dowry among the Tamil middle class is elucidated by the statement of Navaneethan, my neighbor from the Kōṉār caste:

"In villages, we lived in small hamlets. My sister lived by my side; we took turns watching each other's children. My daughter went there, their daughter came here. Mutually, we shared responsibilities. So, as long as we were together, we are mutually interested in the well-being of each other's family. There is not such a question of taking and giving. We just give and take the responsibility of the systems. But now, my daughter goes out and away from me, and I say 'you take these things with you' ... This is how the gift system started. Along with the bride, we send it to the groom and his family. So many offerings are gold and sometimes dowry."

For Navaneethan, "the principle of dowry is love". For his daughter, they deposit the money into an account that she can exclusively access. Dowry therefore provides the daughter with a certain amount of self-esteem: "If the bride brings so much dowry or gold, she will be proud and have the upper hand. She may think, 'I have brought everything from my family, so why should I go work in the kitchen while others shout at me?'".

A third category of dowry is represented by the term *varataṭcaṇai* which refers to those goods and cash directly given to the groom (Zeff 1999: 44). Such items, typically a cell phone, costly watch or a motor bike are exclusively for the

13 One problematic effect of this potential of dowry were unreasonable demands by young brides and conflicts between and within families if some siblings received more dowry in their marriage than others did.

benefit of the groom. The primary function of such offerings lies in emphasizing the concern of the bridal family for a good relationship between both spouses. Those goods shall satisfy his demands and ensure that he properly takes care of the bride.

Picture 8: Transfer of cīr to the groom's house with the help of friends

How are dowry practices evaluated among South Tamil's young generation? MKU students understood dowry primarily in the form of an investment strategy. Suresh and Prasenna equated donations with "giving a price". Following this anthology, parents supply a high quantity in order to produce a successful alliance for their daughter, notably an educated groom with promising career opportunities who, however, expects an adequate amount of dowry from the bride's family. Prasenna explained those reflections in detail:

"They would think like this: (The groom) is educated and has arrived at this status. If she wants to enjoy his standard of living, she must pay a certain price for that. The parents demand and the bride's parents also think, 'My daughter will become wife of the collector, so I will give 10 lakhs as dowry.' If you go to the same sort of people[14], the dowry system does not exist. If status differs, the dowry system becomes relevant."

A similar view has been disclosed by the Osellas (2000) regarding the Izhava community. Although in this setting, such a view evokes the pejorative

14 This expression refers to close kin marriages.

connotation of 'purchasing' husbands, the authors find that the value of the bride, which becomes publically exposed through this process, depends on the groom whom she can 'afford' (ibid: 97).

While the parental generation described dowry practices as an act derived from attachment and responsibility, for the students, it remains a delicate and ambivalent issue. To avoid the impression of greediness, most declared their skeptic view about dowry practices, such as Ramesh: "I actually don't bother about dowry ... Are parents who give birth to a girl sinners? They also spend the same amount of money to educate them like my parents do. So ... it is not fair to ask for money as dowry from the bride." When I asked him whether he would refuse dowry, he replied that he would accept whatever the bride's family is ready to give. To underline his statement, he referred to one encounter with a bridal family: "I didn't even ask her how many sovereigns of gold they would give. Even now, I do not know how much gold she has from her parents. I am only interested in the girl." This expressed reservation about dowry forms part of a discourse associated with the image of an 'enlightened' and 'decent' attitude of the South Tamil middle class. With reference to observed strategies of class distinctions among Brahmins in Madurai, Wilson regards the "outward denial of material and monetary excess in the form of dowry" and it's "function of India's formal outlawing of the practice" as "indicative of contemporary middle-class identity construction" (2013: 41). Graduate students therefore explicitly opposed excessive exchanges and prestations that they regarded as 'immoral' and a violation of their ideals and values related to marriage. This attitude has infiltrated marriage negotiations. While educated people deliberately present themselves as humble and noble during matchmaking conversations, a demanding behavior is equated with 'backwardness' (*piṉtaṅkiya*). During initial negotiations with his in-laws, Nataraj even refused to invite his father's younger brother (*cittappā*), who he considered a challenging character: "I don't want him to be involved in this meeting. If he and other people involve themselves, they might talk about dowry and make demands. This behavior may ruin the whole marriage arrangement and make us look like we have the attitude of 'village people' (*kirāmattu paḻakkavaḻakkam*)."

All in all, dowry has advanced to a pragmatic strategy to meet economic requirements in the course of contemporary transformations in Tamil marriage practices. Attitudes towards the question of dowry are expressed in conjunction with values of modern middle class society, although they reveal a contradictory inter-generational discourse. Parents articulate their offering as an indicator of prestige, responsibility and gender equality in familial life. The present generation that aspires to get married assumes a critical view in regard to dowry practices – at least excessive demands – that do not conform to the image of the prudent appearance of educated people (paṭiccavaṅka).

6.3 GOOD LOOKING OR PRETENTIOUS? IDEALS OF BEAUTY AND PHYSICAL COMPATIBILITY

While involved and authoritative family members evaluate most of the criteria during the selection of a potential mate, the future bride and groom assess physical appearance themselves. Principally, they make their decision based on the photo attached to the profile. After rejecting a range of candidates, Suganth, the youngest daughter in my host family, looked at one picture and agreed to the alliance by emphasizing that she immediately felt in love. When I asked her how she can judge merely by seeing a photo, she stated, "No need to see him in reality. After seeing his photo, I am entirely convinced." Rather than rating the physical appearance as attractive or handsome, most students articulated their judgment with their impression of the spouse's decency and respectability. A frequently discussed and – according to most assemblers – entirely underestimated detail, therefore, is the visual depiction of the spouse. In order to convey his educated background and advanced lifestyle, for instance, an aspiring groom presents himself in a 'natural way', typically a casual posture, such as leaning against a wall or holding the handle of the motorbike. Usually, men wear casual clothes like jeans and a shirt, women a well-fitting chudidar or Western outfit. Passionate sentiments are accompanied by moving postures, presenting the person in a course of action. Be it a quick head shake or a melancholic view, such photos capture the depicted character in a unique and individual manner. The particular mood of the scene, portrayed through a smile or pose of concentration, provides the spectator with a personal impression of the potential mate. Characteristically, the photos situate marriage aspirants in natural sceneries, which according to Zeff (1999: 127) "stand in for romantic action never shown, particularly kissing and sex". Since the exposure of love and romantic feelings is associated with 'modernity' (Donner 2012), such a personalized technique of photography is assumed to be practiced among educated people. In contrast, extravagant clothes with dazzling colors, combined with oversized jewelry, are placed in the category of 'backward people': without any atmospheric background, those pictures bring into light the main physical features such as face, hair and body shape. Moreover, such postures are often made in front of a mirror to be visible in all angles. In Suganth's view, those candidates appear as mere objects of desire.

Apart from the photography, further information specifying physical details facilitate the exterior match between spouses. In her presentation under the title "He's too Dark, She's too Fat: Middle Class Matchmaking in Tamil South India", held at the Annual Conference of the Association for Asian Studies, Wilson (2012) demonstrates how the contemporary matchmaking process in Tamil Nadu follows its "own unique language, complete with acronyms and English words with nuanced meanings," as for example the desired "wheatish complexion". Beyond skin texture, classified in categories like bright and dark, the candidates insert their height and weight. It is important that the woman not be taller than the man and that the difference between the couple be moderate.

Picture 9: Profile of paṭiccavaṅka
(Paṟaiyar caste)

Another precondition for a positive match relates to the age of the couple, determined by two factors: first, the wife ought to be younger than her husband (Daniel 1984: 166); second, the age difference should not exceed three years. Especially with the increase in nuclear families, the wife needs the support of her husband in the household. This is one of the reasons why most middle class families do not support an alliance between a woman and her maternal uncle who is usually substantially older than his sister's daughter. Nowadays, such prescriptions vary according to caste, class, gender and education. Families usually wait until their children complete their exams before searching for profiles. The average age for female degree-holders is 24-27 years, while male university graduates marry in their late 20s. Pursuing a PhD, therefore, appears problematic, as it prolongs the marriage and limits the choice of equally qualified husbands. Although the match is primarily determined by social and economic criteria, the indicated physical attributes hint at considerable preferences for certain exterior features.

6.4 ASTROLOGICAL COMPATIBILITY: THE SIGNIFICANCE OF HOROSCOPES AND *JŌTIṬAR*

"Earlier, marriages were fixed at the moment the baby was born. A woman would choose her own brother's son for her daughter. There was no need to compare *jātakam*. But nowadays, the practice of these kinship marriages is declining. So the need of comparing jātakam arises more and more."
(Gomathy, neighbor and wife of Navaneethan)

In the course of non-kin marriages, astrology has advanced to a primary criterion for defining the match (poruttam) of bride and groom. Today, the information about *irāci* (zodiac, planet constellation at the time of birth) and *navāmsam* (planet constellation at the present time) comprise important components of every profile. Indeed, comparing the horoscope (*jātakam*) represents a precondition for the matchmaking process because it predetermines the prospects for the conjugal life and cautions against inauspicious elements. Astrology has an impact on the qualities of each individual and is utilized to diagnose the oneness, happiness and the fertility of the couple. Taking into account the planet constellation at the time of birth and the present, astrologers identify certain 'good' planets (*nalla kirakam*), considered particular advantageous for a functioning conjugal life. Fundamental for a marriage are rays of *viyāḻaṉ* (Jupiter), which encourage two individuals to arrange the marriage. A decisive planet is *cukkiraṉ* (Venus): if it is located in the suitable house, the respective person is predicted to be blessed with a beautiful spouse, prospering married life, and an extravagant wedding ceremony. If it is in an imperfect house, however, then he is determined to receive an ugly and quarrelsome spouse; males will have two wives, lead a life with struggles and the wedding will be conducted in a modest fashion.

Beyond the astrological data in the profile, most families additionally consult professional astrologers (*jōtiṭar*) who diagnose a possible match with the help of the horoscope by *naṭcattiram* (star), *rāci* (star constellation at the present time) and *lakṉam* (star constellation at the time of birth).[15] Each of the 27 stars has its specific time within the 24 hours of one day. The star combination of both spouses defines their compatibility as a couple. *Tiruvātirai* Star (Betelgeuse, male dog) and *hastam* (female buffalo), for instance, present a good match since dogs and buffaloes do not fight with each other. Dog and deer in contrast constitute a rather unfavorable combination, because dogs hunt dears. Neither is the constellation between a buffalo and tiger desirable, since the tiger is assumed to attack the buffalo. Moreover, the calculation of stars indicates the nature and quality of a person, which helps predict positive or fatal consequences for a future life together. A woman born at *āyilyam,* for example, is said to affect the life of her father-in-law. If her star is *kēṭṭai*, she endangers the life of the groom's mother. In general, stars might have a negative impact on the groom's family, but never on the bride's family. Thus, astrology places the bridal family into a slightly inferior position, as wife-takers are continuously anxious to satisfy the concerns of their in-laws.

The various constellations of stars and planets at the time of birth and at the present time can be calculated in ten possible matches, out of which at least six should exist among the couple as a precondition for a successful conjugal union.

Examples for combinations

1. Tiṉapporuttam:	health and everyday life/this match indicates who will die first.
2. Kaṇapporuttam:	physical match and the joy of the couple
3. Makēntirapporuttam:	wealth/fertility
4. Stirī tīrkkapporuttam:	life of the wife
5. Yōṉipporuttam:	sexual relationship/satisfaction between the couple
6. Rācip poruttam:	healthy and joyful relationship between the couple
7. Rāci atipati poruttam:	prosperity of the couple's family life
8. Vaciya poruttam:	mutual attraction
9. Rajjūp poruttam:	lifespan of the husband
10. Vētaip poruttam:	pleasure and frustration

15 Astrological compatibility not only refers to the well-being of both partners, but can be placed in a wider context: Daniel (1984: 176f.) describes that planets present an influencing factor for the compatibility of body fluids which enhance the health of the child.

Mushrooming offices in every part of the city, horoscope sessions in television channels and promotion stalls in shopping malls visibly indicate the increasing importance of astrology for matchmaking. Regarding the overbearing presence of astrological offices, booklets and software programs, it proves worthwhile to concentrate on the strategies, functions and impacts of the professional astrologers during the matchmaking procedure. Originally perceived as mountebanks who exhibited local authority, today the astrologer advanced to a skillful businessman with commercial practices and influence. In contrast to their ancestors, who held their sessions in remote areas, a range of astrologers today offer their services in central offices, malls or fairs. Correspondingly, astrology has advanced to a respectable science, offered by MKU as a diploma course through distance education. The variety of consulted astrologers varies from erudite Brahmins who share their advice with a limited number of customers, to the well frequented jōtiṭar, conventionally from the *Vaḷḷuvar* community, who practice their job as a caste-based occupation (*kulatoḻil*).

On the road running parallel to my house, I had the opportunity to witness the growing success of Sri Guru, an astrologer from the latter category, who attained great affluence through a well-functioning service system. In his own words, he gained increasing influence within his neighborhood: "People from all social sections give respect, response and honor to me. It is because of my behavior towards the people. Even the sweepers respect me. When neighbors ask them to clean the dirt, they never listen. But whenever I say something, they immediately do it." Sri Guru experienced his elevated position in the ritual context, notably during temple visits: whenever police men recognize him, they immediately bring him to the front of the cue, where he receives a *puja* free of charge.

At first, I visited him together with Suresh and his parents and later on I returned on my own to gain insights into his methods. In order to manage the rising queues in front of his office, clients have to register in a nearby shop. The shopkeeper strictly inspects whether the customer holds a proper *jātakam notebook* before he issues a token number. This screening process facilitates the entire procedure, as a considerable percentage of clients does not document the birth details correctly and turns up with an incomplete horoscope. The office hours are regulated from 9 am to 2 pm, during which time he receives between 20 to 40 customers depending on the season. Inside his entrance hall, clients sit in an ordered row to consult the astrologer one after the other. Usually, the session for one client lasts between 10 to 15 minutes. The way to convey the message requires the appropriate sensitivity, which finally determines the image of the astrologer. Contrary to other astrologers who define the horoscope match by standardized computer software, Sri Guru conducts exclusively personal conversations. He addresses his customers with respectfully familiar terms. If he detects any dangerous signs, for example a mismatch between two spouses, he chooses a cautious and suitable way to convey his evaluation. Typically, he prepares his customers by mentioning positive signs. Smoothly he turns to delicate issues, but ends his session by presenting the prospect of a remedy. This strategy, described as "giving a banana with a needle inside" implies regular calls by the customers to clarify preceding conversations.

Picture 10: Sri Guru, prescribing remedies

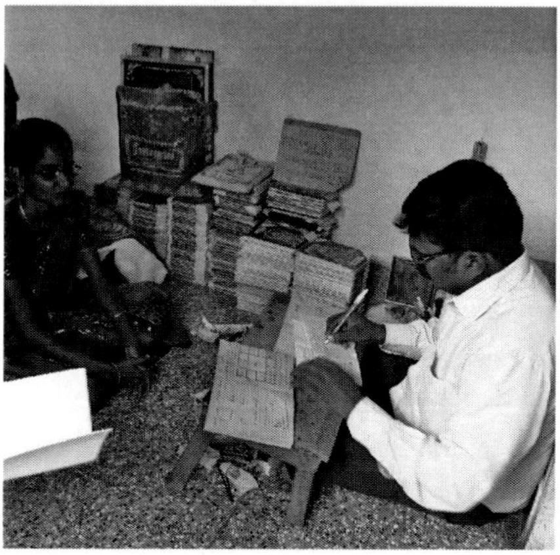

For the graduate students, astrology plays an essential role to confront several hurdles within the matchmaking procedure. The following cluster reveals peculiar explanation patterns for comparing horoscopes and elucidates the strong demand for astrology.

Security: In light of declining family bonds, a jōtiṭar provides a scientific validation for the match between bride and groom, as Sinjuta explained, "Earlier, the marriages were organized among cross cousins. In that period, the marriages were fixed at the moment the baby was born. But now ... marriages are among non-relatives. So the need to compare jōtiṭar arises more and more." For Prasenna, the diagnosis of an astrologer helps "to satisfy the mind". Confused by various contradicting opinions within his family about potential brides, he feels safeguarded if astrologers diagnose the matches in detail. Given the exhausting procedure of viewing profiles, astrologers serve as a professional and competent consultant for arriving at a decision.

Moral support: When faced with dangers and misfortune, astrologers serve as sagacious and reliable navigators. The tactic of "circumventing" presents a popular strategy for addressing a predictable disaster found in the horoscope: if Sri Guru previews an accident for instance, he advises the client to sell the vehicle and buy a new one. Ideally, by that time, the danger is gone. Equally, this method is applied by recourse to ritual activities: "Housewarming parties, ear piercing ceremonies or offering some sacrifice distracts the people – then, they won't think about the bad happenings in their life."

The case of Suresh's younger cousin, Kirthi, exemplifies how Sri Guru applies this strategy to prevent an inauspicious coupling. Her mother handed over her horoscope after the young woman had fallen in love with a young man. Sri Guru could not find even one single match. Further, the horoscope revealed that if they got married, the groom would die after six months. He was reluctant to divulge his diagnosis directly because he knew the young woman to be adamant and feared she might commit suicide. Therefore, he recommended taking the horoscope to other astrologers and coming back for further proceedings. After other astrologers gave a similar evaluation to the family, Kirthi locked herself inside a room for two days. Afterward, however, as the entire process was extended by consulting several opinions, the passed time helped her to finally calm down. Sri Guru designates this method as "shock-avoiding treatment": "If I tell her straight the bad news, she will be too dazed. So I have to carefully deal with these kinds of cases. But if I send them to other astrologers, they will slowly get prepared for the negative happenings. Till now they are not married, but slowly their relationship is diminishing." Beyond merely diagnosing horoscopes, the challenge for astrologers lies in considering the individual situation of the particular client.

Influence: If families explicitly support the relationship, the horoscope presents a valid confirmation of the alliance. In the case that other criteria such as education and economic background seem promising, astrological mismatches are creatively circumvented. One possibility lies in the simultaneous consultation of several astrologers until one among them gives positive and encouraging statements. In turn, graduate students in search of a partner frequently use astrology as a popular excuse to reject a profile. Sasi consulted his own astrologer as soon as he received a profile. Since he was born under an unfavorable star (*rōkiṇi*), the astrologer dissuaded him from continuing the matchmaking process. Given his advanced age, his parents urged him to see one of the proposed brides, but he remained relentless and rejected their suggestions. In fact, astrology serves as a welcomed justification for adducing evidence of the incompatibility with a potential spouse and cancelling the marriage while remaining courteous and not offending the in-law family.

Middle class asset: To a large extent, my conversation partners expressed an ambivalent view toward astrologers, as Rajendran explained, "A horoscope is a material which we never know. When people start to believe, then it is important for them. Others who don't believe also live happily. It depends on each personality." Skeptic about its increasing popularity, he and his peers equated astrology with superstition, which stands in contrast to the rational attitude of paṭiccavaṅka who question the background of established norms and customs. With an enlightened mind-set, they are supposed to evaluate a conjugal union in terms of 'important' facts, such as wealth or family constellations. The sober appearance and techniques of the astrologers, however, transformed the field into a middle class asset that stands for an educated background, integrity and exposure. The consideration of horoscopes advanced to an elaborated strategy for evaluating the viability of a match. Such a perception is linked to the fact that the science represents secret knowledge from ancient literature, which is only accessible to literate Brahmins. This specific approach to astrology by middle class sections of the population has been adopted by astrologers themselves who enhanced the separation between 'educated' and 'non-educated' customers. Sri Guru illustrates the changing ambition among his clients: "Being that we are diagnosing the horoscope in the right way and promoting it properly, it is attracting the educated also. Paṭiccavaṅka require solution-oriented answers." Appearing as a proficient scientist, Sri Guru applies new strategies and methods to convey his diagnosis. Instead of presenting his assessment in a great length, he provides precise prescriptions, packed in limited quantities, as he elucidated, "Before, I used to diagnose each and every aspect – lifespan, job, family, child birth and so on. When I speak about all issues to analyze one horoscope, I need half an hour. Nowadays, because of my experience, I can directly identify the problem and suggest the *parikāram* (remedy). This attracts the educated." The consultancy became output-driven. For Prasenna, it is "like a medicine", as he explained, "Doctors and astrologers are the same. Doctors diagnose the disease by asking us questions. For astrologers, as soon they see the horoscope they will know the person's whole life: problems, caste, future remedy and so on." Thus, despite their ambiguous attitude toward astrologers, the students recognized astrology as a distinctive and efficient form for evaluating the compatibility between bride and groom.

6.5 CONCLUSION

Assuming the perspective of the students, this chapter outlined the aspirations of the Tamil middle class with respect to their future conjugal life. Its principal focus lay in the way education, class consciousness and vocational prospects have shaped priorities and notions of compatibility. In fact, my respondents do develop an alternative view of conjugal life by aspiring to an ideal union that approaches the form of a *companionate* marriage – a model that brings acquired 'modern' values of autonomy, individual desires or gender equality in line with social standards of Tamil caste society.

Contrary to the Western concept, the compatibility between two spouses is not defined by personal characteristics, but rather by "social categories that stand for individual qualities" (Zeff 1999: 68). As a facilitating service, professional brokers structure key factors of compatibility via standardized profiles. Social and familial constellations are matched by pursuing an ideal of togetherness on an equal level. Those considerations include principles of mutual understanding, strength of character and responsibility toward their social community. Vocational and economic background is valued in accordance with harmonious gender relations, while compensation payments in the form of dowry serve the function of empowerment and investment strategies. Physical attraction is expressed in comparable terms and reveals a distinctive appearance and taste of the South Indian middle class. Finally, astrological compatibility in the form of horoscope matching satisfies the practical interests of marriage aspirants and its status has advanced to comprise evidence of a good match, determined through pragmatic and thorough proceedings. So far, students' expectations of their future spouse and their understanding of a suitable match are orientated toward progressive ideals and partly differ from those of the more senior generation. However, their explications do not confront imposed social categories. Rather than rejecting established matchmaking practices, the present generation applies acquired ideas of maturity, responsibility and decency in accordance with principles of endogamous Tamil marriage and status aspirations.

7. Peers as mediators in matchmaking and pre-wedding ceremonies

The present matchmaking process, striking due to the proliferation of matrimonial websites, assembler bureaus, mediators, meetings and related ceremonies, has not always formed such a crucial part of Tamil marriage practices (Wilson 2013: 37). Through the example of selected case studies involving my host family and other MKU graduates, I outline contemporary strategies and challenges with respect to finalizing the alliance. Observing the rising popularity of pre-wedding ceremonies, I explore the importance of initial remedy and matching rituals and subsequently identify the forging of the marriage alliance as an indigenous performance that follows its own rules. Supporting the statement of Clark-Decès that matchmaking is not to be confused with "dating savoir-faire" (2014: 159), I concentrate on the role of involved family members and trustworthy acquaintances.

Regarding the participation of family and external members in the search for an appropriate spouse, I highlight the supportive engagement of non-kin friends. Against the background of recent, 'modern' trends including technological advances, behavioral norms, self-determination of the younger generation, the emphasis on personal compatibility and mutual attraction of the spouses (Donner 2008: 72), this chapter offers a meticulous description of the structure, organization and dynamics of today's matchmaking ceremonies.

7.1 DELAYED MARRIAGE AND REMEDY RITUALS

Manju[1]:	We know our destination when we get married;)
(sent a proverb via text message)	
Charles:	Great ...
M:	Today is not April 1st: Get married soon, I am going to search a girl for my son.
Sasi:	When is your marriage, *da*?
Ch:	It comes when it comes.
Nataraj:	We are getting bored repeating the same thing, waiting for your marriage, don't delay Charles.
Sasi:	There is tension!
Ch:	I also have tension.
Sasi:	Once he is old we'll have to feed him.
(In between there were other exchanges of funny pictures)	

Manju:	Charles, did you find a life partner?
Ch:	U just committed to find a partner, what happened?
M:	Please don't joke.
CH:	You're not a good friend Manju.
M:	Now I will say one thing as u think of me as a good friend...
CH:	Please go ahead
M:	U go to church everyday to find yr life partner. Do it like a part time job. Or else, I will bring you to *Thirumananjori* to conduct puja!

Despite several transformations in marriage practices in India, a normative consensus about marriage as a necessary fulfillment for every human being persists (Chowdhry 2009: 291, Skoda 2002: 3).[2] "Living as a sage does not add

1 Fellow female classmate whose caste and age are unknown to me.

2 Sharada Srinivasan (2014) compared the situation of male bachelors in Punjab and Tamil Nadu at the 43rd Annual Conference on South Asia. Concentrating particularly on the development, gender discrimination and social exclusion, she listed explanation patterns that rationalize their unmarried status. The study revealed that none of their study participants regarded his situation as a self-chosen state so that Srinivasan concludes that life as a bachelor is not an approved concept of life. Even more precarious is the situation for unmarried women. Susan Seymour (1999: 201) outlines

value to the human life", assembler Ganesh explained to me, "if we plant a tree, it must grow and yield fruits, otherwise there is no use out of the plant." Pressure to get married emanates not only from parental or family influence, but also from peers who frequently persuade their friends to settle down into family life. This nudging occurs especially toward the numerous long-term bachelors and spinsters among academics (see section 5.2). Peers repeatedly compel and admonish their fellow classmates in everyday communications, as presented in the above sms chat between Charles, Sasi, Nataraj and Manju. Moreover, locals consider ongoing failures in finding a suitable spouse dependent on astrological auspices (*tōṣam*). *Māṅkalya tōṣam* therefore presents an unfavorable hindrance for getting married and *tāra tōṣam* a hurdle to finding a bride. Such difficulties have lead to an increasing recourse to remedy ceremonies (*parikāram*) to alternate and overcome such unfavorable factors.

Most long-term unmarried degree-holders visited Kalyanasundarar temple, a famous site for conducting a *māṅkalya tōṣam parikāram*. The sanctuary presents the place of the divine marriage between goddess Parvati and Lord Shiva who are worshipped as Gokilampal and Sri Kalyanasundarar. This temple is located in Thirumananjeri, a small village in Nagapatinam District. The temple was erected 3000 years ago and owes its present architecture from 1500 years ago to Chola Queen Sembiyanmadevi. According to the *Puranas*, ancient Hindu texts, six places are connected to this temple, in which Parvati resided while pursuing an earthly marriage with Shiva: Therazhundur, Thiruvaduthurai, Kuthalam, Ethirkolpadi, Velvikkudi, and finally Thirumananjeri. Angry about her impatience, Shiva delayed the wedding and transformed her into a cow at Therazhundur where Parvati's brother Vishnu became her shepherd. At Thiruvaduthurai, Shiva allowed Saint Barathamuni, who had no children, to remove her curse so that she reappeared as his daughter, worshipping God Uthvaganathar. She grew up in Kuthalam (today Thiruthuruthi), in Bharathamuni's house. Barathamuni approached Shiva to fulfill Parvati's wish for an earthly marriage and received him at Ethirkolpadi. The marriage rites took place at Velvikkudi. Finally, the gods conducted their wedding ceremony in Thirumananjeri according to the local formalities. Because this place represents the ultimate fulfillment of desire and the satisfaction of the goddess Parvati, she henceforth blesses those aspiring to get married.

Today, the Kalyanasundarar Temple advanced to one of the most important sites for accelerating the matchmaking process. Further, it provides a sanctuary for recently married couples who come to complete their prayer and express

---

the social consequences for spinsters in Orissa. Since they are not accompanied by their men to family events, they remain continuously excluded from public functions.

their gratitude for having obtained the desired conjugal unity. Every year, several thousand people frequent this place. Worshippers who come from all communities, religions and provenance arrive in hired vans and organized busses, accompanied by their parents, relatives and friends. Especially within the last 30 years, the place became such a popular attraction that it created a range of employment opportunities for the 360 resident families from Thirumananjeri. For Murthy, who has carried out the transfer between Kuthalam and the temple for the last forty years, astrology and media publicity has enhanced its popularity even more. In fact, under the title "Marriage will be fixed here,"[3] the magazine Aval from August 14, 2012 described the high impact of parikāram, held at the temple. Other advertisements, broadcasted via the internet and international TV channels, have attracted migrants from Malaysia, Singapore and Sri Lanka.

I accompanied Charles on a two-day trip, together with his parents, older brother and David, my host brother. The worshippers approach the temple on its eastern side, where they face the main entrance. In the south, Shiva blesses the devout in the form of Sri Kalyanasundarar, while Durgai Amman resides in the north. In the west, Raghu Bhagavan receives those who are praying for the birth of a child. In front of the temple, there are eleven shops, established by the local authorities. Here, the visitors can find all the necessary ingredients for the ritual: two garlands, two coconuts, turmeric, cumcum, camphor, ghee, sandal powder, ve<u>rr</u>ilai pākku (betel leaf with a nut inside), kalkaṇṭu (byproduct of sugar), lemon, banana, yellow thread (mañcal) and tīpataṭṭu, a plate with a lighted candle and clay lamps.

Inside the temple, archana tickets are offered at the counter. The temple is open to visitors from 6.30am until 1.30pm and again from 3.30pm to 8.30pm. Pujas are conducted continuously throughout the day, depending on the crowd. Since the ceremonies receive worshippers from every caste and religion, the temple is not restricted to a specific puja schedule. A central ingredient for the ritual, therefore, is lemon juice, which all religions drink and offer to the gods. Notably, the ceremony desists from idol worship. Having entered the temple, the visitors pray to Selva Ganapathy on the left of the Sanctum. Next, they worship Sri Kalyana Sundareswar and turn to Amman ca<u>nn</u>iti, the altar on the right. Here, Meenakshi Amman presents the thirteen year-old Gokilampal with three bends.

The principal ceremony takes place in Kalyana Sundareswarar Hall, where the deities are exhibited in a marriage kolam, a posture in which Shiva places the cumcum on the forehead of Parvati. The visitors enter the main hall where they find a huge mirror to their left, on the backside of the hall. Here, they approach a god in the form of light: through the glass, the worshipper has a direct

3 Translation from Tamil.

connection to the divine, not distracted by the presence of other people. After lighting the clay lamps (tīpam), marriage aspirants take a seat on the floor. Unmarried women and men are seated inside the enclosure: women on the right side and men on the left. Accompanying parents and relatives stand outside, surrounding the enclosure. Symbolically, they surrender their children to the goddess. Married couples sit in the space between the single men and women. Again, the wives sit to the right of their husbands, a required constellation for all auspicious functions, following the goddess Meenakshi who stands to the right of Shiva.

The three brothers Raju Gurukkal, Swamynathan and Ayyappan serve as priests in Thirumananjeri and have conducted the ceremonies since 1999. Having given their instructions through a microphone[4], they collect the garlands and place them in the palms of the god and goddess. With this gesture (caraṇākati), they surrender all struggles of the unmarried men and women to the god. By receiving and handing back the offered garlands, gods remove the curse of the participants. Meanwhile, the participants conduct caṅkalpam, a process in which the devout meditate and concentrate on the marriage. The priests take the tīpataṭṭu. Before they return the garland to the visitors, their parents keep it in their hands and recite the name of clan ancestors (gothram) as well as the name and star of their child. During archana, coconuts are broken. Finally, the priests hand over the taṭṭu after aarti, the fire ceremony. During all stages, local saints, the Siddhars, are present to bless the unmarried men and women.

Because visitors remain together during the entire prayer, the ceremony is called kūṭṭu pirārtaṉai, a collective praying ritual meant to enhance the results. In contrast to individual prayers, joint worshipping is considered more effective. The priests therefore appeal to the released energy:

---

4 "Following the prayers, *vipūti* (sacred ash) and cumcum have to be used, for one *mandalam* by the concerned men and women. The next morning after taking bath, they should pray, wearing the garland, and then drink the lemon juice with a little water, but without adding salt or sugar and before eating any food. Until the marriage is done, the garland should be kept in a mañcal pai (yellow cloth bag) in the puja room. After the marriage, the couple brings it and finally puts it in the temple tank here. With this action, the prarthanai (prayer) is completed. While those instructions shall be followed merely by the concerned participants, the remaining coconuts can be used by the entire family for cooking."

"We are so patient in the theater where a movie is displayed for three hours. Do we deviate and speak to others? We do not. But here, in the temples, when we are sitting here we do not concentrate and we start looking around. The puja conducted here is important for our life. Life begins here. Hence, you must remain silent without speaking to each other and concentrate on the puja. This is a *kūṭṭu vaḻipāṭu* (particular path for a joint prayer). You have to concentrate on your desired life partner, how to lead a successful family life, and pray to Sri Sundareswarar. You will get your spouse very quick only if you keep silent with fear of the Lord and concentrate on what I said. Hence, please concentrate and remain silent for the next 20 minutes. Kindly switch off your mobile phones and concentrate on your prayers."[5]

"When numerous people gather and pray for the same cause", Sri Gurukkal explained to me in a later conversation, "more auspicious aura arises to fulfill their wishes. The main effect, however, is the positive thinking and confidence of the devout. When unmarried people see the couples in the middle, they gain energy, hope and their concentration enhances the success." This energy is assumed to overcome external influences. In contrast to other pujas, after which the visitor returns home straight away to avoid further distractions, this ceremony is believed to release so much power that participants may visit other places before returning home. After kūṭṭu pirārtaṉai, the visitors exit the Kalyana Sundareswarar altar and leave 10 rupees for the musicians. In the adjacent shrine, they repeat the prayer to Shiva. Those couples who desire children may conduct a prayer to Raagu at the Mangala Raagu.

If the parikāram is successful, marriage should take place within 90 days. The married couples are required to come back and visit the temple at least once to express their gratitude and complete their prayer. For this ceremony, each of them has to buy two packs of garlands (*mālai*) and the ingredients used for the kūṭṭu pirārtaṉai. One set of the garlands remains at the temple. The newlyweds each take the other set home and exchange the garlands with each other on the next day after drinking lemon juice. Finally, they leave the mālai in the nearest water stream, for instance a well or a water tank. In case the visitors do not find a spouse despite the ceremony, the candidate has to return with his garland, which he places inside a temple tank, and subsequently breaks a coconut. The priest then hands him a second one so that he can conduct a new remedy ceremony.

5 Extract taken from the initial speech of the priest and translated.

Picture 11: Instructions in the Kalyanasundarar Temple

While temple rituals advanced to an integral part of the contemporary matchmaking process, the practice of conducting private functions became equally popular among long-term spinsters and bachelors. A wide-spread domestic parikāram is the *tāra tōṣa cumaṅkali pūjai.*[6] The exorcism of bad spirits from a previous life that hinder the successful search for a spouse form a central part of this remedy ceremony.

Picture 12: Tāra tōṣa cumaṅkali pūjai

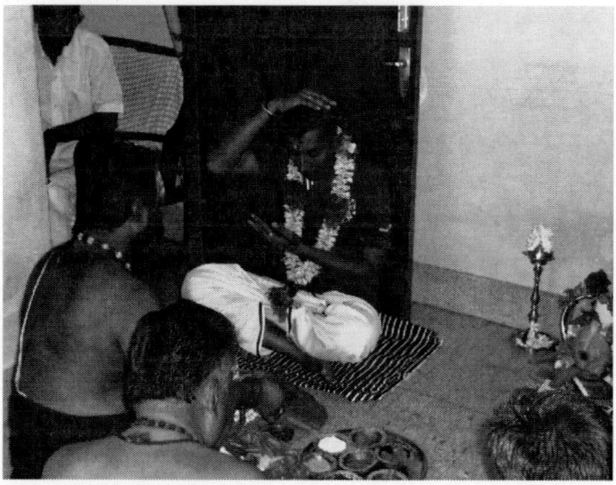

6 *Tāra tōṣam cumaṅkali pūjai* can be translated as 'wife ceremony' and is conducted for a male. If it is conducted for a female, the name of the ceremony changes into *Māṅkalya tōṣam cumaṅkali pūjai.*

The description of that ritual for Sasi illuminates its significance in the contemporary matchmaking process: the 38 year-old Akamuṭaiyār, originally from Madurai, works in Erode, 200 km away from his home as a branch manager in a finance company. For more than ten years, he and his family have been searching for a bride. With his unfavorable rāci (*riṣapam*) and star (*rōkiṇi*), he attributes the failure to find a bride to his unfavorable horoscope. Thus, he has consulted his own astrologer in Erode, a professor who dissuaded him from previous bride profiles. Although his parents would accept a bride from other Tēvar castes (Piramalai kaḷḷar and Maṟavar), they preferred an alliance with the Akamuṭaiyār, who are placed at the top of the Mukkulattōr. A marriage with their cross lineage is considered too complicated. Even though Sasi developed romantic feelings for his second cross cousin of the same age, they were not regarded as an appropriate match. Apart from a star mismatch, the main reason lay in a long-standing conflict between their relatives. In addition, his family considers his mother's younger brother's daughter, another potential partner, too young to be matched with Sasi. During her schooling and college, she stayed in Sasi's parents' house in Madurai together with her sister. By that time, the cross cousins developed an intimate relationship, however unsuitable for a conjugal union, as Sasi assumed a fairly authoritative role. His mother described this constellation as a "father-child" relationship. An ongoing fight over landholdings between her younger brother and Sasi's family constituted a further factor weighing against the alliance. His mother's own marriage to her tāy māmaṉ (Sasi's father) presented yet another problematic issue for a marriage among relatives from these two lineages; their conjugal life appears dysfunctional, as they have not spoken to each other for several years. As Sasi's father is the eldest family member, there is no senior authority to pacify their quarrellings. Additionally, she recalled genetic defects within their family – all together bad signs for a cross-kin liaison. Regardless of whether those concerns constitute cogent reasons against a consanguineous union, her explanation supports the observation of Clark-Decès (2014: 164), who highlights the dynamics in contemporary cross-kin marriages and the relevance of particular relations between *contam*.

Prior to tāra tōṣa cumaṅkali pūjai, Sasi and his family already organized a number of parikāram. Three years before, he had visited the Kalyanasundarar temple. In Erode, Sasi conducted different rituals in his office. Every Saturday, his family performs an *annadhanam*, a food donation rite, for which Sasi's family spends 1000 rupees. The futile search for a bride has induced participation in several remedy rituals and aggravated relationships between family members. Sasi's father accused his son of exaggerating the importance of astrology in his search, going so far as to suspect him of using it as a pretext to reject unwanted matches (see section 6.4). He complained that for five years, he collected suitable profiles for him and contacted promising brides working as doctors or in the government sector. Even though several bridal families have accepted Sasi's profile, his son takes the horoscope to the astrologer who advises him against the match. Upset with this development, Sasi's father denounced astrologers as "money makers".

After the efforts of Sasi's family remained unsuccessful, they carried out the tāra tōṣa cumaṅkali pūjai, in which I had the opportunity to participate. The event took place in Sasi's parents' house in Madurai, where participants were welcomed in the entry hall with turmeric (*mañcal*), cumcum powder, jasmine flower and betel leaf with sugar, placed on a small table. The attendants included Sasi, who served as the groom (*māppiḷḷai*), two priests (*Brahmin* and *Ōtuvār*[7]), Sasi's parents and seven cumaṅkalis – elder ideal women, who had lived a prosperous family life with children (and grand children) for many years. In contrast, the presence of spinsters, widows or divorcees is said to have a destructive effect. Likewise, people presenting non-ritual constellations such as peers, should not participate in such a ceremony. Particularly unmarried males of the same age should keep their distance, since they are considered inauspicious and suspicious of causing rumors. Curiously, three peers and colleagues were present, although for non-ritual purposes: David took pictures for Sasi and his family, Nataraj helped the priests facilitate ritual duties and one classmate waited in the adjacent room as "moral support".

Initially, the priest prepared the puja in the hall. At the back of the hall hung a *mūṉ mūrtti* with a framed picture of Ganesh and his parents Shiva and Parvati, generously decorated with flowers. In this ceremony, participants should praise a single Ganesh figure before starting the ritual, as it presents the god of all good ventures and the remover of obstacles to finding a spouse. With his elephant head and corpulent body, he is said to appreciate offerings in the form of fruits, sweets and other food. On the floor, the priest places nine plates with garlands, fruits and betel leafs, jasmine flowers, *katampam* (a bunch of the flower arali, nandiyavattai and tulsi)[8], tīpataṭṭu, mañcal with cumcum powder, flowers for the groom and betel leafs. Additionally, he provides water, an oil can and a banana with incense sticks. Facing the god statue, he places a *kalacam*, a pot of water

---

7 Non-Brahmin priest who learned the Tamil version of mantras and is mainly responsible for the organization and a correct procedure.

8 The selection of flowers serves to enhance the matchmaking process: Arali is a popular flower for most female goddesses; nandiyavattai is used for better sight; tulsi contains oxygen which enhances blood circulation.

where positive spirits are believed to enter and remain, together with booklets[9], bananas, rice, a dhoti[10] and an oil lamp on the left side.

Meanwhile, Sasi's mother gave instructions to the cumaṅkalis about how to order, keep and fold the Sari. Together, the women prepared the gift boxes for themselves, which symbolically endows them with positive energy for blessing the aspiring groom from the bottom of their hearts. The Sari and blouse, together with bangles, comb, mirror, mañcal thread, betel leaf, a note of ten rupees and a one Rupee coin[11], flowers and a banana, which is considered to be a precious and strengthening fruit, represent the principal gifts. Additionally, an oil lamp, a *kuthu vilakku,* can be found in the center of the gifts, which the wife must light after marriage in order to fulfill the most important duty of showing appreciation to the god. It is decorated with jasmine flowers, an item underlining and decorating the beauty and virtue of a *Madurai poṉṉu,* an ideal woman who adheres to female virtues. Later, during the ceremony, cumaṅkalis will pray for a wife who will light the kuthu viḷakku in the groom's family. Next to those gifts, there is a picture of Sasi's paternal grandparents, who are decorated with flowers in order to symbolize their approval as well.

Before the ceremony began, Sasi received the blessing of his parents in the corridor between the hall and the kitchen. To initiate the function, both priests started announcing instructions. The Ōtuvār priest addressed the aspiring groom formally, "This is a Puja conducted for you. Do you want to have everyone around?" Sasi nodded his head. The priest further instructed the cumaṅkalis to think about their *kula teyvam*[12] of their husbands' family, then about Meenakshi, Sundareswarar, Adhi Sivan and additionally about two goddesses. The actual ceremony took place in the main hall, where the priest prepared one banana leaf with mango and the sweets *laṭu* and *cakkarai poṅkal*. The Ōtuvār priest called Sasi's mother to light the oil lamp and she followed his instruction. The priest then began reciting the mantras. Sasi and his father stood in the adjacent room of the hall to pray while the cumaṅkalis remained in the corridor on the right side. While the first priest invoked the gods, the second instructed and continued to

9 Among the books are Ganapathy mantras and stories about Māriyammaṉ, the South Indian rain goddess and role model for a good cumaṅkali who keeps the husband in a good health. Usually, they are distributed to the ladies after the ceremony.

10 This gesture stands for a reciprocal act: first, the god receives the dhoti that facilitates acts of love-making and has to hand it back to the groom as soon as possible to accelerate the time until the first night.

11 In Tamil Nadu, giving one rupee as a gift serves to enhance the further accumulation of wealth.

12 Family god, divine ancestry.

guide the participants. First, the cumaṅkalis entered the room and took a seat in the corners on the right-hand side. When Sasi entered, he placed a towel on the floor to sit to the left of the god, facing the priest.

The priest hung the pack of garlands around the neck of the aspiring groom, who sprinkled water from the can over himself. While Sasi formed the god Karpaka Vinayakar out of turmeric paste, both priests continued to chant mantra, followed by praise to Karpaka Vinayakar. The bachelor started his prayer by calling upon other related gods and goddesses. He blessed the god with oil, decorated it with flowers and fanned it with incense sticks. The priests sprinkled water and lit the fire on the tīpataṭṭu to perform aarti, a worship ritual in which fire is offered to the divine in form of a flame. Circulating flowers above the fire, the priest again placed flowers on the god, reciting all of the divine names. After putting yellow thread on the deity, the priest raised the plate and repeated placing flowers on the god.

This praising act is followed by the offering (*prasadam*), in which the bachelor blesses the sweets and changes his place by sitting directly in front of the god. Forty pieces of *koḻukkaṭṭai*, the favorite sweet of Vinayakar, have to be placed on a big leaf and offered to the god. The Brahmin resumes placing flowers on the god, followed by the priest once again circulating the tīpataṭṭu and sprinkling water, first on the god, then on the sweets and finally on the remaining participants. He subsequently conducts the ritual fire ceremony, *hōmam*[13], for the gods Perumal and Mahalaxmi. Additionally, the priest conducted a second *hōmam prasadam* in which a laṭu was distributed to the guests. Sasi then positioned himself in front of the god and offered a coconut, lit incense sticks and sprinkled water over it. Again, he received blessings from his parents. In the next sequence, the elder women brought the Saris inside the room and placed them in front of the god. With this gesture, they consider god as their spouse and implore him to induce a quick marriage for Sasi. Moreover, they offered one Sari to the god, which the future wife has to wear during the wedding before she enters the stage. The Brahmin priest then placed a praying booklet on each gift box.

13 The *hōmam* is also conducted at Sasi's place of work in Erode. The priest traveled with him to his office wherehe distributed jasmine flowers to the mother of a colleague.

Picture 13: Blessings by cumaṅkali

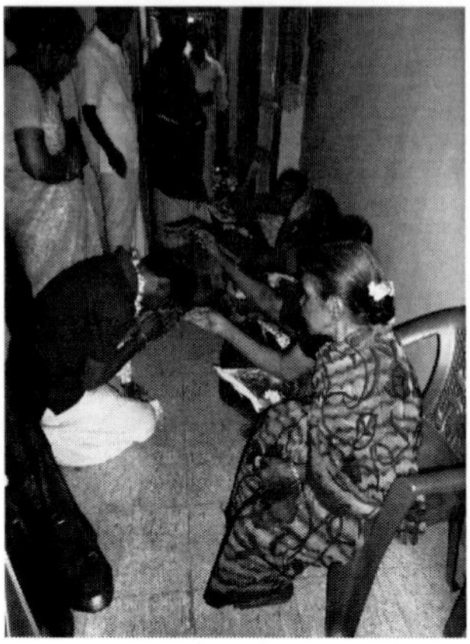

For the collective blessing, the cumaṅkalis sat in the threshold between the hall and the kitchen. Entering this corridor, Sasi received the benevolent energy from all cumaṅkalis while the priest held the plate. In turn, Sasi handed the Saris to them as presents for their transferred power. The priest gave rice to the women, which they threw over Sasi to bless him. Back in the main hall, the priest tied a towel around his neck, blessed the aspiring groom with cumcum and handed him a plate, containing water, betel nut and cumcum. This gesture signifies the bachelor's liberation from any bad aura previously inhibiting him from finding a bride. Sasi's father then entered the room and relieved the participants from their duties. He then received another blessing from the cumaṅkalis. Finally, food is served, first to the cumaṅkalis, then to the rest of the participants.

The inability to find a partner remains an inacceptable state. South Indians explain a delayed marriage through cosmic causes, which creates a great demand for remedy rituals. Both pujas presented in this subchapter aim to appease the god with the salutary energy of the married woman. In this context, the relationship between humans and their divine ancestors plays a prominent role while that between the individual seeking a match and the parents or relatives assumes a marginal one. The positive female energy of a cumaṅkali provides the source of inspiration in these ceremonies. For instance, in the Kalyanasundarar temple, the goddess Parvati holds the power of giving a blessing, demonstrated by her persistence in demanding an earthly marriage with Shiva: she persevered in the face of all hurdles, including Shiva's anger, his curses and the tedious existence as a cow in order to successfully achieve her desire. During the ceremony, the married couples positioned in the center of the crowd embody and release this power, transferring their positive energy to the singles in the audience.

Similarly, the power in the domestic ritual relies on the influence of the auspicious cumaṅkali. The principal purpose of this remedy ritual lies in the elimination of inauspicious elements in order to restore the ritual order. In that stage, parents do not actively involve themselves, while other kin and anti-hierarchical constellations remain entirely absent, with the exception of executing practical duties. Their emerging presence, however, becomes salient in the subsequent steps of alliance-making, which take the form of "long-term reasoning and mutual dependency within a given social setting" (Donner 2008: 88).

7.2 First encounters

The forming of an alliance, as a "key point in which family status is negotiated, effected and displayed to the social public" (Lamb and Mines 2010: 199), does not exclusively take place between two individuals, but involves a wider circle of family members, kin and selected acquaintances. Not surprisingly, profiles often provide columns to indicate the names of relatives or important friends. Since assemblers remain unreliable as contact people and are suspected of "boast[ing] about wealth and status" (Osella & Osella 2000: 98), most families rely primarily on so-called mediators, *terintavaṅka* or *teriñcavaṅka* (Wilson 2013: 43). This term derives from the Tamil word *terinta* (known) and reveals an outstanding negotiating competence. Typically, terintavaṅka entertain continuous connections within and outside families and clans because they exert authority as well as a deep understanding of familial relationships. Usually, older relatives, preferably married siblings or the maternal uncle, assume this position. A recent trend is the participation of non-relative mediators, so-called 'well wishers of the family' – a frequently used expression to describe one's sympathy and trust for reliable acquaintances, neighbors or friends and local authorities like village heads or pastors. Additionally, educated sections of the population increasingly draw upon the help of office colleagues, teachers or professors.

Today, terintavaṅka mostly represent the key actors in establishing an alliance between two families. As a first contact to the in-laws, most families prefer an informal meeting between selected members, which generally takes place in a neutral location, typically in an office, temple area or a church. Those meetings are arranged as casual talks about the family's place of origin and family-related issues. The main purpose of this meeting lies in confirming data stated in the profile, obtaining a clear picture of the family ties and background, vocational or educational intentions, avoiding negative surprises and reducing uncertainties. Additionally, the participants acquire a first insight into the demeanor and reputation of the in-law family. If they arrive late, cancel the meeting, forget the profile or make inconsistent and contradicting statements, they will leave the impression of having a dubious character or lacking respect. The required code of conduct is further motivated by South Indian gender norms. Although Clark-Decès (2014: 172) points out that wife-givers often suffer from severe humiliation at the hand of wife-takers and remain deprived of rights, influence and power, my observations reveal that unlike the process for forging alliances in North India, where the groom's family assumes a superior role, in South India the bridal family exerts a great deal of influence by determining the outcome of a potential match. Graduates and their families agreed that they expect the groom's side to make the initial effort in promoting the alliance through prescribed gestures. Thus, wife-takers must hand in their profile first instead of requesting the data from the bride.[14] In contrast, if the bridal family were to take initial steps to approach the groom, they would expose their inferiority and place their prospective in-laws deliberately in a dominant position. This notion is exemplified by the explanation of my host father, who insisted on conducting the wedding ceremony in his own church: "If they have some friction later on, the groom would say, 'You are the one who came to our church and got married to me. So now don't make any complaints!'" The precious role of the bride as well as the horizontal relationship between families reveal the particular image and status of the South Indian woman.

In the following, conventional methods and duties of mediators shall be exemplified through the experiences of Periyasami (Peri) and Ranjith (Ran), who act as terintavaṅka in the matchmaking process between my 31 year-old host sister, Suganth, and Joseph, both Christian Paṟaiyar. Periyasami lives in the adjacent village of the bridal family. He became familiar with the groom through one of his own relatives, Ranjith, a faculty member in the department of economics at MKU. Ranjith suggested Joseph, a classmate and very close university friend, as a potential groom for Suganth. Peri initiated a first encounter between himself, the bride's maternal uncle (MB) and her older brother (OB) in his house near the university campus. In this meeting, Peri acted as a terintavaṅka for Suganth's family members while Ranjith provided the information about Joseph. The conversation between the participating members and Ranjith took place via phone and served to acquaint the families with the

14 Equally, the *poṉṉu pārkka*, described in the following section may be regarded as an approaching of the bridal house.

idea of the match. After comparing assets, both parties inquired into the background of the parents, followed by listing degrees and acquired titles. The recorded fragments shall elucidate the nature of such initial meetings:

Ran:	He is an assistant professor. His father is a doctor and his mother works as an assistant manager in the Reserve Bank of India in Chennai.
MB:	Ok.
Ran:	What does the bride do?
MB:	She did her MSc, MEd and MPhil and is completing her PhD part time at Pondicherry University.
Ran:	Is she doing her PhD or yet to register her PhD?
MB:	She is doing her PhD. I am her tāy māmaṉ only. You can speak to Peri.

As soon as further questions surfaced with regard to the prospects of her PhD, the conversation was interrupted and passed to the mediator, who is supposed to handle the conversation:

Peri:	She works at American College.
Ran:	How long she has she been working there?
Peri:	She has been working there for about four years and she will become a permanent staff member. Her parents are all important people. The father was an auditor ... Sir, what is his age?
Ran:	He is 30. And what is her age?
MB (steps in):	She is 27 years old (which is a lie).

The conversation continued by speaking about the salary and the prospects of the job. As a mediator, Ranjith makes an effort to convince the family about the virtues of the groom with designed phrases:

"He is a very god guy. He listens to me ... He is like my relative. He is like your family and our family ... If they like the bride, then they won't ask for this and that. As soon as the marriage is complete, they would go to Chennai. They have many properties in Chennai. They already saw three bridal families. He is not satisfied. But when I spoke about this family, he was impressed."

Ranjith not only presents the advantages of the groom, such as his good character (good guy), economic wealth (properties) and similar background (like your family). Furthermore, he points out his own strong influence on the groom and his family – a crucial requirement concerning the future conjugal life of the couple. In some cases, such exaggeration even results in incorrect information, as the following passage between the bride's older brother and Ranjith demonstrates:

OB:	Do they have their own lands?
Ran:	The whole family struggled to get education.
OB:	I heard that all houses are bought by the older brother, who works as a break inspector in the RTO?[15]
Ran:	yes
OB :	So the properties that you were talking about before are the properties of the brother and not of the groom.

Beyond avoiding unwanted surprises and assuring a suitable match, the mediator remains an accountable person in the event of later frictions in conjugal life, as my host father explained to me, "If some things go wrong, we can easily sort out the issues with the help of common friends and the relatives. It would be easy to contain the problem and find a solution. If we look for an unknown person, it would be difficult. These issues would end up in serious struggles." In sum, the duties of terintavaṅka are held in high esteem, although this position implicates a serious obligation. As the principal representatives of one or both families, this person initiates the contact, monitors all relevant negotiations and mediates familiar conflicts throughout different stages of the matchmaking process.

Following initial encounters, further demands, discussions and arrangements are usually organized via phone. By that time, the matchmaking process requires not only the role of terintavaṅka, but also the efforts of other participants. The engagement is conducted according to prevailing gender norms. Male family members usually are responsible for the verification of the spouse's background by confirming data, ensuring the economic situation and evaluating the reputation of the in-law family. Fathers, brothers and male parallel cousins inquire into the nature of the spouse's profession by visiting offices or calling colleagues. During these interrogations, men cooperate predominantly with other male authorities as Prasenna explained, "Men can go around asking others for their opinion about the character and habits of a potential spouse – so we can inquire and give our appraisal to our parents. Women accept or reject that person

15 Regional Transport Office.

depending upon his character. So they make their decisions based on information from men."

Female members, in contrast, engage themselves with investigating the *personal* side of the spouse: particularly the sisters of aspiring grooms, female parallel cousins and mothers entertain direct conversations with the bride or with her female relatives. This exchange takes place through regular, casual phone calls or informal meetings in order to evaluate her character. Additionally, they convey feelings, wishes or doubts with respect to the potential spouses to the male members or mediators. Ilakiya, one female parallel cousin from my host family explained to me how she negotiated her alliance through her sister: "My sister asked me whether I am interested in Stephen. I told her she should talk to our parents. But I asked her about Stephan's job and so on. Then she spoke to my parents and then they did all the proceedings." Similarly, male grooms stated to me that in case they are unsatisfied with the profile, they do not express their reluctance openly; instead, they indirectly entrust their doubts to close, mostly female relatives.

Beyond familial contacts, the increasing complexity of the matchmaking process urges both sides to draw on social networks in order to receive reliable information. Usually, families of aspiring brides and grooms initiate such an inquiry by contacting distant relatives or trustworthy friends. College mates, teachers and colleagues serve as key agents for verifying information related to education and career as well as judging the spouse's integrity and family reputation. [16] Educated relatives frequently visit places of employment, departments and hostels to form an impression of the social environment surrounding the groom or bride. Importantly, these investigations involve distant relatives or acquaintances without confronting the family directly, as Suresh's father explained, "We will touch the outside circles but not the family itself. We do not approach the closest inner, circle. Instead, I ask someone who has a close contact to the family to find out about their character and reputation. This is more comfortable for both." 'Modern' challenges in marriage arrangement enhanced the involvement of such non-familiar participants and altered the established position of older authorities. Even though Fuller and Narasimhan (2008: 749) emphasize that most young people leave the task of searching a partner to their parents, who they expect to have greater expertise in arranging a suitable match, my own observations revealed that senior authorities increasingly struggle to meet the requirements of today's matchmaking rules.

One hurdle is the capacity to handle new forms of media: in order to select a suitable partner, it is useful to have experience with relevant matrimonial web

16 See section 5.2 for the importance of family *māṉam* in alliance making.

pages and to be firm with the digital forms of the profiles and e-mail correspondence. Thus, the younger generation increasingly assumes responsibility for a substantial portion of the procedure. Moreover, modern values, transmitted in educational institutions are adopted and exerted within the matchmaking procedure itself. Not only do young people in Tamil Nadu refuse to enter an unwanted marriage and openly oppose the expressed wishes of older authorities (ibid: 745ff.), but according to my observations, respondents often even criticize the behavior and demands of senior kin, which they designate as "out-dated".

This inter-generational discord becomes evident through the situation of Mishak, one colleague of my host brother. The 33 year-old Paṟaiyar is a former graduate of MKU and works in the IT sector in Chennai. Despite having submitted his profile to C.S.I. in Madurai, the alliance-making process turned out to be endless and tiring, lasting more than five years. As he belongs to the "IT people" with exposure to a modern lifestyle, in-law families became suspicious about his attitude and made careful inquiries about him. He recalled one vivid incident in which the father of a potential bride from a 'rural' background travelled to Chennai, entered the new company and began to question the doorman. Mishak narrated the encounter with the father, after the doorman called him in his office, "When I recognized him as the father of a potential bride, I went to the reception and took him around. We both went to the cafeteria. He asked me about the family and so on. Then he saw that the staff members were mingling in couples." In this setting, men and women join together to have coffee, which represents unusual conduct in Tamil everyday life. Mishak's illustration about the reaction of the potential bride's father in that situation reveals the gap between *taṟkālattavar* (modern attitudes) and *piṉ taṅkiyanilai* (non-modern attitudes): "So the bride's father was shocked when I explained that they are not couples and that they are not in relationships. Given that they work in the same department, they discuss work issues. But he is from a southern village (near Dindigul) and he does not understand this culture." As expected, the father did not continue to pursue this alliance, which Mishak attributed to those unusual scenes that he believes scared him away. Evidently, the father expected a small office where he would be able to gain an overview and make a straightforward assessment and the experience during his visit overwhelmed him enough to dismiss Mishak as a prospective groom for his daughter.

While that incident may largely be attributed to a different place of origin – the rural versus urban context – 'depreciated' attitudes often result in an inter-generational struggle over codes of conduct as shall be illustrated by the following example in my own host family: David, the older brother, found the profile of Rajiv and deemed him a suitable groom for his youngest sister, as the profile data suggested he would prove a promising match: he came from the same community, was a distant relative and three years older than Suganth. His professional aspirations seemed propitious, as he had completed his PhD in physics and spent time abroad at a European research institute. Suganth liked him and considered the prospective groom handsome. In the first meeting, however, both senior kin raised a delicate affair, namely the fact that Rajiv has an unknown father. The bridal father and his younger brother (*cittappā*) made uncomfortable comments about the strange exterior of the groom – behavior, not only considered inappropriate and indiscrete, but evidence of their lacking *decency*. Consequently, Rajiv and his family members designated Suganth's family as "backward", which finally lead to the rejection of the alliance. Due to such inconsistencies in values and appropriate behavior, most academics expressed their reluctance to involve elder authorities in the matchmaking process because it often causes severe generational conflicts. The fear of loss of status and control is an increasing problem expressed by many elder authorities, who respond to their limited power by degrading educated mediators as *veḷaṅkātavaṉ* (unlucky fellows).

This sequence shows that today's matchmaking is accompanied by newly imposed codes of conduct: marriage aspirants of the educated middle class demonstrate their integrity through decent behavior, reflected in a respectful and humble attitude. Delicate topics include caste, dowry or family affairs, about which families should inquire cautiously. A direct confrontation is considered 'backward'. This attitude comes to light in the statement of the younger host brother: "We see if these girls suit our family and whether she fits into our family, attitude and other things ... But we inquire into this in a discreet manner – we cannot directly go to the bride and ask."

Among the young generation, non-kin friends give emotional assistance and discussions within college friends circulate around personal and intimate feelings of the prospective spouses. Generally, the role of friends in partner selection revealed a gender-related difference: while men are likely to help and support their friends during weddings (especially in the case of love marriage, as will be shown in the following chapter), female colleagues function as moral support for each other's desires and doubts. This tendency is reflected in a statement by Soundariya concerning the input of her 'university friends' in marriage practices: "There is a difference between male and female friends. Regarding male friends, they participate and have more work in the process, but women also participate in the decision–making process." Female graduate students stated that they consulted their friends about their opinion of the groom and share their hopes and anxieties with them. Among male friends, the emotional support remains rather restricted. Suresh explained the character of his interaction with his classmates, "Mostly I don't discuss so much with them. I would say, for example, 'Now my family is looking for a girl. I hope that she is from that part of Madurai'. But that's it."

Notwithstanding the supportive role of academic friends, the formalities of the matchmaking process remain an enclosed, intimate affair of the domestic sphere. The principle reason for this privacy stems from the constant fear of damaging the family's status in case of a sudden cancellation. While neighbors and 'village friends' are common participants in matchmaking, non-kin friends remain often excluded during the principal steps. Graduate students fear teasing comments, jealousy or a bad reputation as Anitha explained, "If I tell my friends that we are looking for a groom and he doesn't like me, they will reveal that the guy rejected me. So they may spread rumors about me. We tell them only if the alliance is fixed that he likes me and I am going to get married." A cancellation after the public announcement causes severe humiliation, particularly for the bridal family.[17] To reduce the risk of getting rejected, families set up a regulation stipulating that the family of the groom has to pay a fine if the match is cancelled at a certain time. While justifications for suddenly rejecting a match seem to be subjective and contradictory (Wilson 2013: 35), a selection of case studies among the marriage aspirants and their families reveal some common reasons for cancelling an ongoing arrangement:

Rudeness: Rude gestures include any deviations from the accepted matchmaking procedure, for example by neglecting formal address or disregarding the prescribed order. Most families commonly felt offended when they received the profile late or if in-laws failed to attend the meetings on time. Similarly, many families considered it 'rude' to disregard local gender codes. Such a situation occurs, for example, when wife-takers demand the profile of the bride without disclosing the data of the groom. The demeanor of family members presents one of the principal reasons to continue or cancel an alliance. Deepak, one younger classmate of my host brother complained about the awkward behavior between the bride and her siblings, "Her older sister was so dominant. This girl did not speak herself. Whatever I ask her, she needed her sister's permission or opinion

17 Clark-Decès (2014) postulates how wife-takers hold the power to degrade wife-givers: "They certainly complain a lot. The bride is too short, the food served at the marriage feast is skimpy or not good, the gifts of the wedding [...] are of mediocre quality and so on" (ibid: 172).

to give an answer. This is not good. A girl should be independent. She (older sister) was so dominant. So I rejected her."

Materialistic, demanding attitude: One of the most frequent causes for cancelling a match is the insistence of the groom's family on receiving a higher dowry, which reveals a 'demanding attitude'. In turn, parents of the groom are scared away by financial claims of the bridal family concerning the expenses for the ceremony or the value of the *tāli* (bridal neck ornament), usually purchased by the wife-takers.

Non-transparency and deviation: Sudden changes or alterations to former agreements raise suspicion of in-laws and present a frequent reason for a sudden cancellation. After finalizing his alliance, Ramesh was told by his future wife that she decided to resign her job and asked him to conduct the marriage sooner. This was against their former agreement when she assured him she would continue her work and support his PhD studies. Ramesh suspected her of having an affair and only getting married to him to save her reputation. He lost trust in her and cancelled the arrangement.

Finding another spouse: While in kinship marriages, the alliance is fixed from the childhood of both spouses, nowadays forging an alliance requires exhausting efforts to find a suitable match – an endeavor which pushes the families into a permanently unsatisfying state until the official agreement on both sides is finally confirmed. On the one hand, parents have to fear that the in-law family searches for another alliance; on the other hand, they might be tempted to see if they could arrange a more prestigious alliance for their own child.

Internal conflict among family members: Another common reason for an unforeseen cancellation stems from conflicts not between but *within* one family. Typically, such frictions arise if the established social position of one family member is endangered. A new alliance usually signifies power redistribution within the family and a threat to former status constellations. The fear of losing one's position explains why certain kin may try to sabotage the proceedings. Again, the case of Suganth illustrates such a situation, notably when her family members found Jananeshan to present a promising alliance for her. As a long-term spinster, Suganth provided her older sister Angel indispensable help in the household and regularly took care of her daughter. Angel and her husband maintained the principle authority in important financial and family-related decisions. This privileged position might change with the marriage of her younger sister, whose husband could acquire certain rights due to his status as a family head. Since Angel had eloped with her husband, Suganth's alliance with Jananeshan is ranked higher, so that this union would exert a stronger influence. To save her position, Angel started to spread rumors against her own family members in order to impede the arrangement.

Irrespective of the manifold reasons, cancelling the alliance presents a difficult and most unrewarding task requiring a great degree of tact. Therefore, annulment is usually entrusted to very select members of the intimate family. Instead of stopping the marriage bluntly, the cancellation should be conveyed cautiously. Typically, families simply cut off contact after the first encounter. They might also communicate disinterest through certain gestures during the meetings; while serving tea signifies rapprochement, cool drinks indicate alienation. A mismatch of horoscopes serves as a popular pretext for stopping the process. Some families claim to have misunderstood the profile and begin to suddenly emphasize their preference for a particular caste or religious background. Further conjured reasons to end a match include an unforeseen misfortune, as for example financial loss, an accident or sudden death. The delicate implications of the procedure are further reflected in the subsequent ritualized encounters that constitute complex behavior determined by a range of rules, regulations and codes of conduct.

7.3 EVALUATING THE SPOUSE: *POṉṉU PĀRKKA* AND *MĀPPIḶḶAI VĪṭU AṟIYA*

If the initial encounters result in the satisfaction of both families, they proceed to the next step, the "bride viewing" ceremony (coll. *poṉṉu pārkka* or *peṇ pārkka pōratu*). This event constitutes a first personal encounter between the wider family circle, a "setting in which first impressions are made between the potential bride and bridegroom's families, impressions that often determine the likelihood of a match" (Wilson 2013: 42). Particularly in non-kin alliances, this ceremony becomes a principle performance that serves to establish a harmonious connection between the potential spouses. Following its meaning, notably "seeing the bride", the primary aim of this ceremony lies in a detailed evaluation of the physical appearance, behavior and social environment of the female spouse and her family.

The detailed description of the poṉṉu pārkka for Suresh's younger male parallel cousin, Mani, shall elaborate its crucial significance for the matchmaking procedure today. The ceremony always takes place in the bridal house. The number and function of the participants are regulated: the parents of both marriage aspirants and important kin such as the maternal and paternal uncles (*tāy māmaṉ, periyappā, cittappā*) as well as their wives (*attai, periyammā, citti*) are present. Relatives of the same age such as siblings and cousins only take part if they have a close relationship with the bride or groom. However, they should be already married to avoid the risk of attracting their relative's prospective mate. The ceremony starts with a 'warm up session', which serves the purpose of creating a relaxed ambiance between both sides. Usually male members of both families sit in chairs, remaining silent or exchanging small talk. Female relatives on the groom's side continue chatting with each other on the floor opposite the men, while the mother and sisters of the bride serve tea and snacks or busy themselves in the kitchen. Importantly, the hosts do not dish up any food, which is a sign of welcoming and comforting guests. As long as the outcome of the ceremony is unclear, there is no space for intimacy or emotional content and both parties remain aloof.[18]

This initial stage culminates in the appearance of the bride – the central purpose and focus of the meeting. Made up in an elegant dress, maquillage and jewelry, she enters the room and places herself in the middle of the attendants so that she remains visible to everyone. In some cases, she also engages in a physical activity, for example by serving tea. Since Mani's family members liked her, they accepted the tea as a sign of their goodwill. The aspiring bride should neither rise to speak nor look up directly into the eyes of her prospective in-laws. This would evoke the impression that she would be disobedient in conjugal life and moreover that she disregards her ritual role, unable to show respect.

That key performance and its implication for matchmaking shall be elucidated from several perspectives of the participants. Suresh's father explained this decisive moment for evaluating the spouse:

"During poṉṉu pārkka, we will ask her everything, where she works, what she does, just to confirm the data. Then we will check her walking, eye sight, voice, her behavior and the way she respects the elders. As parents with our experience we can easily judge the character of the girl. When I ask her to bring water, it is not because I am thirsty, but to make her walk and check her way of walking. One bride I asked to sing, so I could listen to her voice. This we do, because in that ceremony, brides are seated, even before the groom's family arrives. So, the visiting family is not able to see her movements."

18 This ceremony was the first situation during my stay in India that I was requested to refrain from taking pictures.

Suresh, who played a central role in the decision-making process for his own brother, Prathib, illustrated his impression of one bride through her gestures and facial expressions: "I could feel something... fishy... when I spoke to her, something... see like this, no?" In that moment, he pointed to his mouth, making an exaggerated huge smile from one ear to the other. "It was very wide on her face. So I felt that she was more talkative ... even though when we were watching her she was silent ... And for that reason, I concluded that her family would not be good."

Young women undergoing the ceremony were aware of the required performance as Soundariya stated: "See now I am talking very frankly. Whatever I have on my mind I will just say. And this is ok with my partner. But during poṉṉu pārkka, I have to be silent. If they ask something I should answer with a word, that's it."

After an adequate amount of time, the bride may express an emotional reaction. Typically, she demonstrates shyness by disappearing. Mani's future wife suddenly started to cry. Her outburst caused a rush of female relatives from the groom's family who brought her into a separate room to comfort her. This reaction serves to establish a close link and an emotional relationship with the bride and also gives a direct insight into her personality. Meanwhile, the remaining male participants continued to discuss further proceedings. Since they were interested in the bride, the terintavaṅka, the maternal uncle, and the father fixed a date and locality for the next meeting. This agreement is ritually accompanied by a cloth, which is usually brought by the wife-takers. As a response and sign that the bridal family accepts the groom, they kept this cloth in their house.

So far, the observations reveal a prescribed role for all attendees at the poṉṉu pārkka. The principal task for elder male authorities lies in evaluating the spouse. Hence, they remain largely passive and should be addressed in a respectful manner. Moreover, the ceremony offers an occasion for the prospective spouses to exchange a glance, although the groom is not supposed to overtly gaze at the potential bride. Mani took a seat behind the other participants and observed her in a decent way.[19] Younger members play an increasingly active role in carrying out pragmatic inquiries concerning educational and professional plans. Finally, terintavaṅka are responsible for the organizational process and discuss the date and place for upcoming meetings. Women, similarly to close friends, attempt to persuade the groom to select the bride. I present an outline of a chat between Mani and his female relatives. On the way back from

19 In some cases, grooms even persuaded me to take a secret picture of the potential bride.

the ponnu pārkka to his house, he sat in a van, together with his older brother's wife (W 1), other female relatives, myself and my research assistant. The cited comments shall demonstrate the particular methods applied to present the bride as attractive.

(Women are teasing Mani):

W 1:	This bride is good, we should show her to others.
W 2:	We won't show anyone
W 1 (to Mani):	This girl is too good for you
W 2:	This black guy, you think he deserves a fair girl?
Mani:	Is black an ugly color?
An elder woman:	Do you (all sisters) like the bride?
W 2:	We are just women, we are not going to live together with her.
W 1:	For us the girl is ok. We have to ask Mani, if she is ok for him.
She turns to me:	You like the bride?
Stephanie:	No, she is ugly. (making fun)
All women are laughing.	
W 1:	You're right! She fits Mani
W 3:	Mani has to live with her, so he has to like her.

These statements present formalized teasing to convince and support the groom about the choice. In this case, the women already accepted the bride and organized the date for the next visit, to finalize the match. Mani himself realizes they are joking; since he likes the bride, he joins in the humorous conversation.

Mani:	Now I am saying yes only because you all like her. You only decided.
W 2:	See, we show you the bride and you like her.
W 1:	I can get you her mobile number. Not immediately, but after the pū cūṭṭu viḻā[20].
W 2:	I took some pictures of the bride... I had a mobile with me, I must have deleted the picture.
W 1:	Let this poor boy enjoy the pics. Leave him...
W 3:	I spoke to the bride. Someone was telling the bride to look at you. She was so shy.
Mani:	So they have to give me ten Sovereigns of gold.
W 1:	what, ten Sovereigns...

20 See section 7.4.

Mani (making fun):	She has done her 10th standard only, that is why ten Sovereigns.
Elder woman:	If her elder brother calls, what should I say? (This questions serves for finding out if he likes the bride or not)
Mani:	I will talk to him.
Elder woman:	Do not involve me in those things. You talk to him clearly.
Mani:	Ok. Aṇṇaṉ (his older brother) and you (W 1) have to go and ask.
W 1:	But now you said that you don't like the bride. Then why should they go and see her?
Elder woman:	It is decided that, on Friday they will come here (to the groom's house).

These conversation sequences illustrate how the compatibility of the spouses is negotiated in consideration of the groom's perspective. After mentioning the beauty of the bride, the women continue to claim that she is not suitable for Mani and that they might stop the procedure. These comments are meant to provoke an emotional reaction from him. If both families agree, the encounter that follows the poṉṉu pārkka is *māppiḷḷai vīṭu aṟiya*, the bridal family's formal visit at the groom's house. Derived from the words māppiḷḷai vīṭu (groom's house) and aṟiya (to learn), the purpose of this event is the evaluation of the male spouse's home, which presents the prospective future environment for the bride. Usually, the bridal family inspects equipment, wealth and makes inquiries into the groom and other members of the neighborhood. This event challenges the groom's family, since they are in charge of demonstrating their ability to take proper care of the bride. In contrast to the northern part of India, where young married women move to an unknown residence, bridal relatives in South India ensure by several visits that the bride is well settled in her new home.

Māppiḷḷai vīṭu aṟiya does not require the presence of all relatives, but mostly remains restricted to the parents and a few selected relatives from both sides. Normally, the bride does not attend this visit, avoiding any risk of attracting male family members. Compared to the poṉṉu pārkka, the procedure resembles a cosy get-together, containing few ritualistic elements. While tea is served for the bridal family, both sides sit together and clarify further formalities, including financial transactions, professional prospects and family planning. If the bridal family is convinced about the groom's home, both sides celebrate the agreement by handing over a sari to the bridal family. In case any doubts remain, the encounter may be followed by a third meeting for further clarification.

The period between those two ceremonies constitutes an uncomfortable situation of uncertainty and tension because a constant fear of being rejected prevails for both families. The bridal family in particular remains in a nervous condition during that period. In Kerala, Osella and Osella describe that wife-givers find themselves preoccupied with the hectic maintenance of the house in order to be prepared for the bride viewing ceremony or unforeseen visits by the groom's side prior to the ceremony (2000: 98). During this precarious period, young brides are exposed to constant interference and restrictions in their habits, movements and contacts. That stage reveals strong inter-generational disagreements about suitable behavior, patterns of dress or adequate conversational topics with in-laws. In my own host family, both older brothers persuaded Suganth to start fasting. Additionally, she was pressured not to have long conversations on the phone or invite unknown people to the house. Interactions deemed too close to her peers could create the impression of entertaining many dubious contacts or even an affair. In turn, young brides find those precautionary measures exaggerated. Moreover, they reject recommended clothing such as saris as old-fashioned (Wilson 2013: 34). Among wife-takers, similar disputes transpire. Thus, young grooms consider it vulgar to pressure the bridal family by making open demands (see also Osella & Osella 2000: 99).

Contradictory attitudes and individual desires of marriage aspirants enhanced the recourse to egalitarian ties, made in external contexts. So far, non-kin friends seem to play a marginal role in pre-wedding activities. A closer look, however, revealed that they exceed the role of mere moral support. In fact, peers assume a crucial position in evaluating the personal traits and reputation of the prospective spouse. Through daily interactions, they indicate whether the groom or bride is polite, trustworthy, and gentle or whether (s)he behaves rudely, suspiciously, has a short temper or bad habits. Furthermore, they enable personal encounters between both spouses, which remain neglected during official ceremonies.

The increasing function of peers becomes apparent through the example of Mishak and his present wife Cynthia, a Christian Paṟaiyar couple from Madurai. The 27 year-old bride had befriended several of Mishak's female and male peers through an affiliated MKU college. Since they were in regular contact with Mishak, her friends seized the opportunity to observe his behavior and inquired about his personality and habits. Repeatedly, they confirmed to Cynthia that he is a "good guy", i.e. responsible, caring and abstinent with respect to smoking and drinking. While the family members of both were occupied with formal proceedings, friends acted as key organizers of the first opportunity for the future spouses to approach each other. That encounter took place after a service at C.S I. and was initiated by Ruby, Cynthia's former college friend who contacted Thamba, Mishak's senior in college. Thamba went with Mishak to the church courtyard. Inside, Cynthia was attending the mass together with Ruby and her mother. After the service, Thamba called Cynthia on her phone to inform her that he was standing outside with the groom. When Cynthia stepped out of the church, both bride and groom were aware of the other's presence and took the opportunity to take a glimpse at each other. This contact took place without any direct interaction while both were accompanied by close family members and friends. After this instance, Mishak called Thamba to inform him that he was interested and ready to continue the matchmaking process. Thamba passed this statement on to Cynthia, who replied that she also approved of the groom.

Mishak's explanations during a clarifying conversation suggest that it is not the individual sympathy of bride and groom but the 'external' judgment of the social environment, which proves paramount for the procedure: "My *ṭēy naṇpar* Thamba and Ruby were talking about her like my cousin's wives.[21] Pressure came from different directions. So I decided to go and see her. I saw her photo before I met her. I liked this profile and everything seemed to suit my expectations." Similarly, Cynthia revealed to me that she did not consent merely due to this instance, but that her close friends convinced her: "Thamba and Ruby were talking to me, saying that there are no parents-in-law, so I would not face any pressure. Mishak is such a nice guy. He doesn't have any bad habits and so on. Now it is me who has to decide and tell them my decision. I did not see the groom properly on the first meeting so I was not very serious about it. But everybody told me that he is a very polite fellow and trustworthy."

In some cases, friends become active in cultivating the contact between both future spouses. To enhance the communication, her former college friend, Alice, took Cynthia's mobile from her. By that time, Mishak's friend's wife, Suganthini, called her on her mobile and Alice attended the call. Both Alice and Suganthini knew each other from primary school. They spoke to each other and both passed the phone to Mishak and Cynthia. In this way, a connection was established and opened the opportunity for further contacts between the future groom and bride. Cynthia described her experience as such: "Suganthini insisted that I talk to Mishak afterwards. I accepted, but I did not ask for his phone number. On the next day in school, Victoria (another friend) and Suganthini were waiting for me and scolded me because I did not call him. Victoria took my phone and made a call to her own mobile to get my number. She gave it to Mishak. Then he started calling me." When I asked her what they spoke about, she replied: "He talked about his job and asked about my work. He wanted me to live with him in Chennai. He insisted that I learn to cook. These are all the talks we had through phone."

21 The expression *tēy naṇpar* and the comparison with female cross kin emphasizes trust and influential position.

To conclude, matchmaking ceremonies present decisive events in today's spouse selection process, which attests to a required performance involving all relevant participants. It is a peculiar moment for the spouses and their families and therefore excluded from public and non-familiar contacts. In the course of a wider and more complex radius of the matchmaking scene, however, friends increasingly assume roles traditionally reserved for kin. Their involvement does not counteract, but facilitates the proceedings of matchmaking ceremonies. The example of Cynthia and Mishak demonstrated how friendships forged in the educational context supplement the formalized actions of familial and kin authorities. Taking account of individual needs and desires, this engagement is socially recognized and complements the alliance making.

7.4 FINALIZING THE MATCH: *PŪ CŪṭṭU VIḺĀ* AND *NICCAYATĀRTTAM*

While poṉṉu pārkka and māppiḷḷai vīṭu aṟiya focus on the acquisition of information, evaluation and negotiation, the *pū cūṭṭu viḻā* (Flower Ceremony) marks the official confirmation of the alliance. This peak ceremony transforms the matchmaking status from a secret and pending state to public disclosure. Hence, beyond the spouses, parents and related kin, for the first time family acquaintances and neighbors are present. If families are not entirely convinced about the match, they postpone the date of the pū cūṭṭu viḻā to allow more time for their final decision. Likewise, if they become very concerned for the alliance, they insist on conducting the pū cūṭṭu viḻā as soon as possible.

Usually, the Flower Ceremony takes place in the bridal house. Parents, siblings and relatives of the groom bring jasmine flowers, a sari, fruits, coconut, betel leaf, betel nuts and sweets. As soon as wife-takers enter the house, coffee or tea is served to the guests. Corresponding to its name, the culmination of this ritual lies in the continuous exchange of flowers by both families to signify the common agreement for the alliance. This process is initiated by elder cumaṅkalis of the groom's family: they tie jasmine garlands to the bride, together with the groom's sisters. The flowers symbolize attachment and energy from the female relatives and express their willingness to support her in future duties as a married woman. Hence, this part of the ritual represents an act of strengthening the bridal position in her conjugal life. Having received the flowers, the bridal family in turn gives flowers to the female members of the wife-takers. This exchange not only symbolizes love and the happiness of both sides about the arrangement; most importantly, it signifies that the alliance is ritually confirmed and henceforth both families do not look anymore for an alternative match. Correspondingly, pū cūṭṭu viḻā presents the first occasion, in which both wife-givers and takers eat together. Any skepticism and distance that once existed become replaced by a mutual attachment between all participants, finally celebrated by a joint feast.[22]

Another indicator for the public recognition of the alliance is the official approaching between the bride and groom. Up to this point, the contact between the two has been restricted. During the initial rituals, the presence of spouses plays a minor role, with the exception of the bride viewing ceremony. If the confirmation of the alliance is imminent, the bride and groom receive a space to talk to each other during the Flower Ceremony. While a direct encounter between both partners was restricted until recent years, families increasingly support an intensified relationship between the spouses before the wedding. Here, modern communication technology provides a welcomed channel by which to enhance their connection. As observed in similar studies (Wilson 2013: 45), partners utilize available internet technologies or cell phones to cultivate their relationship, as Mishak explained, "After the Flower Ceremony, we made phone calls. We start speaking at 10 o'clock until we get tired. We speak about the family and the job and relocation. Sometimes she speaks to the female family members. They prepare her to be able to give respect to the parents. And boys will give advice to the groom: 'Behave like a man, don't let her do this and that'." Further, both meet each other in public places, preferably shopping malls or coffee shops.

Importantly, those encounters reveal an entirely different character than romantic affairs within the college campus. While such unofficial liaisons take place in a secret manner, unrelated to the domestic context, the 'privacy' between future spouses is ritually negotiated and monitored by the social environment. These meetings require a socially accepted and expected behavioral pattern. Here, close family members and friends are considered responsible for maintaining the positive feelings required for a functioning conjugal life and avoiding the risk of an unforeseen cancellation during the final pre-marriage arrangements.

Subsequently to the FWC, the engagement ceremony (*niccayatārttam*) is the key event in which two families confirm the alliance in the presence of relatives and a wider circle of guests. Because in contemporary weddings the engagement

22 Margaret Trawick (1990: 52) states that the mutual feeding stands for the exchange of body fluids and signifies an indigenous form of love and affection.

becomes more and more relevant, it is often conflated with the pū cūṭṭu viḻā.[23] As a distinctive criterion, the Flower Ceremony presents an 'oral confirmation', a ritual which exclusively takes place in a private context. Niccayatārttam instead fixes the alliance officially by the involvement of related functionaries and the signing of marriage documents. With reference to 'modern' influences, Fuller and Narasimhan (2008) regard this event as a "recent development resembling a wedding reception [which] is distinct from the traditional 'betrothal' (niccayatarttam) ritual" (ibid: 746). My respondents in Madurai expressed a similar view: in their parents' generation, the engagement ceremony presented a setting for negotiations, carried out at least one year before the wedding itself. Nowadays, however, it transformed itself into a time-consuming life style event which requires huge financial investment. Middle class members tend to organize it one day before the wedding itself. Preferably, families rent a hall (*maṇṭapam*) for both the engagement and the wedding so that those guests who arrive from distant places have the opportunity to participate in both events during one stay. Beyond this practical concern, a shortened time lapse between niccayatārttam and the wedding further reduces the risk of an unexpected cancellation.

However, the niccayatārttam of Suresh's older sister, Nandhini, took place in the bridal home. As will be shown in section 8.1, the maṇṭapam represents the symbolic home of the bride and is chosen and selected by the wife-givers. Since niccayatārttam is entirely prepared and conducted by the family members of the bride, they find themselves in the challenging position of satisfying the expectations of the in-laws and the guests. Importantly, it is the first event in the matchmaking process where not only close relatives, acquaintances and neighbors are officially invited, but also non-ritual contacts such as friends, colleagues and official personalities.

The ceremony is initiated by the family members of the groom, who serve an odd number of dishes (minimum seven) with presents like flowers, fruits, sweets and a new sari. This is a gesture that attests to their wealth and readiness to welcome the bride. Sisters of the groom, or alternatively the father's sisters (*attai*), accompany the bride to the dressing room in order to help her to put on the given sari – this also provides an opportunity to evaluate her body. The presentation of the dishes is followed by a mutual tribute between both maternal uncles and the spouses by exchanging flower garlands. This honor follows a prescribed order and takes place between (1) *tāy māmaṉ* of *poṉṉu* and *māppiḷḷai* (2) poṉṉu and māppiḷḷai (3 times) and (3) the bridal tāy māmaṉ and the poṉṉu as

23 In some cases niccayatārttam replaces the FWC, or both events are held together.

well as the groom's tāy māmaṉ and the māppiḷḷai. Through this action, the tāy māmaṉ relinquishes his conjugal rights to his sister's daughter.

Picture 14: Plates for niccayatārttam in the Kōṉār community

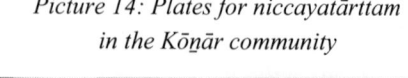

A related ceremony that was carried out for Nandhini is *kāppu kaṭṭutal,* in which the tāy māmaṉ ties the *kāppu*, a yellow thread around the wrist of the bride. He symbolically transfers his sister's daughter to the groom and relinquishes his own rights to marry to her. The tying of the kāppu represents the last occasion in which he can touch his niece. This ceremony is likewise conducted for the groom and has a protective function for the couple: it serves to eliminate any bad will stemming from jealousy or external desires toward the spouses. When the groom is bound with a thread around his wrist, he should refrain from any risky activity, as for example riding a motorbike or eating non-vegetarian food to avoid the risk of an accident or sickness before the wedding ceremony. The kāppu will be removed when the couple enters the room on their first night.[24] Subsequently, the engagement ceremony is followed by a *parucam*, a function to enhance the physical contact between bride and groom. For this ritual part, both spouses touch each other's body by exchanging chains (Hindus) and rings (Christians). With this action, bodily contact becomes an acceptable gesture within the ritual sphere and therefore socially approved. This confirmation of

24 A frequent ritual, practiced among most non-Brahmin castes is the *Kaṉṉiyatāṉam*, which represents the gifting of the *kaṉṉi* (virgin). During this ritual, the father of the bride places her in the hands of the groom. For a detailed analysis see Michael Allen (1986: 81ff.).

social status is followed by the official part when both families register the date of the marriage on a stamped paper. The event is closed by a joint meal to demonstrate mutual affection.

7.5 CONCLUSION

Particularly among the highly educated middle-class in India, matchmaking strategies become increasingly challenged by influences attached to 'modernity'. Some of the main alterations include advanced techniques in profile design, changes to the prescribed codes of conduct, a visible engagement of the younger generation and greater attention paid to the personal and physical attraction between spouses. In particular the trend toward non-kin alliances intensified the amount of effort necessary for identifying and confirming an adequate marriage alliance. Moreover, this change has rendered the process a delicate and exhausting affair, which dominates the routines, demeanor and relationships of the family members. The precarious and crucial significance of finding a spouse is reflected throughout all observed stages. An increasing demand for remedy rituals demonstrates the recourse to spiritual support, ritually symbolized by the female power of the auspicious cumaṅkali and appealed to with the goal of enhancing positive energy for conjugal life. The search for a partner follows a prescribed order and is only disclosed to selected persons, such as relatives, neighbors, local authorities or intimate friends, as an unexpected cancellation might destroy the image of the family. During private negotiation rituals – poṉṉu pārkka and māppiḷḷai vīṭu aṟiya – all participants perform a prescribed role in evaluating the suitability of the match. The turning point is ritually celebrated on the pū cūṭṭu viḻā, a ceremony that conveys the union between both families, expresses the joy about the successful match and restates the ritual position of established authorities through honors and blessings. Due to practical reasons, this custom is increasingly substituted or even conflated with the engagement (niccayatārttam), despite considerable differences in their formalities and respective connotation.

As a response to the complexity of contemporary matchmaking, selected kin and acquaintances constitute an elaborated network that helps to acquire relevant information about the prospective spouse. In this context, social constellations, formed in the academic context gradually become integrated into marriage practices and take over duties formerly ascribed to family members. Equipped with skills in modern technology and exposure to the modern sphere, former university friends and academic peers not only choose contemporary tactics of finding a spouse, but also propagate a suitable and decent attitude amongst their friends seeking a spouse and advocate for them in the presence of potential mates. Moreover, banter and jokes between male groups and intimate conversations between women constitute an additional domain in which youth can articulate personal desires and doubts. Hence, although excluded from initial meetings, non-kin friends do retain a considerable scope for practicing solidarity among their peers. Rather than constituting a contrasting system of anti-hierarchy, peers adjust their forms of interactions such that their engagement considerably facilitates and complements marriage arrangements. The behavior and significance of non-kin contacts shall be further illustrated in the following chapter, through the example of designated middle class weddings in the town of Madurai.

Table 5: Marriage rituals and central events (example: Paṟaiyar Caste)

Ritual	Activities	Place	Participants	Position of non-kin friends
		Matchmaking rituals		
Remedy puja *parikāram* (practiced initially to enhance the match-making process)			Bride (*poṉṉu*), groom (*māppiḷḷai*), parents (*ammā, appā*) *pūcāri, ōtuvār*	Not present, except for practical reasons
māṅkalya tōṣam parikāram	Removal of inauspicious *tōṣam*	Bridal and grooms' home		Escort, information about the puja, procuring ritual items
tāra tōṣa cumaṅkali pūjai	Praying to Karpaka Vinayakar, blessing by cumaṅkali		Above persons plus seven elderly married women (cumaṅkali)	
kūṭṭu vaḻipāṭu	Joint worship	Temple	Above persons, plus close kin	
Bride viewing *poṉṉu pārkka/ peṇ pārkka pōratu* (first official meeting)	Presentation of the bride, distribution of tea and snacks, mutual evaluation of both families, organization of the subsequent meeting	Bridal home	Bride, groom, parents, parental authorities from both sides: *tāy māmaṉ, attai, periyammā, cittappā, periyappā,*	Indirect support in between the meetings by obtaining information, advising, listening, joking

Visit at the groom's house *māppiḷḷai vīṭu aṟiya* (1-2 weeks after poṉṉu pārkka)	Evaluation of the groom's house (usually the future home of the bride), further negotiations concerning dowry and wedding conduction, fixation of the wedding date	Groom's home	Groom (rarely) parents and parental authorities	
Pre-wedding rituals				
Flower Ceremony *pū cūṭṭu viḻā* (several weeks after mutual con-firmation)	Official agreement Grooms family brings flowers, sari, fruits (banana), coconut, veṟṟilai pākku, Groom is gifted cash and clothes Tea/coffee is served Grooms' sisters/attai help the bride put on the sari and evaluate her body. Mutual exchange of flowers (first by female relatives of the groom, then by the bridal side) Joint meal, planning of engagement	Bridal home	Bride, groom parents, parental authorities, young generation: sisters and brother of both spouses, few close neighbors	Only close friends attend occasionally

Engagement *Niccayatā-rttam* (originally few weeks before the wedding, today often at the night before)	Grooms family brings at least seven plates of jewels, fruits, sweets and a new sari, official registration of the alliance, Mutual garland exchange, blessings by elder authorities, congratulations by guests, Joint meal	Bridal home, alterna-tively: *maṇṭapam* church (Chris-tians)	Priests (pūcāri, ōtuvār), bride, groom, whole family, whole community, limited number of friends and neighbors	Invited occasionally, Congratu-lating, gifting presents
Binding ceremony *kāppu kaṭṭutal*, (3-1 days before the wedding)	Tying of *kāppu* (holy thread which symbolizes god) around bride's and/or groom's wrist and gifting new dresses. Hereafter the groom is not supposed to eat non-vegetarian food to maintain his health	During niccayatār-ttam or in the spouse's home	Groom, his sisters	
Bride's departure *poṉṉu āḷaikka pōratu* (practiced occasionally, one night before the wedding)	Relocation of the bride to the groom's house to reevaluate her new home and give her moral support. Welcoming the bride with an oil lamp and a	Groom's home	Bride, groom entire bridal family, groom's family for welcoming	

	common feast. Accommodating bridal female members			
Rituals on the wedding day (*kalyāṇam*)				
Gifting the virgin *kaṉṉiyatāṉam*	father of the bride gifts the virgin (kaṉṉi) to the groom	maṇṭapam	Priests (Brahmins, pūcāri, ōtuvār), bride, groom, both families, whole community, neighbors seized number of friends, colleagues, public personages like politicians	Male peers: Organization of the wedding, negotiations with hall owners, caterers, distributing marriage invitations. During ritual activities, they keep physical distance, but provide services, like distributing food. Female peers: moral support for the bride, accompa-nying the bride to the parlor
tāli binding *tāli kaṭṭu* (culmi-nating event)	The *tāli* (ornament, on a yellow thread) is tied around the neck of the bride. Through the tāli the poṉṉu obtains the status of a cumaṅkali. The placement of the tāli is also significant as it is understood that she carries her husband in her chest.			
Bangle wearing *vaḷai kāppu*	Groom's sisters hand over bangles to the bride. Purpose: sound of the glass bangles is compared with the laughter of a girl, so it should keep the bride in a good mood.		Bride, sisters of the groom	

Joint ride	Ride by car or chariot: horses demonstrate a high economic status; secondly it distracts negative sentiments and the evil eye.	in front of the maṇṭa-pam	Married spouses	
Post-wedding rituals				
Feast at the groom's house *māppiḷḷai vīṭu cāppāṭu* (on the next day)	Groom's family prepares a feast	Groom's home	Married spouses, parental authorities	
Visiting the bride *vīṭu aṟiya pōratu* (7th day after the wedding)	Visit by the bridal family to the groom's home to inquire into her well-being. Handing over sweets, rice, spicy snacks, *dhal*, and meat. Wife-takers prepare food for the bridal family.	Groom's home	Bridal family, groom's parents	
Reception *varavēṟpu* (occa-sionally a few weeks after the wedding)	Bride is acquainted with family and friends, speeches of thanks by groom's parents and mantras of priests, blessings by wife-takers	maṇṭapam groom's house	Married spouses, both families, community, neighbors and peers of the groom	Handing over presents, occasionally preparing sketches or speeches

Prestations on holidays (within the first year)	offering sweets, new dresses and spicy snacks to the groom and his family	bridal or groom's home	married spouses and their parents	

8. Peers in wedding ceremonies

The wedding ritual in India constitutes a family affair, in which peer groups usually play a marginal role – a contrasting phenomenon to marriages in other ethnographic contexts where weddings may turn into a "youthful event" (Roche 2014: 182). Yet, an increasing commercialization of marriage practices particularly among the middle class has led to a new image of its participants. As evidence of social influence, goodwill and reputation, non-kin contacts have become established as consistent guests in the audience at wedding ceremonies. Such guests include not only well-known personalities, but colleagues and friends made in the educational context.

The Tamil wedding market transformed the wedding ritual (*kalyāṇam*) into a display of family status and economic success. Its influence becomes evident in everyday life, where the wedding industry has enhanced the vibrance of Tamil towns and cities: wedding planner bureaus, stores for silk saris and dhotis, bridal shoes and other related accessories have overrun the streets. Beauty parlors and jewelry stores attract young brides with fancy make-up, hairstyles and glittering ornaments. Glossy magazines and wedding journals advertise scripts for eccentric activities for bachelor(ette) parties, eve-of-wedding-parties and the honeymoon. While each wedding ritual varies according to locality, caste, familial participation and economic resources, professionals have introduced standardized trends across different communities in the town of Madurai. Usually, the kalyāṇam takes place in a hall (*maṇṭapam*), which is accessible to several communities and religious groups. The date and place are publicly announced via invitation cards and banners. While until a few centuries ago, the preparation of the bride presented an exclusive activity between female kin, the visit to one of the many newly founded beauty parlors has advanced to a common event between the bride and her peers. Caterers prepare wedding menus as an indicator for the bridal family's status, hospitality and respect towards the groom's family. Concerning the marriage ritual, its procedure and exertion is gradually 'determined' by photographers and videographers. Marriage albums and videos have become obligatory as documented evidence for the wedding procedure and its online version is accessible to an unrestricted audience.

The booming wedding industry has set up designated classifications among its customers whose consumption patterns disclose caste status, economic background and taste. In fact, Osella and Osella (2000) contend in their observation among recent wedding practices of the Izhava caste in Kerala that

> "[...] there exist [...] clear signs of distinction, looked for and understood or decoded by the guests [...]. Certain practices of styles are associated with certain communities and hence hold negative or positive prestige connotations, while also suggesting a families particular orientation and strategy and would-be identity" (ibid: 102).

In urban Madurai, the transforming wedding market enhances a distinction between 'decent' or 'cultivated' and 'tasteless' weddings. Those evaluation criteria emanate from the notion of decency as a crucial characteristic for the self-image of the educated middle class (see section 1.3). Distinctive criteria of a middle class lifestyle include a neutral decoration style, respect toward the groom's family, an organized procedure and particularly the correct conduct of ceremonies. The stage inside the wedding hall constitutes the setting for displaying ritual integrity, where scale and style of the performance specify the status of the family in caste, class and economic terms. Typical "low status marriages", for instance, are defined by disorder and uncertainty, by a chaotic mess of people who give contradictory instructions. In Kerala, Osella and Osella observed that the conduct of the ceremony designates the "family's culture or prestige level" (ibid: 101ff.), rising according to the priest and other ritual elements such as *prasadam*. A ceremony dominated by drunken senior members for instance, arguing about the right procedure is equated with 'low caste behavior' (ibid). Likewise, weddings deemed "uncultivated", which my respondents associated with the Piramalai kaḷḷar community, incorporate neither priests nor musicians, but perform jāti identity by provoking fights.

In contrast to these scenes of 'low cast' behavior, a 'typical' middle class wedding of 'advanced' and 'modern' personalities (*taṟkālattavar*) is characterized by clear hierarchical structures corresponding to *Vedic* custom. While until the beginning of this century, wedding ceremonies were conducted by local priests (*pūcāri*) or elder authorities according to local traditions of the *jāti*, nowadays the middle class prefer for a Brahmin priest to exert the rites.[1]

1 "If the marriages are conducted in the right way by a Brahmin", Suresh's father explained to me, "the conjugal life will prosper." While most of the host families

Respective ethnographies have argued that the conduct of Vedic rituals designates the social standing of the family. Elucidating class consciousness among the middle class in Madurai, Sara Dickey (2012: 581) states that the descended knowledge and performance of ceremonies stand for financial power as well as an enlightened lifestyle. This contention corresponds with Brosius (2010: 276f.), who suggests that in elite weddings, participants take recourse to indigenous practices and customs, in order to appear modern and chic – and thus offer a countervailing model to a strange and Western culture. Wedding rituals among upper classes in India therefore advanced to an exercise in conspicuous consumption, knowhow and status (ibid: 293).

Picture 15: Piramalai kaḷḷar wedding

Contemporary marriage practices offer considerable space for the involvement of non-familial contacts. In the course of increasing commercialization of lifecycle events, friends of different castes assume duties formerly exclusively reserved for kin. This chapter discusses both the overt and indirect support of non-kin friends, who serve as 'organizers' and 'facilitators', but also as intimate listeners. Those insights are principally based on my observations of five

stated that they hope for positive energy concerning the future life of the couple, Brahmin priests expressed an ambivalent opinion about the reorientation towards Vedic scripts. Most of them even doubted the knowledge of their clients concerning performance and the meaning of rites as Iyangar (Vishnavite) Sridhar pointed out: "They think that, if the marriage is conducted with the Brahmins, it would be better. But they don't know the details. They are incapable of understanding any rituals."

'middle class' weddings among my study participants[2]: Nataraj, Prathib and Tenmozhi (Paṟaiyar), Selvakumar (Ceṭṭiyār), Muthu (Prakash's younger brother, Piḷḷaimār) and Ajitha (Muslim). Beyond these observations, I conducted interviews with young people prior to their marriage, their family members and representatives of the wedding industry. The first subchapter defines the role peers play in the marriage hall, the preferential location for conducting the ceremony. Here, the focus lies in their function and interaction before, during and after ritual activities. Their ambivalent status becomes further evident through their demeanor during the wedding feast. A particular section is dedicated to female peers: beauty parlors present a popular space for cultivating female friendships as they turn into exclusive sites that transcend ritual caste and gender restrictions. Moreover, the status of non-kin friends is evaluated through their representation in invitation cards, banners, wedding photos and videos. Finally, a digression on love marriages discloses a unique sphere of influence for anti-hierarchical constellations. In self-selected alliances, non-kin friends assume a crucial role throughout all stages of the wedding – from the matchmaking, to the confirmation of the arrangement and finally the preparation of the ceremony.

In a first step, this chapter highlights the limited presence of peers and supports the theory that those constellations occupy a low rank within the ritual order. A closer observation, however, reveals essential duties of egalitarian non-kin friends during marriage as a principal lifecycle event. Their involvement becomes especially visible through their handling of contemporary challenges presented by the wedding market that overwhelm domestic authorities and senior kin. A particular focus centers on the capacity to alter egalitarian interactions in accordance with ritual practices. This chapter therefore intends to stress the dynamic modes of behavior in anti-hierarchical friendship constellations.

8.1 STATUS AND 'HIDDEN' SUPPORT ON STAGE

"People want to show off; the whole city must wonder what is happening. It is like a festival."
(Ramalingam, owner of Menaka Ramalingam Arangam about the mushrooming of marriage halls)

The marriage hall (*maṇṭapam*), the most popular location for an engagement, wedding and reception not only provides room for a sizeable number of guests; it

2 I list only the name of the spouse who invited me and the peer groups.

comprises a vivid example for a new public space in which, according to related studies, "social moral and cultural values as well as identities could be negotiated" (Brosius 2010: 281). Until the beginning of the last century, weddings in the region of Madurai took place on a central village square (*mantai*), temple or in the bridal home (Zeff 1999: 42). With an increasing audience in the early 1970s, families began to conduct weddings in larger localities, mainly in abandoned houses. In the past few decades, halls began to mushroom and surpass former marriage locations.

In the city of Madurai, halls split into different categories concerning size, design, location and booking prices. While the largest maṇṭapam in town, the Raja Muthayar hall, mostly frequented by high income portions of the population, can accommodate more than 1000 people, the average size of a hall provides space for approximately 600 guests. Caste or religiously oriented maṇṭapam are decorated with corresponding symbols, signs or goddesses and booked by the respective community. Neutral halls without a specific orientation attract a broader spectrum of customers. In their study about Izhava weddings in Kerala, the Osellas (2000: 102) identify a further distinction: "city marriage halls" describe a spacious maṇṭapam where everyone is served food in one dining room. Smaller halls (*gurumandiram)* in contrast remain associated with a low caste status, as they require the family to channel their guests through small corridors, one after the other, due to lack of space. As style and category of the hall shape the reputation of the family's taste, the selection and decoration of the wedding is increasingly left to the younger generation.

Menaka maṇṭapam is one highly frequented hall into which I gained insight. It was selected for a Hindu Paṟaiyar marriage of Nataraj, whose parents assigned their son to negotiate the terms of use. Nataraj asked David and his younger brother for support. The hall owner, Ramalingam, runs Menaka maṇṭapam in Kamarajar Salai, a street regularly frequented by wedding processions, which at the time of my research was bordered by 48 halls. The former rice mill owner and paddy cultivator had been running his business for the past ten years. Sensing the promising boom of those buildings, he invested 85 lakhs of rupees to establish his hall. Menaka maṇṭapam is average in size and can accommodate an audience up to 700 people. Following a pragmatic business concept, he provides access to all communities and religious groups. He chose neutral decorations without jāti-specific or religious symbols and permits his clients to consume all sorts of foods. Due to these techniques, Menaka advanced to one of the most frequented marriage locations for a variety of customers. Even though the maṇṭapam may be used for other occasions like conferences, anniversaries or birthday parties, the 60 to 65 weddings per year account for the biggest part of the events. To handle the rising demand, Ramalingam introduced several rules for facilitating the booking procedure: Clients have to reserve and pay in advance. On auspicious days, he charges 35 000 Rs for 24 hours, and 20 000 Rs on non-auspicious days. His staff includes one doorman, one watchman and one cleaner.

The involvement of David and his peers presented a considerable relief for Nataraj's parents. Weddings that are not conducted in marriage halls usually take place in the house of the bride, or if both families are from different towns, in the bride's place of origin. Since the maṇṭapam functions as a substitute for the bridal house, wife-givers are responsible for the choice and maintenance of the hall, while only in rare cases does the groom's family bear the expenses for food and other necessary components for the wedding.[3] Consequently, parents of the bride are often under pressure to find a suitable location and to satisfy conflicting demands by family members concerning the number of guests, atmosphere and locality. Moreover, the requirement to display an 'enlightened' family status causes a slight imbalance between wife-givers and wife-takers. Notably, adequate respect toward the groom's family is considered "cultured behavior" (Osellas 2000: 103). Hence, on the wedding day, cousins and sisters of the bride find themselves assuming the duty of continuously attending to the needs of the groom's family. In addition, wife-givers remain responsible for the safety of the guests and their belongings – a challenging task considering the increasing threat of uninvited participants or even thieves. Among a crowd of roughly 600 people, the maṇṭapam presents a welcomed opportunity for pick pockets who steal jewels and presents from the gift table or sandals in front of the door. Other risks consist of the possibility of duplicating the key to the dressing rooms in order to gain access and steal belongings. Regularly, uninvited intruders take the opportunity to enter the hall and take advantage of free food.[4] Consequently, most hall owners hire watchmen or install video cameras, lock the dressing room or close off the gift table. At the same time, the bridal family has to be extremely prudent in questioning the attendants as to whether they belong to the invited guests. In the case that the person is an important guest, such inquiries not only signify an insult for the guest, but cause humiliation for the groom's family.

3 Against the background of growing expenses, some of the families share the costs. After fixing the alliance, families usually wait until both sides are financially sound. This development is rationalized by economic reasoning and demographic trends towards nuclear families.

4 This opportunity was adopted in Tamil movies, as depicted, for example, in the film naṇpaṉ, where the protagonists, a circle of college friends, sneak into the maṇṭapam to enjoy the wedding meal.

David, therefore, insisted on safety arrangements. Moreover, he was in charge of suitable decorations that met contemporary middle class standards.

The decoration of the stage is usually entrusted to professionals. Menaka Hall maintains a fixed contract with Jeeva, a decorator from Nagercoil, who set up his office at the nearby donkey bridge and has been operating his business for the last 25 years. A second long-term partner is Selvam, a florist, who has been running his business for twelve years. This mutual agreement between decorators, florists and hall owners is advantageous for both sides. While the two service providers receive regular orders, Ramalingam can count on them for diligent and reliable work. Likewise, young people, including friends of the spouses, increasingly take on the duty of deciding on the right decorations. Against the background of recent trends toward endless varieties, most parents feel overwhelmed by the task of selecting the hall adornments. Decorators and florists provide a large selection of *ceṇṭu* (flower bouquets), *campaṅki* (tube roses) or *cāmanti* (marigold). Taste is defined not least by jāti and religious custom: while Hindus prefer to decorate the entrance in the style of a temple gate, a *gopuram*, Christians mostly choose modest flower bouquets in soft colors. Muslims usually opt for carpets. According to decorators and florists, ornaments and flower arrangements do not have an exclusively decorative character, but indicate the family's taste, progressiveness and group membership. Whereas the upper classes select costly *pū maṇavarai,* a coherent arrangement of jasmine flowers adorning the entire rear wall of the stage, excessively flashy decoration is associated with a wasteful attitude or vain attempts by lower economic classes to imitate the lifestyle of the rich. Decorators even mocked the lacking taste of some clients who naively asked for the advertised flower arrangements by under- or overestimating the correct prices. Paṭiccavaṅka in contrast, demonstrate a sense of moderate style, for instance through cosy furniture or plastic flowers.

The construction of Menaka marriage hall and its interior corresponds to the architecture of Indian sacred buildings. The main entrance is located in the east, in the direction of the divine. The principal stage also faces east, where the principal wedding rituals take place. A second stage is used for the reception and engagement ceremony. Two tables for each family are arranged at the entrance of the hall with turmeric, cumcum and betel leaf – welcoming gestures which, according to Zeff (1999: 42), "create visual images of themselves as gracious and generous hosts in the acts of greeting, entertaining and feeding the assembled guests in a sumptuous fashion." Behind the reception, a gift stand exposes luxury articles, mostly wrapped in glitter paper. The Osellas (2000) assume that those boards serve as an opportunity to display one's economic status. However, the public registration of cash gifts and dowry, as practiced predominantly in Kaḷḷar communities, is considered 'backward' (ibid: 107).

Picture 16: Interior of the Menaka maṇṭapam

Picture 17: Christian marriage: stage decorated in a 'modern' style

Having passed the entrance, the guests for Nataraj's wedding took place in the main hall by maintaining a prescribed configuration: parents and first-line relatives usually sit in the first row. Additionally, elder authorities, celebrities and renowned Sadhus also sit in the first row. Other seats are reserved for politicians, who sit in the front, although they leave the event at an early stage. Subsequent seats are confined to other kin and long-term friends together with their families. Representatives of economic achievements, particularly professors, employers and bosses, followed by colleagues and business contacts, all of whom occupy the middle rows, also represent integral groups of guests for the wedding. Non-kin guests such as fellow students, classmates and friends sit as a separate group in the last rows. For Nataraj's wedding, approximately 40 friends of other community backgrounds were invited. As they do not command the focus of attention, they gossip, joke and occasionally leave the event to take a ride or have a smoke. Of all participants, peers keep the greatest distance from the stage. They give gifts, but do not participate in ritual activities, as Ramesh explained to me, "Friends are not allowed in these ceremonies."

Picture 18: Peers at the rear of the maṇṭapam

Since the stage itself exhibits ritual activities and serves to demonstrate expertise and economic status, it represents a site for negotiating rank and social standing. Furthermore, any person in contact with pollution is not allowed on stage to congratulate the couple. Such guests include menstruating women, those who encountered an unfortunate incident in their family or widowed persons, with the exception of the parents of the bride or groom. Confronting such restrictions, the stage consistently enhances ego clashes between principal relatives. If a senior kin feels neglected, he is vigilant to regain attention. A popular strategy is the ostentatious refusal to step on stage by indulging only after several requests by other family members.

Picture 19: Honoring of both spouses tāy māmā

Although non-kin friends do not appear officially on stage, they are not restricted in performing their supportive role even during ceremonies. Nataraj reminded David, for instance, that he gets nervous on stage and that he, moreover, feared a physical breakdown. After several hours, the ceremony becomes exhausting for most couples who have to endure the ceremonial activities, follow the orders of the priest and finally stand still in front of the camera in the spotlight, continuously maintaining their composure. With his mobile, he rang David and Prakash from the stage and asked them to stand nearby. His friends occasionally joined him or sent him encouraging text messages, which relieved the groom to some extent. Notably, this support took place "in a hidden way", as Prakash explained. Furthermore, the form of interaction becomes adapted to the ritual event by adhering to socially prescribed behavior. While it is common to make jokes about the beloved one in a campus context or about a young bride on profile pictures, peers cease teasing the groom once he has selected a spouse. "Even if she is 130 kg, we do not say anything", David stated. Further, friends and peers adjust the form of address to the ritual context. Thus, on stage, it is uncommon to touch each other, although such gestures represent a frequent method of expressing intimacy and affection between friends. In Nataraj's case, David and Prakash stood still, apart from handing water to the groom or following instructions of the priest and videographers to facilitate ritual activities.

The above description has outlined the transformation of the wedding ritual into a staged event to display a certain economic status and social standing. While the exertion of rituals has loosened, traditional authorities are reasserted in this process. Within this development, non-kin friends of the bride or groom involve themselves in preparations, negotiations and the design of the wedding. While they keep their distance from ritual events, they play a fundamental role in facilitating the arrangement of a 'modern' wedding and provide moral support to the spouses. Hence, non-ritual peer groups appear in a modified way on stage, where they adjust their interactions to accommodate prescribed boundaries in Tamil Society.

8.2 INCLUSION AND EXCLUSION IN WEDDING MEALS

"For a wedding, all the relatives, friends and others will be invited, so that the new couple will get the blessings from all invitees. Through this event, this family gets an opportunity to give food for many. While serving food, sages and the poor will join the meal. Also, there are business opportunities for the professionals"
(Asirvatham, caterer in Madurai).

The wedding meal, a central event that unites all participants at the wedding, has undergone significant changes during the last centuries. In ritual terms, externally prepared dishes were considered polluted. As described in the previous chapter, food is culturally understood as a transmitter of intimacy. In the initial meetings of the alliance-making, therefore, bridal families symbolize their distance from the groom's family by restricting the food to snacks and cold drinks. During the Flower Ceremony in contrast, both sides invite their relatives and village inhabitants to celebrate the match and publicly announce the arrangement. A culminating feast not only enhances a festive atmosphere, but also symbolizes the bond between both families.

Until the late 1980s and mid-1990s, externally prepared food was only brought for inauspicious or occasions associated with 'pollution', such as funerals and ceremonies that mark puberty. Moreover, caterers operated their business in non-ritual contexts, typically at conferences, anniversaries and university celebrations. In the early 1990s, however, cooking services lost their contaminating image and were hired for life events such as births or ear piercing ceremonies. Initially, only a few individual cooks and professional chefs prepared food as their main form of paid employment. Today, more than fifteen caterers in Madurai, ranging from big entrepreneurs to small-scale providers offer their services to all caste and religious communities. Wedding meals not merely present a feast, but contribute to a generous image of the hosting family. Homemade food may even be assessed as a sign of a "low budget marriage", in which the family restricts their means to mobilizing helpers from the same caste

(Osella & Osella 2000: 103). Hiring a caterer, in contrast, demonstrates economic potential and social integrity, as professional food providers are usually booked as part of an all-inclusive arranged wedding ceremony. This section shall provide further insights into the social dimension of meals in contemporary weddings. Based on my own case studies, I indicate how this gastronomic highlight serves as an indicator of prestige and social rank among guests and defines the behavior of egalitarian friends.

Asirvatham, one of the first caterers in Madurai, operates his business in Arapalyam, Madurai. Initially serving food for death and puberty functions, he started to prepare dishes for marriages in the year 2000. He boasts clients from nearly all castes and religions, with the exception of Brahmins, who hire cooks exclusively from their own jāti. Asirvatham offers two kinds of contracts: as a first option, the food contract includes the food and dishware, based on the estimated number of attendants. The second alternative is a labor contract, which stipulates only the preparation of food. To demonstrate his professionalism, he and his staff members wear uniforms. Interacting with customers, caterers function as experts by monitoring the choice of menu. The process of receiving orders from clients resembles a professional consultation in which caterers even explain the significance of the chosen food.[5] As part of their business, cooks introduce a range of new dishes. Until 25 years ago, the standard wedding meal consisted of rice, soup (*racam*), *sambar*, *dhal*, buttermilk (*mōr*), papad (*appaḷam*) and desert *(pāl pāyācam*). Selected items varied according to caste, religion and region. Lower castes had to restrict themselves to two or three vegetable dishes. The different choices reveal a community-specific attitude towards vegetarian and non-vegetarian food: high castes, particularly Brahmins and Ceṭṭiyār exclusively adhere to vegetarian dishes, as the consumption of meat is considered impure. In contrast, among low castes, Christians and Muslims, non-vegetarian food became a sign of prestige. Especially in Kaḷḷar marriages, it is considered an offense not to provide enough meat for all guests.

Among the middle class, changing trends in food practices reveal a shift from caste to class standards, as stated by Asirvatham in urban Madurai, "In cities, they want to copy the practices of their neighbors or their colleagues ... but we cannot say that low castes are coping higher castes. Nowadays, many of

---

5 One example is the introduction of peanut cake (*kaṭalai uruṇṭai*) served in the last son's marriage until 25 years ago. The purpose of serving kaṭalai uruṇṭai is to convey the message that this is the last marriage in the family. Today, a diminishing size of families has rendered this practice obsolete. Nowadays however, this custom has been revitalized through the efforts of cooks, who sense a promising business opportunity in selling peanut cake.

them (Dalit) are financially in a top position in society. Every caste has the same kind of expenses in the cities. Because we are not living like in villages, so we are not separated geographically." This trend presents a pan-Indian phenomenon among the middle class in India. Observing food preferences in North Indian weddings, Brosius (2010: 289) states that pollution through *kacha* food (typically boiled rice) is declining in favor of exposing economic status and prestige. In fact, the author observes that Indians increasingly tend to play with Western elements, albeit in a restricted manner (ibid: 279). Most meals served in middle class weddings include a range of Chinese, Arab and European vegetarian and non-vegetarian dishes, but usually omit alcohol. The variety of wedding meals further enhances class standards and the classification of modern (*mu<u>nn</u>ē<u>r</u>iya*) weddings, performed among educated sections of the population. For paṭiccavaṅka, the priority lies more and more in variety and originality as evidence of elaborate taste. Ordinary meat curry and rice has been replaced by omelets and chicken or mutton *biryani*, a spiced rice dish. Clients ask for extravagant items like *karaṇṭi*-omelet (egg dish in the form of a spoon), which requires a specific kitchen utensil. Other favorite dishes include fried fish, scrambled eggs or special items that have to be cooked on the spot.[6] Such differentiation not only applies to food, but concerns drinking water as well; whereas water used to be filled into tumblers, today mineral water is served in plastic cups or bottles to display a higher economic standard.

An examination of the joint meal, which always follows the wedding ceremony, exposes the social dimension of the wedding feast. As the designated highlight of the wedding, it presents a focal point around which the social hierarchy becomes affirmed. For the wedding meal, guests are placed in relation to each other – an order that reveals local mechanisms of ranking, inclusion and exclusion. The wedding banquet at Nataraj's wedding took place in a separate dining section inside the maṇṭapam. Catering staff rushed between table rows with long crowded benches to immediately accommodate the demands of the guests. Depending on the size of the dining room, the invitees eat in several sequences. Within the first group, the feasting order is largely determined by caste, kinship and gender norms. Senior kin and important relatives of the groom's family are usually served first. Consequently, catering staff may be hassled if they forget to serve demanding authorities. The prompt satisfaction of

6 As additional indicators of distinction, the Osellas defined refreshments, snacks bought from stores, branded soft drinks and foreign items like Cadbury chocolate (2000: 105).

invitees reduces the risk of fights.[7] Moreover, enduring conflicts about the quantity and choice of food items place considerable pressure on the bridal family. In Kerala, Osella and Osella emphasized that "serving the groom's party first means demonstrating respect" (2000: 103). The social rank of the family is further identified by the numbers of *papads*[8], side dishes and desserts. Gomathy, my neighbor from the Kōṉār community, who recently married off her 22 year-old daughter, illustrated that challenge: "Food must be available for everyone. If there is no food for a few, it is a bad thing. Everyone will talk about it ... so we provided food for 900 people even though there were only 600 people."[9] In the second sequence, food is served to distant relatives, family acquaintances and highly-reputed guests. Usually, they eat in one round without causing much of a stir and content themselves with a limited quantity of food. The third and often last sequence is confined to non-ritual constellations, colleagues, friends and peers.

In most cases however, college friends remain entirely absent by joining together in the rear of the hall or roaming outside. If the hosts provide non-vegetarian food, considered 'impure' in ritual terms, peer groups might even fill buckets with the meat in order to consume it outside the hall in large quantities. The following incident from the marriage of Selvakumar, a Ceṭṭiyār colleague of my host brother, exemplifies a growing, conspicuous preference for meat at weddings: His wedding took place at the same time as Muthu's, Prakash's younger brother and a Christian Piḷḷaimār. The friends visited Selvakumar's wedding, as they had a closer relationship to him and were of the same age group. However, during the meal, they came to visit Muthu's wedding, which took place in Menaka maṇṭapam, 300 meters away. After delivering their gift, they served themselves with non-vegetarian food and immediately returned to Selvakumar's wedding. When I asked David why they did not eat in the hall, he

7 Especially Piramalai kaḷḷar are said to expose their strength and boldness by the popular saying "āṭṭukarikku aṭuccukuvōm kōḻikarikku kūṭikkuvōm" (For goat meat we will fight, for chicken meat we will join and find peace). A vivid scene of their short-tempered attitude during feasting is presented in the blockbuster Kathal.

8 Crisp round flat bread.

9 An alarming outcome of such a development is the excessive waste of food which finally required government intervention: one effort is the food prevention act of 1964 as well as the state-wide regulation by Indira Gandhi between 1975 and 1977, which limited the quantity of food to 250 meals per marriage. A targeted allocation of food presents one strategy to curb lavishness: staff dispenses a huge amount to vigorous customers and rations the portions for skinny people. This tactic proves particularly relevant with regard to luxury or foreign items like meat or chocolate.

explained, "See, meat is something special and therefore finished very quickly. So we take enough for ourselves and hide." This explanation supports the findings of Strümpell (2006: 77), who observes that people connected through constellations of *convivium* conspicuously consume impure substances. Moreover, their get-togethers frequently involve collective drinking. Importantly, those consumption patterns have to take place 'secretly'. Remaining in those secular constellations, peer conversations primarily revolve around delicate topics. Out of ear shot, they gossip about lapses during the event, the body shape of the bride or about sexist attitudes among the male guests.

If vegetarian food is served, however, peers usually eat inside the hall. Here, they form the last group to eat. By that time, their interaction is far more relaxed than that between their predecessors. Usually, the main ceremonies are finished by that time and a substantial portion of the guests already left the event. Peers mutually share the remaining food by eating from each other's plate. This familiar interaction not only presents a contrasting structure to the formerly regulated procedure, but counteracts prescribed limitations of commensality. Importantly, this grouping constitutes an independent constellation and appears as a separate unit of paṭiccavaṅka. In case other family members, women or the married spouse join for food, they restrict themselves in physical contact and limit their conversation to family matters by addressing each other in a polite way or by name.

This section has highlighted the social function of the wedding meal, which has evolved into an evaluation criterion for the reputation of the hosts as well as for the success of the procedure. Status distinction is achieved by meeting contemporary requirements of high quality and acting in a decent manner by avoiding rude gestures and disagreements. Observed food practices reveal how status differences in Tamil society surround the wedding meal. Non-kin friends and peers compose a distinctive category: they reveal a preference for impure substances so that they enjoy their meal last or even remove themselves to separate areas where they exchange gossip and secrets. Only in the presence of familial authorities do they alter their egalitarian forms of interaction.

8.3 *KŪṬṬU NAṬPU* IN BEAUTY PARLORS: WOMEN'S GROUPS

This section focuses on young women who engage in intimate circles to assist the bride in cosmetic treatments prior to the wedding event. Their involvement is related to a feature of recent ideals of beauty and physical appearance of the bride. In Tamil Nadu, Ajitha explained to me that female kin dress and apply make up to the bride, which signifies an act of intimacy: "Due to physical contact, you feel close to each other. So this occasion strengthens family ties among women of both families." Moreover, sisters-in-law use this opportunity to evaluate the physical health of the bride. In the urban middle class, this treatment increasingly takes place in salons, which have mushroomed since the 1970s in order to prepare women for ritual occasions.[10] The culture-specific impact of beauty practices in India becomes especially visible with reference to Western concepts of wellness, which appeal mostly to recreation, comfort and satisfaction of the inner senses. Advertisements of American spa resorts present the wellness experience as a getaway from daily routines. Listing the most demanded spas in America, the website travelandleisure.com, for instance, attracts its customers with the following slogan: "Many stressed-out Americans urgently need to escape their work schedules and address such life issues as aging, dietary habits, and sexuality. What better place to do this than a heaven where that willful child called the Inner Me is given center stage?"[11] This advertisement regards wellness centers as a harbor, a getaway from surrounding troubles and refuge for the 'inner self'.

Picture 20: Preparing the bride for wedding

In India, beauty parlors have implemented the Western concept of wellness as a subjective experience. An elaborate version of beauty parlors has become popularized in the form of expensive spa resorts, exclusively frequented by the

10 Nowadays even many grooms undergo a cosmetic treatment prior to the wedding.

11 http://www.travelandleisure.com/articles/the-best-spas-in-america.

upper middle class. Brosius (2010: 312ff.) argues that this trend enhanced stereotypical ascriptions and class distinctions related to the kinds of salons. Among the Hindu middle class in Indian metropolises, convention parlors even became degraded as 'ordinary', as they exclusively focus on the outer body and a standardized exterior. Following Western concepts of beauty care, more elaborate parlors, in contrast provide a favorable setting for an inner-sensual experience that includes wellness for the body, mind and soul. Brosius regards the rapidly growing beauty business in New Delhi as an outcome of an altered body perception among the urban middle class where "a beautiful body is now a happy body" (ibid: 308). Hence, the consciousness to maintain a sustainably fit body is conceptualized as a newly emerging need that forms a central feature of a middle class lifestyle and component of a 'global class'.

In Madurai, beauty parlors occupy a distinctive space for cultivating anti-hierarchical constellations and infiltrates ritual boundaries that avoid physical contact. *Vinithas*, to which I accompanied Ajitha prior to her wedding, is rated among my respondents as the fanciest beauty parlor in Madurai. My impression highlights the relevance of the salons as a place for intimate exchanges between female peers – in line with Brosius' observations, who describes parlors as a "social centre, where they gather and exchange news, where they are among themselves, in a family-free space, where weddings can be envisaged and criticized, husbands and mothers-in-law cribbed about" (ibid: 310). The attraction of Vinitha, therefore, exceeds the mere cosmetic procedure to offer a popular site for enclosed interaction, disconnected from established social barriers. Daily, the salon receives approximately fifty clients. In the last weeks before the marriage, young brides come to treat their skin, hair and body. At the entrance, the visitors find a guidebook presenting different models and extraordinary varieties of special treatments. Accompanied by friends and siblings, they choose different offers, ranging from body spa treatments and massages to several forms of hair styles and make-up. The common version of make-up consists of applying ordinary facial powder or talc. Pleads and hairpins are used for tying the hair. Next to this standardized version, there are fairly expensive offers including a tailored treatment: affluent customers opt for a professionalized alternative in which the beautician analyzes the face of the woman and adjusts the treatment according to individual traits. This package includes extra features like beautifying the front sections of the hair. Advanced material like waterproof products is used to avoid smudging through sweat or other liquids. Beyond caste or religiously motivated preferences, the choice of make-up is increasingly correlated with class differences. This range of styling enhances the divide beyond economic differences and indicates 'distinctive' tastes. Standard forms of make-up, supposedly preferred by pin̲ taṅkiyanilai, are characterized by garish colors and a lacking of understanding for personal characteristics. A well-tuned style of make-up that accentuates a specific skin and hair type in contrast, indicates the elaborate taste of paṭiccavaṅka.

Importantly, *Vinithas* offers an opportunity to relax and at the same time a protected space to exchange secrets and discuss intimate experiences or familial conflicts with female counterparts. In the words of Ajitha, it presents a "source of gaining strength and confidence". In the main hall, right behind the entrance, female customers sit in front of the make-up mirror and dressing tables, arranged in a circle, and discuss their hopes and worries concerning the upcoming event. Vinitha, the owner of the shop, occasionally participates in their jokes and expressed attitudes. Behind the corridor, small separated chambers are available for make-up and body treatments, including massage and hair removal and also create a space for informal exchanges regarding fairly intimate topics. The conversations openly criticized family constellations, misbehavior of husbands or in-laws and address own wishes, longings and projects.

Picture 21: Chatting at the main hall of Vinithas

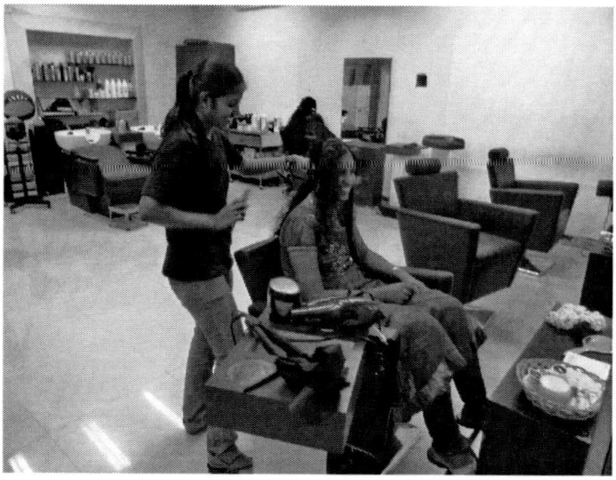

When I underwent a treatment myself, I was joined by Soundariya and Ajitha, who completed one session of her six-month facial treatment. Both took the opportunity to discuss internal family conflicts about pending wedding expenses for Ajitha. Soundariya shared her concerns about her long-term affair with a senior from MKU. This conversation was continuously commented on by Priya, the 23 year-old staff member. This situation revealed to me the peculiar purpose of Indian beauty parlors as sites for an unimpeded female exchange – an intention that replicates the purpose of Western spa centers as an experience of recreation in its own culture-specific way. While social boundaries are undermined, parlors offer space for mutual encouragement and gaining energy. For young women, parlors present an occasion for sitting, relaxing and joking. Such activities stand in vivid contrast to the reality in Tamil everyday life: simply gathering or wandering around in public is a recognized and accepted behavior for men, while women are expected to leave their neighborhood only for a specific reason (Alex 2009: 131). In fact, the social dimension of the parlor has led to such a crowd that staff restricted the number of companions to four persons per visit. This observation not only emphasizes parlors as a space to circumvent social barriers and cultivate intimate female friendships, but buttresses the findings of other studies that have focused predominantly on spaces for male peers, such as tea stalls or river banks (Jeffrey 2010: 99 f, Strümpell 2006: 79). Moreover, the case of Ajitha demonstrates that young female friends assume a supportive function, supplementing networks of female kin during collective treatments for the bride. In contrast to the latter, however, visits to beauty parlors among female peer groups take place independently of wider social or familial control.

8.4 REPRESENTATION OF NON-KIN FRIENDS IN MARRIAGE MEDIA

Having examined several spaces for anti-hierarchical constellations within the ritual context, this section discusses the representation of friendships, kūṭṭu naṭpu, in print and audiovisual marriage media. First, I focus on the categorization of invitation cards, which are utilized to show caste, religious and educational background. Moreover, I turn to the role of banners that became an omnipresent domain for displaying status hierarchies. In the second subchapter, I discuss the role of photo- and wedding albums, where recent developments in printing technology and display formats reconcile 'modern' desires with established restrictions. Outlining the changing significance and usage of marriage media throughout the last centuries, my analysis identifies marriage media as a realm in which social ranks become reasserted. Within this ranking, I examine how the distinctive status of egalitarian friendships is integrated into the ritual event.

8.4.1 'Friends' cards and banners

The usage of invitation cards has proliferated during the last decades. During the colonial period, predominantly higher social classes, royal families and *zamindars* used printed versions of marriage invitations. Until the 1950s they served as an assurance for the financial and communal agreement between two families. *Sambandhapatra* represents the term used to indicate a marriage deed in which both families signed the invitation in front of witnesses, typically elder village members. This function lost significance in the middle of the 19th century in the course of the declining authority of zamindars, urbanization and increasing inter-caste marriages (Majumdar 2009: 245ff.). Gradually, invitation letters were drafted by large sections of the Indian middle and upper classes, which caused a change in its purpose: rather than merely confirming and documenting marriage conventions, cards displayed the status of parvenus, characterized by British influence and an urban lifestyle. Exploring the example of Bengali elite, Majumdar describes how the design of the document accentuates metropolitan areas. An adherence to self-consciousness and discipline is achieved by indicating precise meeting points and time announcements, which resembles the schedule of urban white collar employees and presents the wedding in form of a punctual congregation (ibid: 252). That orientation towards British values was superseded by a strong ambition to represent oneself as a distinctive Ethnic category, a development which is reflected by an altered design. While in the 19th century invitation cards were still composed in English, card formats at the beginning of 20th century reflect a new Indian middle class with their own cultural aesthetic values. The author points out how practices of designing and delivering invitation cards restated local hierarchies among this section of the population: "As printed cards they were commodities, but as designed cards catering to a variety of tastes, they also reflected the contestations through which certain notions of refinement and culture evolved around Bengali marriages" (ibid: 246).

In line with Majumdar's contention that invitation cards are no longer standardized, but rather "expressive of the writer's personal touch" (ibid: 249), in Madurai, they advanced to a medium to express the family's social standing. Technological progress, from manual to offset methods and then finally Litho-printing in the beginning of the 1990s, enhanced creative formats and enabled unlimited multiplication. With the availability of cheaper paper and printers, a great selection of designs in manifold colors, styles and qualities emerged. Different editions of invitation cards become available in high quantities and spread to a wide spectrum of people, a development that responds to demographic trends, such as nuclear families, the separation of clans and migration. Today, it is common to send invitations to each guest directly instead of issuing them through the head of the family or village. The decentralized dissemination of invitations lends itself as a duty preferably entrusted to male peers of the groom, who act as convenient couriers.

Hence, the card shop business is booming, despite the trend to send invitations in digital format, as an e-mail, short message or through social networks. Menaka Card shop in the Majesty Cine Mall, which I visited with my neighbor Gomathy, is one of the most frequented locations for middle-class customers in Madurai and provides a selection of approximately 120 different card designs. The variety of invitation cards range from flashy and elaborate motives to flimsy papers for college friends (Osella & Osella 2000: 100). The standard format of invitation cards, so called "family cards" is used to exhibit the social standing of both families, apparent through the hierarchical status of the involved people displayed on the cards. Usually, they include a certain design, standardized texts and layouts for listing all important relatives or other highly reputable visitors by name and grade.[12]

The choice of cards not only emphasizes the religious, caste, class and geographical background, but considers political involvement and the status of the recipient. Within the variety of presentation forms, religious icons display not only Hindu deities, but motives and symbols of the clan god (*kula teyva*). Gomathy, from Kōṉār Community, selected one of thirty five presentation forms offered of Lord Krishna in different colors and styles. Curious experiments depict the god with six faces, sitting in front of a laptop or tying the tāli. Caste-specific symbols or figures serve to emphasize the jāti identity: a lion depiction and the image of Muthuramalinga Thevar are used by Mukkulattōr castes, while a leopard or the portrait of Ambedkar reveals membership in the Paṟaiyar community. Usually, cards preferred among the middle class are printed in high quality paper out of which one exemplar costs up to 4,5 Rs. A distinctive taste is conveyed through aesthetic parameters, such as dainty designs or fainting colors that present a contrast to the flamboyant motives of 'backward' people.

While the spouses-to-be often invite non-kin friends to their wedding, they usually do not mention them by name on the invitation. In the course of technical changes, however, friends and peer groups comprise a separate category of recipients. As such, a relatively recent category of invitation, the so-called "friends card", provides space for creativity. Designs range from small papers

12 This practice holds mainly for arranged marriages in which the wedding is regarded as a function for reinforcing and displaying social relations. Love-married couples usually do not include any names on their invitation card.

resembling love letters to original forms like a bottle of champagne. Instead of caste, religious or political markers, those cards are dominated by stylish icons mixed with bold comments or poems. The conjugal union appears as a relationship based on a mutual affection, conveyed by slogans like: "Grace us with your presence as we walk out of the pavilion to script the best partnership with booming boundaries and towering sixes. This match doesn't have a replay. Live only at the stadium." This sentence, extracted from the friend's card for Nataraj's wedding creates an idyllic setting (pavilion), places the couple in the center (best partnership) and highlights the emotional content (booming boundaries and towering sixes). The focus on romantic love between two individuals, reinforced by a striking design, content and writing style turns away from ritual barriers towards a celebration of personal fulfillment.[13]

Mushrooming banners offer yet another form of visually displaying ritual rank of family and other wedding guests. In the beginning of this century, a radical shift in the urban landscape became visible through billboards, hoardings, and posters – now digitally produced – dominate walls, buildings and gates of event halls. Banners have gained increasing importance, not only among politicians, fan clubs or other functions (Vāsanti 2006), but also in various academic disciplines.

Working on political strategies of the All India Anna Dravida Munnetra Kazhagam (AIADMK) in South Tamil Nadu, Bernard Bate (2009) posits that the principal effect of banners lies in "saturating the space of the city" with the ideologies of the party leaders (ibid: 132). According to him, they predominantly serve to multiply the principle aspects of Tamil politics: praise, devotion and participation (ibid: 121). Examining several motives of politicians, he identifies a reference to the divine through their salutations. Further, Bate demonstrates that banners create domestic scenes between the local politicians of AIADMK and Jayalalithaa, the party leader and Chief Minister of Tamil Nadu, who appears as an auspicious wife. Analyzing the street propaganda of local politicians in Madurai, the author explores how banners, posters and cut-outs, similar to advertisements, communicate their phrases to the public. They contain the same party slogans printed in newspapers. Multiplicative strategies such as "madukku", the placement of dozens of posters next to each other, have resulted in the omnipresence of banners and posters throughout the city.

Roos Gerritsen (2009: 2) has similarly noted the "evocative effect" of banners. Following a trail of images established by fan clubs, the author regards

13 Analyzing love letters circulating among youngsters in Nepal, Laura Ahearn (2004) demonstrates an association of new technology, literacy and modern ideas, notably in the form of a romantic courtship and unconventional gender roles.

the propagation of banners as a process of democratization, as "the widespread dissemination of visual materials has enabled audiences to shape what they view by their personal and individual consumption of mass-produced materials" (ibid: 5). In line with Bate, Gerritsen indicates coming closer to the divine, as the interaction between the star and the audience resembles the moment of *darshan* – a visual interaction with the deity.

Picture 22: Invitation cards, indicating the status of Piramalai kaḷḷar

Picture 23: Card with film hero Vijay. Above, invited guests are listed by name and grade (left). Picture 24: Invitation card with innovative and unique form and content (right)

How did banners acquire their popularity in contemporary weddings? Gerritsen suggests that the main effect of banners lies in reaching a wider audience by "traversing personal and public spaces" (ibid) and thus opening the wedding event to a broader spectrum of participants. Placed in front of maṇṭapam, they can be traced several hundred meters along the road to announce the ceremony and its participants. Printers summarized their significance in the following way: "It is a kind of happiness ... like making fireworks – to show off the groom and bride and to identify the venue. Also, friends, relatives, and other invitees greet the couple by printing banners. For families, they are a prestigious product."

Due to advances in printing technology at the beginning of the 2^{1st} century, costs for vinyl billboards have considerably gone down (Gerritsen 2009: 6). Selvam, who has worked in his studio for more than ten years, charges between six and ten rupees for one square meter. Relatives, friends or colleagues print up to 100 banners and place them on the exterior walls of houses and halls as well as alongside adjacent roads. Usually, the couple is displayed at the top and the donor at the bottom of the banner. Today, banners and other signs present common gifts that convey greetings and wishes, but also status. A significant purpose of banners lies in their use as advertisement, propagation and image cultivation. In fact, as Gerritsen (ibid: 14) points out, "public visibility and the acquisition of fame [...] works through images, as reflected in the hoardings and posters put up for various events." Most displayed figures are cinema heroes, party leaders and divine symbols. Moreover, the designs of banners are becoming more and more elaborate in their emphasis of jāti identity, political engagement and communal involvement. Businessmen design banners in order to advertise their company or brand.

Banners present a highly contested platform for manifesting hierarchies: Gerritsen has shown how images, defined as "murttis" to praise deities have the effect of elevating the reputation of politicians or deceased relatives (2009: 15). The question of their design and representation, therefore, creates considerable conflicts between and within families.[14] Within my own host family, heated disagreements transpired concerning the order of the displayed persons in the run-up to weddings. Particularly sensitive was the question of who should be presented above or next to party leaders or stars. Using the same medium, non-kin friends have taken up the custom of conveying their regards by affixing a

14 A severe conflict that I witnessed occurred during one inter-caste marriage between a Kaḷḷar bride and a groom from the Kōṉār community. At the beginning of the ceremony, relatives and friends of the groom pulled down those banners presenting Kaḷḷar symbols, such as the lion.

banner of their portraits. This gesture is not regarded as a status manifestation, but rather a supportive act, in which they express their solidarity.

The above descriptions have illustrated the manifold purposes of marriage invitations and banners, ranging from documenting agreements, information regarding time and location and even displays of status. Distributed cards indicate caste and religious status as well as political orientation and class background. In most cases, families choose different formats depending on the recipients and send family cards to relatives, neutral versions to business contacts and fun versions to college friends. Beyond reinforcing ritual ranks, the diversification of cards and banners offers space for promoting an alternative way of communication, new designs and contents. Kūṭṭu naṭpu is cultivated via "friends' cards" or "friend's banners", a separate category of formats in which sentiments and intimacy are conveyed.

8.4.2 Performance in wedding albums and videos

Wedding albums and videos emerged in South India in 1980 and exploded during the 1990s. Displaying predominantly family constellations, locality and segments of the ceremony, these media formats function as evidence of the families' caste and class standing as well as their ritual integrity. More than merely mirroring the actual happenings, their main purpose lies simultaneously in inserting current trends into ritual ceremonies and affirming traditional ranks. Initially, wedding albums used to be a costly affair, confined to well-off classes. The few copies produced served as precious memories of the ceremony and material proof of the economic status of the hosts. Technical possibilities of vinyl printing and digitalization have considerably changed the quality and content of marriage media. Since photographers and videographers capture selected moments of ritual activities without identically reproducing them, marriage albums and videos create a new representation to the viewer. Zeff therefore argues that recordings present a contrast to the "disorganized swirl of action" (1999: 40) experienced by the audience during the event itself.

Notwithstanding the perception of their presence as largely troubling, a wedding without photographers and videographers is considered incomplete. Rajesh, a photographer in Chennai, explained their significance as following: "Making videos and photos is necessary. If there is no photographer and videographer, then guests think that it is not a good marriage function." Right behind the stage, they arrange the composition of the depicted persons, interfere in the ritual activity and determine the later perception of the spectacle. In fact, they seem to have taken over the conducting of the ceremony so that Janaki

Abraham deemed photographers in South India "experts" for ritual activities.[15] In this context, the collaboration between videographers and priests is worth noting: "Priests give the instructions to the people on the stage", Rajesh explained to me, "For example, during the tāli binding, he requests the couple to turn towards the camera. Moreover he ensures that guests do not block the visibility for the camera." Chanting mantras for an extended time helps the photographer or videographers capture gratifying motives and scenes. This collaboration does not always occur without conflicts. Priests often blamed photographers for disturbing ritual practices. Some even accused them of dubious economic motives and suspected them of promoting rituals merely for the sake of designing their videos and albums.

Picture 25: Photographers and videographers in action

The essential function of wedding media shall be elucidated through the perspective of the photographer and videographer, Rajesh, and through a detailed observation of his techniques. Rajesh started out as a helper in 1988 in a small studio in Madurai. In 2004, he moved to Chennai, where he opened his own studio. In addition to wedding pictures, he captures birthday parties, puberty and engagement ceremonies. For one album containing 180 pictures, he charges 500-800 Rs.

15 The presence of photographers was outlined in her presentation *Between the couple and the videographer: ritual, identity and aesthetics in marriage videos in North Kerala, India* at the Annual Conference "Arts and Aesthetics in a globalising world", organized by the Association of Social Anthropologists (ASA) in April 2012.

Additionally, he demands 2500 Rs for the layout and design of the album, which he regards as a particular challenge. The principal purpose of the album lies in depicting established ranks, the correct performance of rituals and economic achievements. Hence, the photographer requires an exact understanding of key figures, hierarchies, caste, religious and educational backgrounds. As part of his business, Rajesh developed a professional sense and experience for "important people", including politicians and authorities. To ensure that he does not omit one of those key figures, he asks the inviting family members to outline the background of the guests and list those to be mentioned. Another method is to observe guests who remain after the celebration and hence are considered crucial to the function. In contrast to popular snap shots in Western countries, in his motives, people do not show any emotions or actions. As a class characteristic, however, lively pictures are becoming more and more en vogue.[16] With regard to such recent trends, the design of wedding albums reflects a class related dichotomy, which Rajesh explained, "There's a clear difference between the educated and uneducated: educated people will cooperate, for example when I say please go there and touch her arm. Uneducated will refuse to do these things." Rajesh affirmed that it is difficult to convince the couple to make a lively pose: "One strategy to encourage couples to give a good posture in a natural way is to take pictures after the marriage when bride and groom know each other better."

Adam Zeff (1999) provides a profound insight into the intentions and particular techniques of videographers. Comparing narratives on a personal level, in movies and in marriage media, the author illustrates how wedding videos reconcile a dichotomy between two conceptual complexes: 'arranged marriage-past-tradition' on the one hand and 'love-present-modernity' on the other. The illustration of *personal* narrative emanates from the conversations with the spouses themselves. Interviewing young couples about their ideas of a perfect match (personal narrative), the author concludes that an ideal marriage is valued socially, based on principles associated with "tradition". Hereto belong elder authorities, rankings, and rites – in sum all elements that symbolize the family harmony of an arranged marriage. In the interview situation, social criteria overwhelm individual identity (1999: 68). Further, the conversations reveal a general concern against love matches. Even love-married couples expressed a "general agreement for the condemnation of love marriage" (ibid: 91). Notably, in their narratives, they distinguished their own liaison from the antisocial behavior of "pure" love matches. They emphasized that they did not

16 Similarly, Brosius (2010: 271) stresses individualistic emotions in pictures, where the woman does not drop her gaze but looks straight into the camera.

act against the will of their parents. In contrast, the narrative conveyed in films centers on individual emotions acted out in idealistic plots. The example of the film Kadhalan (1999: 72), which recounts the love between a young man from a poor background and a governor's daughter, demonstrates that Tamil movies address liaisons marked by an unbridgeable social gap. Zeff's study further shows that usually the content of Tamil blockbusters disconnects individuals from social categories and presents a triumph of personal character over deprivation. Contrary to the personal narrative, blockbusters therefore focus on the two individuals and their mutual affection.

Picture 26: Intimate gestures between bride and groom which convey openness and a progressive family standing

Through the example of four selected episodes portrayed in wedding videos, his study reveals that marriage media succeed in combining those contrasting narratives, mediating between the risks, the promise and emotional content of love matches and the social prestige of the arranged marriage. That intention becomes evident through one episode prior to a Tāli binding ceremony that mainly contains scenes displaying family harmony. Spouses are depicted bowing towards the parents while other sequences focus on praising and honoring authorities or the exchange of garlands. This moment is accompanied by a song extracted from *Chinna thambi*, a movie that shows the scene of connection between the hero and heroine. With this technique, the narrative of romantic love becomes disconnected from its tragic consequences by "joining positive emotional content of love marriage to the positive consequences of an arranged marriage" (ibid: 108). The garland exchange between couples is simulated with "slow-motion" effects, which fade out the background events in order to create and emphasize romantic scenery. The film editing technique of fast cutting, which consecutively flashes several scenes into focus for a short period of time, accompanies the culminating moment of tāli binding in order to suggest an emotional moment. The spouses' unique relationship is created through their isolation from others and a visual dislocation (1999: 120). According to Zeff, marriage videos take on the function of social reproduction by conveying the idea of endogamous marriages as emotionally desirable.

In the aforementioned analysis, Zeff shows how the ritual order is reaffirmed through marriage media, which enhances the continuation of a delineated hierarchy with motives that exceed social barriers. A question, however, remains as to the way in which those audio-visual techniques provide space for representing anti-hierarchical constellations. I trace this question through an analysis of the marriage video of Prathib and Tenmozhi, the female parallel cousin of my research assistant. The introduction sequence corresponds to Zeff's findings: mountain scenery, flower garlands and rose bouquets, followed by a dissolving stream of hearts frame the bride and groom. The sight of the sea breaking on the shore, palm beaches, birds, butterflies and a sunset opens the first episode. Natural landscapes are complemented by presenting well-known sites from Western countries, such as the Acropolis in Athens and skylines of American megacities. In fact, the display of foreign countries creates an atmosphere of cosmopolitanism, augmented by seductive motives including erotic dancing scenes from North India, Cambodia and Arabian countries. The following sequence, however, stands in striking contrast to that idyll and jolts the viewer back into the actual marriage setting. Central motives are banners, the surrounding neighborhood and the procedure of the rituals. The camera traces the arrival of the guests and captures the joy of the participants. Important functions, such as the garland exchange and tāli binding ceremony are accompanied by music and a cacophony of noises. Finally, the video releases the viewer through the gate of India in Mumbai.

The rubric dedicated to "best wishes" from the participants presents the most memorable part of the wedding videos. As the primary intention lies in emphasizing local hierarchies, the videographer captures each congratulant on stage while he delivers blessings and a gift or money to the couple. This record follows a prescribed structure, adhering to local ranks, which are listed below:

1. Tāy māmaṉ of the bride; tāy māmaṉ of the groom,
2. Grandfather of the bride (still alive), mothers' older and younger sisters (periyammā, citti)
3. Invited professors
4. Fathers' older and younger sisters (attai) and their families
5. Paternal uncles of the bride (periyappā and cittappā) and their families
6. Cross cousins of the bride (māmaṉ/maccāṉ)
7. Sisters and parallel female cousins of the bride, brothers and parallel male cousins of the bride (paṅkāḷi)
8. Attai of the groom and their families
9. Periyappā, cittappā of the groom and their families
10. Cross cousins of the groom (māmaṉ/maccāṉ)
11. Sisters and parallel female cousins of the groom, brothers and parallel male cousins of the groom (paṅkāḷi)
12. Second and third line relatives
13. Colleagues, acquaintances
14. Other friends

That order may be altered in the event of individual circumstances, such as personal affection or disputes between the two families. Hence, the ranking varies across the family constellation and external invitees. If the grandfather, for instance, has passed away, the next person on stage might be the oldest paternal uncle. In case the bride or groom does not have a maternal uncle, he is replaced by a second-grade maternal uncle, or even the maternal uncle of the spouse. Irrespective of such variations, the display of congratulants reveals the position of relatives and participants. As Tamil weddings celebrate female power, it is the bridal side and the female family members who are honored before the groom's side. Hence, the maternal uncle assumes a primary position and is captured first in the video. Highly reputed invitees are honored directly thereafter, not only due to their high position, which contributes to a prestigious wedding, but also due to time constraints.

Peers and friends occupy the last rank and further compose a distinctive category. Tenmozhi's and Pratib's college mates are captured as one exclusive group without other guests. That sequence presents a contrasting focus of the regulated scenery. Unlike other participants, who stand immovably, looking straight into the camera, they expose mimics, movements and emotional reactions, such as wiping their forehead or touching each other. Dressed in modern clothes, fancy T-Shirts, well-fitted hairstyles and sunglasses, peers pose with postures that resemble those of film heroes. The videographer captures them in action, turning around, laughing, whispering or speaking on the phone.

A greater presence of non-ritual constellations can be found in recent wedding depictions, which have recently undergone significant changes. Discussing several adoptions of Western elements such as Western dresses, lively scenes of youngsters, drinking and smoking, Parul Bhandari[17] argues that the aesthetics of wedding celebrations not merely focus on ritual functions, but reflect changing identities. Prakash's wedding album contains exemplary pictures. After remaining a long-term bachelor in Madurai, he finally got married at 38. The studio Manassaran captured his marriage ceremony, which took place in Dubai. On his website, the photographer presents himself as "the candid wedding photographers for vibrant, sophisticated and well-travelled couples". Emotional features between the bride and groom, such as intensive eye contact, warm smiling and cautious caressing form a prominent aspect of the video. Emotions are further expressed among the participants through excessive gestures and movements, which replaced the standardized blessing procedure. Male friends arrive in suits and glasses, a dress code which disguises their ritual status. The video captures them in supportive actions, such as arranging the suit of the groom. Moreover, they express amusement by openly smoking cigarettes or dancing together. Similarly, shots of female circles are taken in the hotel room, displaying them discussing, laughing or crying together. Such depictions present a modern version of wedding videos, although they convey a similar meaning as the conventional ones presented above: peer groups appear as an idiosyncratic category, disconnected from ritual activities. Similar to the examples of invitation cards and banners that signify affection, intimacy and moral support, their presence in albums and videos contains emotionally motivated actions.

Using contemporary techniques, photos and videos allow a "temporal discontinuity" (Zeff 1999: 131) by reconciling anti-hierarchical elements with requirements of the ritual order. Lively scenes demonstrate the distinctive taste of the Madurai educated middle class by simultaneously underpinning established ranks. The technical revolution involves egalitarian constellations such as peer groups displayed as a separate category. Indeed, they are captured and incorporated into the videos, albeit visually excluded from ritual ranks. Their exact representation remains dependent on the strategies of the photographer:

17 Her insights were shared in her presentation *From the ballroom dancing to the ghoonghat: Indian weddings and the aesthetics of negotiating identities* at the Annual Conference "Arts and Aesthetics in a globalising world", organized by the Association of Social Anthropologists (ASA) in April 2012.

while in conventional albums they remain marginal figures, recent versions that primarily intend to highlight a distinctive lifestyle provide space even for displaying tabooed activities. Similarly to the examples of invitation cards and banners, this section has demonstrated creative methods of depicting egalitarian constellations as a part of the wedding audience. My observations suggest the dynamic integration of friendships in conjunction with ritual boundaries: they appear to have become a constant within the representation of wedding guests, as their depiction contributes to the accumulation of prestige. Prakash, who appreciated his friends as moral support on stage, explained to me, "Lots of friends show the strength of the individual. All the guests know that my family and I have a good rapport with people." They do not compose an excluded category; however they appear in a restricted form: "On stage and for pictures – this is the maximum role, friends can play."

8.5 FRIENDS, COURTSHIP AND LOVE MARRIAGE

In this final section, I turn to a form of marriage, in which non-ritual constellations function as key phenomena: self-selected and eloped unions, designated as 'love marriages'. Since affairs are openly discussed among friends and within campus borders, love-matches present a popular subject of conversation among MKU students, as the statement of Uma suggests: "We always talk about boyfriends. But we cannot speak about that with parents or other relatives." Similarly, Eashwaran regards self-chosen affairs as a current phenomenon within the campus (modern compartment) and arranged marriage as belonging to the family context (ritual order): "Parents have their own dreams. They might think they will arrange a bride within the family." He connects familial demands in line with social standards that stand in contrast to the ideas and desires of the paṭiccavaṅka: "But the educated guy will have his own desires. He will think that he needs a suitable spouse who will support him. That is why he looks on his own." If a couple decides to get love-married, in his view, the influence of friends increases: "Friends support love marriages ... here youngsters will help the friends because they are youngsters. There is no human life without love in this world."

To specify the significance of self-chosen alliances, the first paragraph elaborates Tamil conceptions of love and examines previous accounts of love marriages. A detailed case study on background, process and ceremony highlights the problematic situation of elopement and makes visible the unique role of peers, who act as principle agents in reconciling the behavior of the couple with the principles of Tamil society.

8.5.1 Love in Tamil Nadu

The experience of love has never been a pre-existing entity, but differs culturally in relation to time and social environment. That approach becomes clearer through classical theories about emotions that focus on how societies perform events or relations and what kind of sentimental content they attribute to their actions. Two principal approaches are contrasted in the pioneering study of Owen Lynch (1990). The "physicalist" theory, based on a descartian assumption, postulates that emotions form an experience to which the individual is extradited without control. This theory regards feelings as a physiological state disconnected from human or social influence and has a considerable impact on Western concepts of emotions. Contemporary anthropological inquiries, however, oppose this ideal by demonstrating that, since behavior depends on the cultural context, emotions need to be located within a particular social setting. Following that view, emotions are (1) not experienced in a passive way and offer a wide spectrum of reactions; (2) natural as well as negotiable and changeable and therefore not opposed to rationality; (3) variable and not to be evaluated (ibid: 10). In India, Lynch argues that emotions are rather objectified, substantialized and not internalized as they are in the Western sense (ibid: 22).

Assuming "love" as a controllable feature, the alliance is evaluated according to social and familial criteria. During matchmaking, the significance of romantic love is largely neglected as is reflected in a comment by Soundariya's father: "Love-marriage does not exist. Love is always subjective ... it is just a matter of compatibility. Say you and me are compatible persons like your earnings are like this, my earnings are like this, your interests are like this my interests are like this, then we get married." By distinguishing local understandings of love among the Tamil population and its role in the matchmaking process, I demonstrate how the concept of romantic feelings is deliberately applied according to the context.

The idea of 'love' in Tamil Nadu reveals manifold forms and meanings. Its purest form is expressed by the term *aṉpu*, which describes the attachment between husband and wife in everyday life. Following Alex, it affects "mainly those who have been married for some time" (2009: 136). Correspondingly, Gomathy expressed mutual feelings in conjugal life as a sentiment that needs to be "cultivated": "here, we love each other, we accept to live and we live." Similar observations of family attachment in North India demonstrate that this intimate form of love is "concerned with obligations, care, concerns and routine devotion" (Grover 2011: 43). Contrary to the Western idea of romantic love, an̲pu composes a predictable attachment, disconnected from sexual desire and instead developed and nourished within family life. Sinjuta elaborated on this understanding, "I expect my husband to teach me many things. If I do not know much, he should not dominate me. I want care and love. He has to show affection towards me. He has to treat me like a little child." In contrast to sexually oriented affairs or romances, spouses do not display intimacy in public. Instead, married couples circumvent affection towards each other. Tamil wives refer to their husbands indirectly, for example as "father of my child" or simply as *avaru* (honorific "he"). This explains confused reactions when I addressed the husband of my female friends directly as *kaṇavar* ("husband"), an apparently inappropriate, if not indiscreet expression. A typical strategy to express and control that feeling of an̲pu is the frequented mockery of the spouse. Chitchatting about the failures and deficits of their husbands, Tamil women act out the proverb of the poet Auvaiyar: "Don't reveal your treasure".[18] Created through consanguinity (Alex 2009: 112), an̲pu further defines the attachment among siblings or between mother and child. Likewise, this concept is expressed in a manifold and oblique manner, for instance by teasing children, creating confusion or simply by hiding one's emotions (Trawick 1990: 39). Exceeding blood or familial relations, the emotion of an̲pu is extended to the divine, friends or peers, which places the term within a "general and inclusive" category (Clark-Decès 2014: 152). All in all, the notion of an̲pu reflects a sentiment that flourishes through a long-term relationship, mutual responsibility, caring and daily practices.

A romantic and sexually influenced form of love is described by the term kātal[19], which represents an uncontrollable obsession and suddenly occurs in someone unexpectedly (Clark-Decès 2014: 153). This concept refers to the principle bond of non-marital affairs and approaches the Western sense of romantic love. Related academic accounts suggest that kātal is acted out in restricted domains. Alex (2009: 137) illustrates how romantic love dominates the themes of Tamil blockbusters, where film plots, music and dance sessions convey a passion between the hero and heroine that surpass social barriers of Indian caste society. The college campus presents another social arena in the form of a modern compartment, which offers space for romances as well as conversations about love, usually while watching movies or listening to film

18 Quoted in Trawick (1990: 44).

19 Academic views on affection in India differ considerably: Ulrike Niklas for instance assumes that since there has never been a Romantic period in India, no genuine notion about romantic love exists (verbal message).

songs with friends. Within an adequate context, such liaisons remain tolerated, as they do not affect the principles of Tamil society. Tamil ideals of love are not exploited by those two expressions: The term *pācam* stands for intimacy and affection in familial circles while *kāmam* defines the mere sexual desire and expresses the lust of the couple (Alex 2009: 137).[20]

In which way are concepts of love evaluated and implemented in Indian quotidian realities? Clark-Decès summarized the problematic experience of romantic love among the present generation in Tamil Nadu: "What complicates the 'modern' love encounter is that nowadays youth from different castes, classes, and localities comingle in public spaces such as schools, streets and malls" (2014: 154). While she agrees that those encounters could be perceived indeed as "stimulating", she objects that "in a society organized by relations of avoidance and deference with elders and superiors and marked by emotions of extreme touchiness when it comes to one's social standing, socializing with strangers can also be a potential of self-doubt and inadequacy" (ibid). In recent decades, the exposure to romantic sentiments and eroticism advanced to a demonstration of the development of individual personhood formed by sexual experiences. Presuming that love acts as a basic catalyst for narratives of class identity, Donner contends that "with the spread of formal education and wage labor, romantic love [...] has become a major arena to define and to perform modern selves and to link a number of spaces" (2012: 3). Analyzing the connection between a middle-class life style, characterized by urbanization, education, elite marriage and sexual behavior, Patricia Uberoi (2011 b: 277) takes the stance that the "deployment of sexual knowledge may have an important connection with [...] the self understanding of the upper middle classes." In Madurai, the exposure of affection and romantic love represents the sophisticated orientation of the middle class, progress and cosmopolitanism. A self-selected marriage, however, and neglectful behavior toward parental authority remains largely condemned among study participants and their families. The above introduction into the terminological differentiation of love served to facilitate my subsequent examination of the reasons for, experience with and handling of love marriage.

20 For a more detailed discussion of different types of love, see Trawick (1990) or Alex (2009: 136).

8.5.2 Self-chosen unions and love matches

The term 'love marriage' is not undisputed. Recent accounts have disturbed the terminological opposition between arranged and love marriage so that Fuller and Narasimhan argue that such a "dichotomy is fluid and fuzzy" (2008: 751). In support, de Munck (1996: 701) demonstrates that both forms of alliances do not contradict each other, but rather remain linked to the same concepts of attachment. His ethnography among a Muslim community in Sri Lanka illustrates that the local construct of romantic love is indeed embedded within kinship alliances and thus compatible with arranged marriage. Regarding current changes among the present youth, an influential contention is the statement of Lamb and Mines (2010), recognizing that "the distinction between arranged and love marriages is in fact becoming increasingly blurred, especially among the urban middle classes, where it is common for young people to participate in choosing their potential partners within the framework of parental approval" (ibid: 6).

Notwithstanding difficulties in opposing both categories, love marriage as an alliance without familial support is consistently considered anti-social across nearly all of my study respondents. In consensus with their parents, most of the youngsters I spoke to associated an elopement marriage with the debauched behavior of "low class" and "uneducated people" who neglect their family duties and engage in unstable affairs. Similar associations and concerns against love marriage are depicted by Donner (2008: 80) among Bengali middle and upper class members. Her conversations reveal that love marriage disturbs the image of the economic elite that locates itself within the established and family-oriented part of the population. Those principles appear to constitute a middle class asset that distinguishes its members from lower classes that allegedly marry for pragmatic reasons, particularly economic pressure or the aspiration of social mobility. Portraying the mate selection process through the example of her host sister, Priya, in Madurai, Wilson identifies the decision to marry outside of one's own community as a "slap in the face of 'tradition' and disrespectful to an 'Indian' model of arranged marriage" (2013: 46). The author illustrates that the anxiety of her family grounded on individual, familial and social reasons alike: "Conceived as doomed and thus as having a damaging effect on her personal future, it attached shame to her family via her connection with an imposing and immodest foreign culture and its concepts of individualism and lack of filial respect, along with stereotypes of disrespectful lower class and caste behavior" (ibid). The condemnation of love marriage further raises the concern that such an alliance damages the family's reputation in general, which in turn could affect the marital prospects of other family members. Moreover, parents fear economic disadvantage as a consequence of previous love marriages within their families, since such incidents place them in an inferior position to negotiate dowry.

Picture 27: Couples in the adjacent park of MKU

With regard to the vigorous resistance to love marriages, most respondents feared tremendous insecurity and the absence of support by their family as expressed by Eashwaran: "I came to see that many love marriages are a failure. In arranged marriages, the family will come and solve the problems ... but in love marriages there is no support."

For Soundariya, the everyday life for love married couples turns out to be exhausting and depressing in later stages: "Whatever happens in love marriage, conflicts, alcoholism and violence, they have to adjust on their own." Such concerns are indeed reasonable. The severe consequences for love-married couples have been pointed out in detail by Shalini Grover, whose ethnography among the low caste population of urban Delhi portrays such constellations as "fragile" unions (2011: xii). The difficulties faced by love-married couples explain why arranged marriages, alliances ostensibly constituted out of respect and responsibility, remain prominent among educated sections of the population (see also Fuller & Narasimhan 2007: 140). Analyzing the image of marriage celebrated in print media, sports, films and television in Northern India, Chowdhry (2009: 7) therefore contends "that the most successful and popular youth icons give preference to persons chosen by their parents to get married." Despite those concerns against self-chosen alliances, love in conjugal life not only becomes increasingly relevant for the spouses, but supports contemporary middle class' rhetoric of an advanced lifestyle. During matchmaking, therefore, parents openly commit themselves to a joyful and harmonious union of their child. In the words of Parry, middle class marriage has developed into "a bond between two intimate selves" (2001: 816). Fuller and Narasimhan capture the present situation for the young generation when they write that "in the Indian middle class, [...], a form of companionate marriage created through arrangement has become the modern ideal, whereas love marriage definitely has not, except in a small 'progressive' segment" (2008: 752).

While the normative aspiration towards arranged marriage remains prevalent, a great part of the young generation opt for self-chosen unions. Particularly educated sections, often distant from their place of origin and caste restrictions, are rather inclined to engage in affairs that are likely to result in elopement. With regard to political democratization, new economic opportunities, resentment and assertiveness of the subordinate castes and classes, Prem Chowdhry argues that runaway marriages and elopement evince a changing mindset and the expression of an "increased sense of self-identity, self-worth, and education" (2009: 233). A rising confrontation with conventional norms has been equally highlighted by Henrike Donner among the young generation in Bengal, where "the allegedly rising number of so-called love-marriages, and the underlying related reformulation of conjugal ideals, ideas of the self and of youth culture, are successfully presented by the media as a trend that threatens established ideas and middle-class ways of life" (Donner 2008: 80).

Notwithstanding the various forms of love marriages, including non-kin, hyper- or hypogamic alliances, two institutionalized forms in the region of Madurai must be distinguished: love marriage and love-come-arranged marriage. Love marriage *without* the agreement of the parents is usually practiced as an elopement, in which the couple escapes from the parental home to get married in front of public authorities, relinquishing ritual celebrations and familial support. The socially required reaction by the family in the event of an elopement appears as a prescribed opposition: they publicly oppose the marriage, cut off contact with their child or even bring the incident to local court. This public reaction usually culminates in severe consequences for the couple, mostly a long-term rupturing of family ties, which signifies social exclusion, impoverishment and the absence of access to adequate services for birth or perhaps divorce (Grover 2011: 7). Aware of these fatal implications, this sanction presents a necessary commitment for many family members to stabilize their integrity within society (Munck 1996: 704). Those formalized rejections, however, do not discourage close kin from discreetly assisting the couple in their everyday struggles. My encounters with such cases revealed that it is particularly the bridal family that supports the liaison materially and emotionally. Mother and sisters regularly support the 'defector', take on chores and advise her in questions concerning nutrition, family planning or the children's health. In the event of severe economic crisis, they persuade their male kin to support the couple financially. If those efforts remain fruitless, most members are even ready to take away small amounts of the common savings for the livelihood of the couple. This informal involvement, accomplished by female relatives of the bride, is acknowledged as an essential commitment "out of a hidden strength" (Gomathy). Navaneethan, Gomathy's husband whose second daughter had eloped justified the involvement of his wife by the fact that "women are so powerful, while we (men) only think of our pride". This official break usually becomes resolved after the birth of the first child. Such an event reactivates family functions and the liaison becomes socially accepted, albeit lower ranked.[21] Henceforth, the couple reestablishes the contact to the parents and participates in family activities and official ceremonies. Rather than presenting a counteracting constellation to established marriage rules, a self-chosen alliance reflects a culturally integrated phenomenon, as a prescribed social consensus about its status and conduct exist. Eloped couples, who oppose local and familial authorities, remain not disconnected, but incorporated within the principles of Tamil society, as they occupy a subordinated rank. This observation sheds light on a statement by Chowdhry (2009) about run-away couples. Despite composing a "highly individualized resistance against cultural practices located in an iniquitous system based upon assumed hierarchies and status claims [...] they confirm and consolidate those very norms they seek to challenge" (ibid: 12).

The second form, *love-come-arranged marriage*, is an alliance accompanied by parental agreement, at least on one side. Among the educated section of the population, this option is a frequent compromise between the claims of the child and the social commitments, as Soundariya stated: "See, I am in an affair ok? But in my house, they won't accept it. He (my boyfriend) has a socially higher rank than I do. There are some girls who run away from their family, but I am a girl who won't do this. I want my parents to make them understand and I want to have my marriage as an arranged marriage." In contrast to mere elopement marriages, parents have limited space for negotiations as Eashwaran explained: "We sit and talk with the parents and tell them, 'He is my lover and I'm gonna get married only to him. So you can inquire into him or talk to him and decide afterwards. And the family investigates the spouse and asks how he plans his future. Then, they have to accept." Usually, both children stay in their home until the wedding in order to avoid rumors in the social vicinity and damage to the family's status (māṉam). Moreover, parents conduct a public ceremony, though a downgraded version of the usual pomp, in which the number of attendants

21 For a deeper analysis of long-term consequences of love marriage, see Grover (2011).

remains limited. Depending on the community, economic and geographical background, weddings of love-married couples are frequented by the most important kin and follow at least the basic rituals. After this procedure, arrangement is officially accepted and the couple continues to live within their social environment.

This outline has explicated the conceptualization, motives and the contemplative image of love marriages. The field of investigation in the following section relates to the involvement of peers, who act as primary actors within those alliances. The case presented here is a hypogamic elopement marriage between Morali, a 29 year-old Piramalai kaḷḷar and Renufa, 26 years old from the Ceṭṭiyār Community. A detailed ethnography of the entire procedure – first encounters, implementation of the alliance and organization of the wedding – identifies this 'anti-social' act as an institutionalized formula in which peers gain a remarkable significance beyond their assumed marginal position. Since this marriage was eventually conducted by a ritual ceremony, it further elucidates the discrepancy between love weddings and the festivities of arranged marriages.

8.5.3 The case of Morali and Renufa

Morali and Renufa made each other's acquaintance at their place of employment, a textile factory. It was located in Coimbatore, an industrial town roughly 200 km away from Madurai. Morali had not completed his MBA and worked as a machine operator, a job he acquired through experience without a relevant degree. Renufa completed her diploma in Industrial Microbiology at MKU and was employed as a quality checker. Being from a higher caste and a postgraduate, this constellation presented a particularly unfavorable mismatch, in which the bride not only has a higher *ritual* but also a superior *economic* status. The parents of both, originally from the outskirts of Madurai, migrated to Coimbatore for job purposes in the 1970s. By the time of the affair, however, the families already had returned to their home in Usilampatty.

The romantic liaison started by an encounter loaded with emotion: a strong argument about the quality of cotton layers. Renufa, who was in charge of controlling Morali's results, blamed him of having committed 28 mistakes in the production. Morali felt deeply offended so that he made a complaint to the department manager about her. Moreover, he insisted on recounting the alleged errors. In fact, the calculation revealed not more than 18 defects. Following this dispute, both did not speak to each other despite the efforts of the manager to reconcile the quarrelers. Roughly two months later, on *Diwali*[22], Renufa gave Morali sweets as a gesture of compromise, but he rejected her apology. Following this rejection, she attempted to persuade him to have a personal conversation, but he remained firm and refused to talk to her. His strong reaction bothered her so intensely that she confided in her colleague, who eventually called upon Morali herself. In a consolidated conversation, he finally apologized for his rude behavior and claimed that he did not accept the sweets merely because he does not like the taste. Henceforth, Morali and Renufa frequently chatted with each other during their lunch breaks, a contact that evoked their mutual sympathy and gradually romantic feelings. Their affair was cultivated by leisure activities, including visits to parks and shopping malls. Those public areas are frequent places for love-birds, as they remain unimpeded by social restrictions. Both adopted common strategies to escape the surveillance of their families and spare additional time for each other. Renufa deceived her parents into believing that her job had been transferred to a further place so that they would not wonder about her delayed return. Neither she nor Morali disclosed their feelings to each other during their gatherings until she informed him that her parents started to look for a groom. Morali immediately asked her to postpone the matchmaking procedure, which is a gentle way to stop her marriage. His move presented the first initiative toward becoming love married. Both were aware that with such a decision, they risk to damaging their reputation not only within the family and social vicinity, but also in the company. As a precaution, Morali looked for a different employment before making their alliance official. The subsequent happenings suggest that the process for implementing a love marriage follows a prescribed order. The first person contacted was Kannithevar, a police officer from the Piramalai kaḷḷar community (see table 3.3). Kannithevar brought in one of his former classmates, an old confidante and influential person in Coimbatore who maintains close links with police and political institutions. Additionally, Morali divulged his intentions to Pushpa (Paḷḷar) and Murugesh (Kōṉār), both old college friends. Each of them contributed to facilitating the process.

The first required task constituted informing their parents. Pushpa conveyed the message to the father of Renufa, whom they considered more approachable than Morali's parents. In order to inform him, Pushpa dialed his number and asked: "Is this Renufa's house? I heard through some other friends that they are getting married. I don't know if they got married or will get married – I just want

22 Hindu festival of lights.

to inform you, that is why I called you."[23] After this sentence he immediately hung up the phone. On the next day, Renufa's father made inquires about Morali in the police office as well as among the co-workers in the textile factory in Coimbatore. He received the information about his jāti and place of origin, a village where Renufa's father had relatives. Through his second parallel male cousin, Renufa's father inquired into the *māṉam* of Morali's family and discovered their social integrity and strong caste pride. His cousin offered to inform Morali's parents about the love match – a delicate task, since he knew that they would accept only an alliance within their own community. Morali's father even rejected other castes from Mukkulattōr. The situation was aggravated because he envisaged an arrangement for his son with one of his cross cousins. Later on, Morali told me that after receiving the news, his father cried loudly and declared that, "He is not our son anymore!" Morali tried to call his parents three times for a personal conversation, but as soon as they heard Morali's voice they hung up the receiver. The next task consisted in the accommodation of the couple that could not return to their homes. Murugesh lived with his wife, mother and two children in Ganguapatty near Western Ghats. He offered Morali a place to stay since his house contained a spare room. Considering their daily routines, all three friends engaged themselves and purchased containers, cooking utensils, small copper items, blankets and groceries.

Following this task, the next step involved taking care of formalities such as the public registration of the alliance at a government agency. Once the marriage is officially notified, family members are restricted by law from intervening in the alliance – otherwise they make themselves liable for prosecution. Morali contacted Kannithevar to arrange the connection with the police office and finalize the registration. Meanwhile, he called four other peers with whom he hired a car and drove to the police office in Coimbatore. During the entire ride, they kept the windows closed to make sure that no one would see them and inform the parents. At the police station, two officers interrogated Morali and Renufa to evaluate their credibility. They turned to Morali, asking the following questions: "Do you know each other well"; "Have you already lived together?"; "Will you live with her for a long time?"; "Once, you had intercourse, will you leave her?" Likewise, they charged Renufa to be strong in her decision and stated emphatically, "If you go with your parents when they come, then it will be a problem for the groom. This looks like an elopement and he might be put up in jail". Both perceived this interview as a "brainwashing" rather than an investigation. However, the officers insisted that such a cross-examination

23 Since the couple knew about my research purpose, they allowed me to be present during this call.

comprised a necessary act to test the seriousness of the alliance and to avoid judicial consequences. In the case of Morali and Renufa, both stuck to their statement so that the officers registered their marriage.

Meanwhile, Pushpa and Murugesh consulted the police station in Madurai to call Renufa's family and inform them about the registration. When her parents arrived, the police officers instructed them: "Leave them and let them live". Her father replied: "We accept this guy as our son-in-law. But send our daughter to us so that we can arrange the marriage for our future. We need to show our own society that our daughter is home." Moreover, they proposed to accommodate the groom in the bridal home as well. In Morali's view, this idea seemed awkward, as the presence of a couple without an official wedding ceremony caused rumors and a loss of family status. However, the police officer replied, "They already got married, so let them live alone. By law, we cannot send your daughter with you. You organize the wedding – we will advise them to attend the ceremony and follow the prescribed rules."

The official registration was followed by a ceremonial one at a nearby temple.[24] In this religious pendant to the former celebration of marriage, Morali and Renufa confirmed their alliance in front of a pūcāri. The conducting of this ceremony requires the certificate of the former administrative registration and three witnesses for each spouse. This formality replaces the presence of familial authorities. While for an arranged marriage, parents, maternal uncles and close relatives attend the ceremony in person and thereby agree to the alliance, in the case of love matches, priests require the number and photocopy of the registration document. This verification serves as an authorization to conduct the ceremony. The temple wedding must be announced to the priests 15 days in advance. For Morali and Renufa, it took place in a small Shrine, attached to the police station. Six of Morali's peers acted as witnesses: Kannithevar, Pushpa, Murugesh and three other non-kindred friends. One among them, Rajesh a same-aged Paṟaiyar living near the groom in Coimbatore borrowed a fee of 750 rupees in order to pay the priest. The ceremony was held for 20 minutes and merely consisted of tying the tāli. Typically, neither a wedding ceremony nor a reception takes place since love marriages are not accompanied by pre- or post marriage rituals.

Demonstrating their ritual integrity, Renufa's parents and close kin nevertheless organized a function two weeks after the registration at the temple. This wedding presented a downgraded version of the usual ceremony, which resembled in their scope more of a reception than a wedding. Invitation cards were distributed to selected persons and included simple information, void of

24 This act is optional, however accomplished by most love married couples.

familial, religious and political icons. The event was conducted in a small foyer attached to a hotel in an outskirt west of Madurai. Renufa's family provided a small celebration package of 15 000Rs for the entire expenses. This amount accounted for not even a fifth of the costs of her sister's wedding, for which the family spent roughly 1 lakh.

Love marriages are visibly underlined by an unornamented decoration and a limited number of gifts as well as other items that demonstrate status and rank. Usually, the family of the groom is not entitled to claim dowry, especially, if the husband and his family have an ambivalent reputation. For Morali, the bridal family contributed at least five Sovereigns of gold, plus an arrangement of small household appliances, which they gave to the couple on the day of the ceremony. The investment for Renufa's sister had been more than 35 Sovereigns of gold. This gesture was motivated by Renufa's mother, who further convinced her husband to surrender a cupboard, a gas-stove and some cookery items. Clothes and make-up of the spouses emphasize the unfavorable constellation, as elucidated in the observations of Wilson (2013: 46) about her love-married host sister: "Priya, instead of wearing the traditional red nine-yard sari (matisār) to indicate the imminent and auspicious change in her marital status, was presented to her Saurashtra mate in a saffron and green nine-yard sari. This was a clear communication to the wedding audience that compromises had been made and there was something amiss about this match." The atmosphere is neither ceremonial nor festive: Renufa's family invited only a small audience of not even 100 guests. From the bridal side, parents and first line kin were present, but the principal part constituted friends and colleagues. On the groom's side, neither relatives, nor neighbors or other acquaintances attended the wedding. An exception was his brother and a well-wisher from the Kōn̲ār caste, an unmarried elder person who looked after Morali and his sisters when they were small. He explained to me that it is required behavior and the fear of a loss in status that kept Morali's family away from participating in the wedding: "They didn't come because of society. Even if they want to support Morali afterward, they cannot attend the marriage." When I asked Morali why he did not invite at least his friends from the village, he stated, "I didn't inform them earlier. Because if I inform them, most of my friends are from my own caste and it is a small village – the news would spread and it may have stopped the marriage." Family members, neighbors and village friends are excluded as they compose the social radius for the damage to the family's reputation. However, he invited friends from university and co-workers from the factory. The performance of Morali's māman̲ was undertaken by Renufa's maternal uncle, who gave the mālai to the bride and groom alike.

Friends took on an active role, as they monitored the procedure of the wedding ceremony and activities. Together with the few family members who participated, they positioned themselves at the entrance of the hotel to receive the guests with cumcum. During the tāli tying they prepared the wedding meal and served the audience after the ceremony. A professional caterer was not hired. Moreover, peers acquired a greater presence in albums and videos. In contrast to conventional photographing, friends enter the stage first, followed by business contacts, colleagues and professors. Those few family members who attend the marriage appear in later stages. Morali's friends further engaged themselves in the organization of the photo material for the couple. Before the ceremony, Murugesh and Pushpa put them in contact with a studio in Coimbatore where photographers supported the couple, free of charge. With six and seven pictures, those albums serve merely as a certificate for the execution of the marriage.

Picture 28: Evening before a Tēvar marriage: College mates of the bride, gathering in the guest room

Picture 29: Between ritual happenings: male peer groups play cards, in a booked hotel room, an activity often associated with 'rowdy behavior'.

Picture 30: Peers on stage in a love marriage between a Kōṉār groom and a Piramalai kaḷḷar bride

My observations have illustrated the central responsibility of friends within a love match: from encouraging, to arranging the registration and finally ensuring an unimpeded wedding procedure. In love matches, the wedding ceremony constitutes a compromise in which only select kin are present and rituals shortened. Since close kin limit the resources for conducting the event, peers engage themselves in satisfying the basic requirements. The involvement of peers in love marriage underlines an essential function of friendships, made in non-familial contexts.[25]

8.6 CONCLUSION

This chapter has demonstrated the flexible character of friendship (*kūṭṭu naṭpu*) by illuminating the presence of academic peers at ritual events. In a first step, I illustrated how Tamil middle class weddings transformed into a display of economic achievements, caste and class standing as well as ritual integrity. The kalyāṇam is staged in a hall (maṇṭapam), a public place and accessible to all social categories. Choice of the hall, its decoration, ritual performance and the exterior of the spouses advanced to indicators for taste and class belonging. A consistent trend appears to be the orientation toward "decency" as a crucial characteristic for the self-definition of the educated middle class in Madurai. Middle class weddings not only define the reputation of the hosting families, but also the ritual and secular status of the invited guests, which can be found depicted on invitation cards, banners, albums and wedding videos. This hierarchy also respects the status of authorities outside of the family and community such as influential politicians, professors or colleagues.

In this context, I have analyzed the status of peers whose presence reveals a *dynamic* picture: on the one hand, they appear as a separated category of *convivium*, among which different jāti backgrounds remain subverted, as Gomathy explained, "As long as they do not tell us about their caste status, we

25 The salient performance of friends in love marriage is presented in the aforementioned movie *Kathal* when Murugan, the protagonist, receives support from his companions to elope with Aishwarya. His accomplices are undoubtedly presented as an external social category and part of a 'modern' realm of experience. With musical elements and dancing performances, that scene evokes a joyful atmosphere and relaxation for the spectator within the tragic plot. Accordingly, it is shot in Chennai, which represents the progressive part of Tamil Nadu and composes a contrast to the 'conservative' South.

do not know. And we will not ask."[26] Throughout the marriage procedure, their position and behavior indicates their assigned rank which becomes particularly evident through the example of male peers. In most cases, they attend the wedding without their wives[27] and sit in the back of the audience. Peers commonly remain absent during the wedding meal, the central setting indicating the family's standing and degree of hospitality. If they do participate, they are among the very last guests to be served. Likewise, their greeting forms through invitation letters and banners as well as their conspicuous presence in photos and videos depict them as a distinctive *non-kin* category among the wedding participants. The analysis so far shows that their appearance corresponds to Strümpell's concept of *convivial* equality: peers physically and spatially distance themselves to reunite in groups to indulge in contaminative activities. Correspondingly, invited peers explained to me during the wedding events, "We put ourselves back!" Institutionalized breaks with rules of commensality, consumption of meat and alcohol do not oppose the ritual order, but rather remain 'compartmentalized' within principles of Tamil caste society.

On the other hand, a closer observation challenges the idea of peers as a 'marginal' cluster, since their performance before and during ritual events illustrates a persisting supportive function. First, the emerging wedding market opened space for cultivating *kūṭṭu naṭpu,* during which non-kin friends appear as an integral part within the organization and preparation of the marriage event. Beauty parlors, for instance, constitute enclosed spaces transcending social restrictions of Tamil society. Herein, female peers of the bride constitute circles of intimacy, in which they exchange feelings of joy and sorrow. Male peers, increasingly involved as organizers, negotiate with agents of the wedding market as Eashwaran explained to me: "We youngsters hunt for different locations and then the only thing we leave to the family is the final selection and negotiation of

26 Notably, this subversion of caste rules only counts as long as their educated background conceals the ritual status. Repeatedly, peers told me that sometimes the caste background becomes disclosed; less by obvious but rather ascribed features. Dalit members, for instance, may be recognized by 'inferior' glances and Tēvar castes by dominant gestures. At Nataraj' wedding, I witnessed one form of caste related discrimination when the host family welcomed certain peers of the groom in a reserved way and even restricted his intake of the food during the wedding meal. Later on, they explained to me that those guests acted in a typical 'rowdy attitude' of Piramalai kaḷḷar. Particularly in middle class weddings, however, caste discrimination is largely avoided since it does not fit the image of tolerant hosts.

27 Only if the wife entertains a close relationship to the marrying couple, she joins the wedding.

price." This involvement presents not only a facilitating moment of support for the family, but forms an essential part in today's wedding practices. Second, their behavioral patterns revealed adaptability according to the immediate social situation. Despite the inauspicious status of their constellation, non-kin relations may be present on stage or during the wedding meal. In the presence of parents and authoritative kin, they alter their interaction by refraining from physical contact or egalitarian address while still serving as respected supporters of their friend. Third, the subsequent case study regarding the love-married couple Morali and Renufa highlights another form of active engagement. As self-chosen alliances occupy a low status within society and lack the support of family members, peers of the spouses involve themselves in reconciling the decision of the couple with the principles of Tamil caste society. Even though the exposure of mutual affection indeed represents a sign of sophistication and progressiveness, an elopement marriage without the agreement of the parents is condemned as irresponsible and anti-social behavior. The alliance between Morali and Renufa presents an undesirable but prevalent phenomenon of Indian caste society that nevertheless follows a prescribed procedure. The arrangement, organization and exertion of a love marriage is facilitated by state institutions as well as the required performance of the couple, family members and non-kin friends, who predominantly take on the organization of the wedding. In sum, I argue that beyond the educational context, friendship and solidarity between graduate students retain an essential function in further stages of life and ritual occasions.

9. Conclusion and outlook

Do peer groups of graduate students and degree-holders represent a social category to be conceptualized within the framework of an external educational regime? Or, alternatively, are they determined by the ordering principles of Tamil society? These questions have constituted the crucial impetus for examining the status and maintenance of egalitarian friendship constellations among academics in South India throughout several stages of life. This case study assessed the assumption that the actors, mostly degree holders in the first generation and members of the lower middle class stratum, adopt 'modern' ideals in an educational sphere that embodies class mobility within a wider social context. My observations referred to the example of peer groups among students at Madurai Kamaraj University – a site where egalitarian friendships appear to be a typical feature of college culture. Data collection in multiple settings outlined modes of peer group interaction within and beyond the campus. I suggest that anti-hierarchical constellations do not present a campus-related phenomenon, but continue to remain active beyond 'modern compartments'. Moreover, the behavior of peers in their home villages and ritual activities revealed that the experience of friendship extends beyond university and proves meaningful as well as life-affirming. Nevertheless, egalitarian configurations require a particular environment to develop. Peer groups of students oscillate between principles of Tamil society, such as kin relations or caste and gender norms and ideals of equality and modernity. I therefore conclude that even though a 'modern' context is needed for such friendships to exist, peer groups do not constitute an external social phenomenon, as they contain the potential to transform themselves and assume a social function in other life stages.

Part I located the research question in a respective ethnographic debate: controversial reflections on the term 'modernity' were described in chapter 1, which further highlighted the impacts of modernization processes for India's middle class. The second chapter defined the university campus as a 'modern' compartment, determined by secular state ideals. Educational and economic achievements as well as anti-hierarchical friendships offer a counterbalance to established boundaries in Indian society. According to classic theories that draw on Louis Dumont, those egalitarian interactions take place on a *secondary* level. On a primary level however, this sphere remains encompassed by a structuring, hierarchical precept. In the words of Uwe Skoda, "hierarchy as a principle of order sets the position of the elements in relation to the whole, which is well founded in the necessary and hierarchical and complementary coexistence of the pure and the impure" (2002: 141).

Building upon the theoretical debates outlined in part I, part II showed that peer groups comprise more than an egalitarian phenomenon of a 'distinctive' modern sphere and stand in ideological relation to wider social networks in Tamil Nadu. Outwardly, peers embrace secular ideals and form groups, to which they attach an emotional connection. A closer look, however, reveals internal status segregations, based on differences in age, gender, success and subjects of study. Those mechanisms of inclusion and exclusion emanate from a separate educational regime, but are circumscribed by kin terms and caste characteristics. Chapter 3 therefore demonstrated that university friendships do not exist in a 'vacuum', as an isolated 'modern' category. Instead, internal and external boundaries permeate peer groups, in which the actors express their status, for instance by means of respect, the need for protection or dominant behavior. Daily practices on campus do not compose a distinct social model, but involve roles and relations of wider circles.

Chapter 4 analyzed peer performance in the village and domestic context. I identified social, political and moral niches, through which peers maintain and cultivate their solidarity. Notwithstanding other friendship ideals, which can be found in relationships among neighbors or kin, university friends retain a special bond and an identity-establishing function. Friendships rest on a common foundation through their distinctive status of *paṭiccavaṅka* and particularly shared experiences or aspirations of social advancement. However, this level of understanding as a bonding principle needs to be culturally understood. In contrast to Western societies, South Indians in Tamil Nadu perceive class mobility as a collective affair of the family or a wider social group, rather than as an individual achievement (Dickey 2010: 201). Thus, paṭiccavaṅka do not relate to each other as entirely equal individuals on a secular level, but create networks respecting unequal power constellations, social disparities and dependencies. In order to succeed in their educational environment, MKU students created supportive bonds in which lending money, mentoring or even instructing someone in his life planning constitutes an integrative part of friendship. This ideal of friendship stands in contrast to Western concepts, which perceive such gestures as 'patronizing'. In the introduction, I showed that contemporary approaches regard relationships across social boundaries as a 'modern' form of friendship, primarily grounded on intimacy. However, narratives and evaluations of my respondents revealed that they attribute a rather *functional* character to university friends. In their view, 'intimate' or 'pure' friendships are those long-term relations within their family or respective native neighborhood, which they consider free from the necessity of external purpose or constraint. At the same time, the particular function of university friends is strongly appreciated. Regular exchange of physical or verbal affection, costly gifts or money symbolizes mutual trust and stabilizes those external bonds.

Friendship ideals and the supportive function of peer groups do not dissolve, but become applied to ritual contexts, which formed the central subject of part III with the help of examples from contemporary marriage practices. Matchmaking strategies and wedding rituals among the middle class, which I illuminated from an inter-generational perspective, provided the framework for this section. Both the trend toward non-kin marriages and conflicting status aspirations has transformed the alliance-making process into a complex endeavor. Within that transforming scenario, I revealed spaces for cultivating friendships among peers of both sexes, who illustrate their solidarity through common views on conjugal life. Thus, I challenged the academic assumption that non-familial friends fade into lifecycle events after college. My observations drew a differentiated picture about the status of peer groups that play a greater role in the ritual sphere. Chapter 5 looked at similar research on youth and marriage and dissociated my case study from the assumption of marriage as an incident of 'inter-generational clashes'. Instead, I argued that there is not necessarily a contradiction between conjugal ideals formulated by the young generation, including secular standards or personal fulfillment, and status assertions, pursued by elder kin and parental authorities.

Recent trends in matchmaking do not pursue a departure from endogamy, but have introduced a contemporary ideal of conjugal unions: *companionate* marriage, a model which is compatible with notions of middle class mobility. Indeed, similarities in terms of caste, (sub)caste or place of origin perfectly correspond to that moral concept of companionate marriage as well as, to a certain extent, to widespread Western preferences for marriage partners from a common social background (Fuller & Narasimhan 2008: 752). A striking feature, however, constitutes new explanation patterns that reconcile 'modern' ideals with determining principles of Tamil society. Thus, chapter 6 highlighted the way in which my respondents articulate ideas of autonomy, privacy, individualism and romantic feelings in line with rules of endogamy.

Integration and exclusion of peers in a concrete sense have been analyzed in the subsequent chapters through illustrations of other constraints and challenges that shaped matchmaking rituals and pre-wedding arrangements. The complex and sometimes precarious stages of finding a partner, described in chapter 7, revealed a set of new practices, moral norms and networks. Within that scenario, non-kin friends experience particular appreciation and gain significance through their knowledge of new standards, including technologies as well as altered codes of 'modern' conduct. While matchmaking strategies maintain their position as a family affair, concealed to the public, recent challenges allow space for the involvement of non-familial contacts.

The function and ritual rank among peers was further analyzed through observations of wedding rituals. Chapter 8 outlined the way in which the ceremony advanced to a public manifestation of family standing. Evaluating the Indian wedding market, I illustrated how ritual practices serve to consolidate ranks in terms of caste, class, educational and economic achievements as well as to reaffirm taste and 'decency' as a constituting element of middle class identity. Several case examples illustrated how the presence of actors like wedding planners, caterers, photographers and videographers assume the function of conferring status on hosting families. The wedding stage not only presents a site for exhibiting the social integrity of the family, but indicates the ritual and economic standing of the audience – a hierarchy depicted in wedding media, particularly albums and videos. The representation of invited peers of the spouses revealed forms of integration and exclusion alike: the presence of anti-hierarchical configurations raise families' prestige, as they symbolize a good social reputation; at the same time they retain their inauspicious status in ritual terms.

As standards beyond caste boundaries shape marriage practices, spaces for cultivating anti-hierarchical friendships emerge. Appearing as an external social category, peers do not take part in ritual events. However, they remain involved as an 'indirect' support by taking on duties that arise, which previously were reserved for kin. I have recounted examples of male peers, who assist their friends on stage, and female circles, gathering in beauty parlors, which constitute a site of transcending ritual boundaries. In sum, the wedding ceased to present an exclusive familial event and has began to involve significant others, whose function and interpretational sovereignty have been highlighted throughout several stages of the marriage process. The most active form of involvement of egalitarian friends becomes visible in courtships and love marriages, as highlighted through the example of Morali and Renufa.

In sum, part III illustrated the conjunctive development of youth aspirations, desires and worldviews as countervailing social principles of Tamil society. Notwithstanding inter-generational divergences, the perspective of the younger generation does not intend to 'override' established principles, including endogamy and local notions of respect and dignity (see also Clark-Decès 2014: 160). In a broader sense, this section depicted the dynamic character of egalitarian friendships in Tamil Nadu and shed light on the capacity to integrate 'modern' influences into marriage practices. Curiously, the ritual procedure allows breaks with caste rules, for instance by inviting peers from other castes on stage. Their presence, however, does not present a contradiction to hierarchical principles, but is even considered as prestigious in secular terms and rationalized by their supportive function. Marriage, therefore, turned out to be particular illustrative for that dynamic picture, as it presents a site that, according to Donner, "[...] is after all, subject to the sometimes contradictory ways of reasoning implied in relationships more generally" (2008: 88).

Finally, I turn to the analytic task of reviewing whether the ethnographic concept of *convivium,* introduced in chapter 2, holds for my example of friendships between peers made in educational regimes. The approach introduced by Christian Strümpell derives from Dumont's theory that all forms of social interaction can be reduced to one Indian hierarchical principle, based on a pure-impure divide. In that sense, convivial equality between actors of a different ritual status nevertheless forms part of a consistent culture-specific system. Observations of campus life and further activities suggested that peer groups compose an egalitarian configuration, in which the ritual status is temporarily subverted. Hence, those friendships require a certain space to exist and develop. Indeed, the isolated campus, a modern compartment in which equality, economic accomplishments and individual emotions are overtly acted out, constitutes a representative setting, similar to the industrial power plant of Christian Strümpell's research. As indicated in chapter 3, ruptures with established boundaries are common and socially accepted within the campus. In accordance with the culture-specific view, I reject the idea of modern compartments – including the urban sphere, working places and educational institutions – as a wider sociologic phenomenon in a universalistic sense. College culture and relationships among students appear to be permeated by internal segregations and counteracting social norms of Indian society. Moreover, I have shown that although the respondents continue to maintain networks based on a distinctive status, they face restrictions within the domestic sphere. Common activities are primarily tolerated when they reveal a reasonable purpose and educational impact, for instance by jointly providing lessons or assisting in translations and academic exercises. In contrast, 'pure' friend activities that occur merely for pleasure, including hanging out, common feasts and drinking rounds usually take place in separated areas. Mixed-gendered groups present a particularly delicate constellation: in order to spend leisure time without a specific reason, young men and women communicate in a discreet way via mobile, and reunite in isolated localities.

In the same way, peer behavior in ritual contexts corresponds with the approach of conviviality. Observing the performance of egalitarian friends in later stages of life, I found that they persist, but remain low-ranked participants in life cycle events. Throughout matchmaking, pre-wedding and wedding rituals, the presence of anti-hierarchical constellations is physically and visibly restricted. Status and performance of egalitarian friends in alliance-making demonstrated that peers are officially excluded from remedy rituals, *poṉṉu pārkka* and further negotiations. Their solidarity takes place in a rather informal way. Male friends actively participate in the preparations, including purchases, negotiating prices or arranging decorations and designs. As *terintavaṅka*, they mediate between the groom and bride, the spouses and parents, or among other related kin. Female friends preferably support the spouse through listening and encouragement. Despite this involvement, peers are confined to the organizational aspects of the wedding, while they do not actively participate in ritual activities on stage. Indeed, during the wedding itself, the restricted scope of action for peer groups foreign to the ritual sphere remains paramount: on stage, they mainly appear only in order to deliver their gift and otherwise remain seated in the back of the hall or withdraw themselves, often to engage in polluting activities that symbolize the inauspicious status of their group. Moreover, egalitarian friends expose their rank through unfitting gestures in videos and albums. Rather than a separate social category, however, peer groups constitute part of a cumulative cultural system. Thus far, I agree with the concept of convivium, which regards egalitarian constellations as contextually integrated within prevailing social principles.

Nevertheless, I should mention several points that distinguish my case study from Strümpell's analysis of industrial workers at the power plant in South Orissa. First and foremost, I extrapolated the ability of peer groups to switch across several contexts. Thus far, the approach of convivium has presented anti-hierarchical constellations as a static group, ranked at the bottom of the hierarchical Indian value system. Yet, my observations suggest a rather dynamic model of friendship groups, ideas and qualities which become altered and adjusted to the social environment. Instead of a fixed category of unambiguous terms, peer groups adjust through their interactions and demeanor in accordance to ritual boundaries, including kin relations, caste rules or gender norms. Beyond campus borders, I revealed alternative modes of conduct in the domestic and ritual context. Thus, the actors cease to expose their symmetric relationship and refer to each other by name, a gesture conveying their respect for existing social principles. Egalitarian patterns do not exclusively take place within a 'modern' context, but continue in an altered form within the private sphere and life-cycle events. I argue that, more than being aware of an inauspicious status, as Strümpell suggested, peer groups are aware of differing environments and adjust their interactions within wider social systems.

A second difference to Strümpell's research is the multifaceted scope of action observed among peer groups. My observations have shown that social constellations of same-aged friends cannot be reduced to one social category. The concept of peers as convives is only *one* model among others. Yet, further modes of conduct exist. More than an 'anti-hierarchical' group, peers appear as paṭiccavaṅka who maintain cross-caste and cross-gendered friendships by exposing educational success and retaining an appreciation for equality. In the ritual context, they act as terintavaṅka, an integrative position – originally confined to family members – that involves a high level of authority and responsibility. Solidarity among academics is not only maintained but gains an influencing role beyond ritual boundaries within the familial and ritual domain. Assuming a formalized function, they are not considered inauspicious and do not endanger the ritual order.

That last aspect brings me to a third statement that refers to Strümpell's assumption that convivial friendships rest upon ritual impurity (2006: 218). The author postulated that convivial groups demonstrate their inauspicious status through activities that transgress the ritual rank and break with rules of commensality (ibid: 76). Typical behavioral patterns are the joint feasting from the same plate and the consumption of beef or alcohol. My observations have shown that the subversion of caste rules may be further regarded as a *superior* attitude. By neglecting caste boundaries for instance, groups of students and former graduates do not deny, but rather rearticulate local divisions. Young educated people question hierarchical constellations and reformulate caste characteristics in line with the educational context, as demonstrated in chapter 3.5. In other words, egalitarian friendships are not necessarily ranked as impure per se, but only in connection with disfavored activities, including excesses or affairs.

A final critic points to the neglect of convivial patterns among women: Strümpell has argued that convivium fades in the presence of wives. My observations, however, have illustrated several forms of egalitarian female and mixed-gendered friendships. Moreover, I disclosed spaces for cultivating interactions and behavioral norms between young women, which subvert existing gender norms. Those spaces are not necessarily restricted to the campus context, but extend to domestic and ritual domains. Admittedly, women do not have the means of practicing friendship activities like their male counterparts: moving around takes place in a restricted way and remains externally controlled.

Principally, my concerns focus on the assumption of convives as a rigid social fabric and I emphasize that peers, in fact, continuously change and alter their way of interacting according to the context. Certainly, the convivium approach offers an explanatory model for the maintenance of an anti-hierarchical configuration within a society, shaped by rigid social barriers. However, it is important not to underestimate the significance of anti-ritual constellations. Egalitarian friendships are more than marginal groups; they are experienced as a beneficial, meaningful element in the social universe of Tamil Nadu. Importantly, recognizing that peers display their own morality does not designate them as a countervailing model that stands in conflict to established norms by surmounting social categories. My research defines them as a supplement or alternative category, compatible with the ritual order. The interaction and influence of convives take place in a context-related way. Beyond common activities within the campus, they create supportive networks in vocational fields and take on an integrative function in marriage practices, through active services, encouragement and by contributing to the accumulation of prestige. Indeed, their presence on stage becomes increasingly relevant for the purpose of enhancing the rank, integrity and reputation of 'modern' middle-class families.

Those creative movements of egalitarian constellations within several social systems suggest that it would be too simple to draw a line between layers considered 'modern', 'traditional', 'local' or 'backward'. Rather, this ethnography has shown how 'modern' patterns and behavioral forms of interaction are integrated into farther-reaching social environments. In accordance with theoretical reflections on the terms 'modernity', presented at the beginning of chapter 2, I suggest redefining the distinction between 'modernity' and 'tradition'. It seems that, rather than 'overcoming' social boundaries through the establishment of a surmounting value system, the 'modern self' in India is defined by the ability to navigate between several systems. Skillful adaptation in distinct contexts appears as an aspired competence and constituting element of class mobility.

Far from being an enclosed independent sociological phenomenon, 'education', as representative for the 'modern sphere' in India, has to be conceptualized by culture-specific parameters. Similar to the flexible character of peer groups, I have presented education as a dynamic concept, which becomes continuously reproduced in relation to the social and cultural environment. Thus, peers define their educated status by embodying educational goals (on campus), by serving as role models (in the domestic context) and via distinction through status symbols, codes of conduct, behavioral norms, taste, ritual knowledge, and the construction of caste and class identity (on ritual occasions). Despite the implementation of secular ideals, I have shown that education, representative for externally driven, state-wide developments, does not imply a transformation of wider social networks. My argument supports the anthropological postulation that pan-Indian or global trends do not compose a consistent phenomenon and cannot be analyzed isolated from the cultural context. Observing increasing priorities toward intimate relationships and nuclear family structures among the urban population in northern India, Henrike Donner has stated that "equally as prominent as such global transformations are locally constructed, class-based practices and identities which emerge in conjunction rather than against older patriarchal arrangements based on marriage and joint family life" (2008: 180). Similarly, tracing changing interpretations, new desires and altered forms of status expressions in South Indian marriages, Clark-Decès emphatically rejects those anthropological approaches as "naive" which assume an evolutional movement of a society, "organized by kinship, endogamy, and patriarchal norms to some kind of 'modernity'" (2014: 171).

I close the discussion highlighting areas for further research. In the introduction, I pointed out the lack of academic research on non-kin and anti-hierarchical constellations. My ethnographic data assessed peer groups of academics as a representative sample of the educated middle class in Madurai. Admittedly, I adopted a rather consistent concept of the term 'friend', which counts only for a particular constellation. Although multiple and transforming friendship ideals in other contexts have not been the primary focus to my study, their topicality cannot be denied. A rewarding subject for future studies relates to the significance and performance of friendship patterns in other social forms. In addition, a further demanded area of research lies in the analysis of solidarity among friends in vocational domains or later stages of family life and particularly the articulation of intimate ties in digital media. Final fields that I consider relevant, are prevailing inconsistencies in friendship ideals and limitations, either through external barriers or internal conflicts. I have depicted peer groups as a category in which the members exhibit their own concept of morality. So far, I highlighted the way in which those constellations are adjusted in accordance with established boundaries. That analysis is sufficient for pursuing the ambivalent impact of 'modern' influences, using the example of educational ideals. Yet, having identified several spaces for cultivating friendships, I neglect to elaborate on other boundaries where friendship constellations are circumvented. Certainly, it would be worth concentrating on clashes and investigating in which way altered forms of interaction within anti-hierarchical groups violate socially established values and cause social cleavage. These prospective areas for further investigation go beyond the scope of this thesis, but present interesting questions for further research. Focusing on a particular section of the population in the experience of friendship, I intended to furnish the reader with a range of ethnographic material, to inspire related project ideas in Tamil Nadu and other ethnographic contexts.

References and literature

Ahearn, L. M. (2004). Invitations to love: literacy, love letters, and social change in Nepal. New Delhi: Adarsh Books.

Alex, G. (2009). Learning and embodying caste, class and gender: patterns of childhood in rural Tamil Nadu; ritual, kinship, gender, and education among Vagri, Mutturājā and Kaḷḷar. Chennai: National Folklore Support Centre.

Alex, G., & Heidemann, F. (2013). Tamil Nadu: Inequality and status. In P. Berger, & F. Heidemann (Eds.), The modern anthropology of India: ethnography, themes and theory (pp. 260-275). London [u.a.]: Routledge.

Allen, M. R. (1986). The cult of Kumārī: virgin worship in Nepal. Kathmandu: Madhab lal Maharjan.

Appadurai, A. (1976). The South Indian Temple: Authority, Honour and Redistribution. Contributions to Indian Sociology, 10(2), 187-211.

Appadurai, A. (2004). The Capacity to Aspire: Culture and the Terms of Recognition . In V. Rao, & W. M. (Eds.), Culture and public action (pp. 59-84). Delhi: Permanent Black.

Appadurai, A. (2010). Modernity at large : cultural dimensions of globalization. Minneapolis, Minn. [u.a.] : Univ. of Minnesota Press.

Appadurai, A., & Breckenridge, C. A. (1996). Public Modernity in India. In C. A. Breckenridge (Ed.), Consuming modernity: public culture in contemporary India (pp. 1-20). Delhi [u.a.]: Oxford University Press.

Aristoteles. (1972). Nikomachische Ethik. München: dtv.

Arya, D., Arya, J., Arya, D. G., Arya, A., & Kanika, A. (n.d.). Madurai: The cultural capital of Tamil Nadu. Jodhpur: Indian Map Service.

Assayag, J., & Fuller, C. (2005). Introduction. In J. Assayag, & C. Fuller (Eds.), Globalizing India: perspectives from below (pp. 1-16). London: Anthem .

Bate, B. (2009). Tamil oratory and the Dravidian aesthetic: democratic practice in South India. New York: Columbia Univ. Press.

Berger, P., & Heidemann, F. (2013). Introduction: The many Indias: the whole and its parts. In P. Berger, & F. Heidemann (Eds.), The modern anthropology of India: ethnography, themes and theory (pp. 1-11). London [u.a.]: Routledge.

Béteille, A. (1996). Caste in contemporary India. In C. J. Fuller (Ed.), Caste today (pp. 150-179). Delhi: Oxford University Press.

Bhargava, R. (2001). Are there alternative modernities? In N. Vohra (Ed.), Culture, democracy, and development in South Asia (pp. 9-26). New Delhi: Shipra Publ.

Böck, M., & Rao, A. (1995). Aspekte der Gesellschaftsstruktur Indiens: Kasten und Stämme. In D. Rothermund (Ed.), Indien: Kultur, Geschichte, Politik, Wirtschaft, Umwelt. Ein Handbuch (pp. 111-131). München: Beck.

Brosius, C. (2010). India's middle class: new forms of urban leisure, consumption and prosperity. London [u.a.]: Routledge.

Bunting, A., & Merry, S. (2007). Global Regulation and Local Political Struggles: Early Marriage in Northern Nigeria. In S. A. Venkatesh (Ed.), Youth, globalization and the law (pp. 321-353). Stanford: Stanford Univ. Press.

Chakrabarty, D. (2000). Provincializing Europe. Princeton: Princeton University Press.

Chowdhry, P. (2009). Contentious marriages, eloping couples: gender, caste, and patriarchy in northern India. New Delhi: Oxford India Paperbacks.

Clark-Decès, I. (2014). The right spouse : preferential marriages in Tamil Nadu. Stanford: Stanford University Press.

Cooley, C. (1929). Social organization – a study of the larger mind . New York: Scriber.

Daniel, E. V. (1984). Fluid signs: being a person the Tamil way. Berkeley [u.a.]: University of California Press.

Das, G. (2000). India Unbound. New Delhi [u.a.]: Viking.

de Montaigne, M. (1909-14). Of Friendship. In C. Eliot (Ed.), Literary and Philosophical Essays. The Havard Classics (p. vol 32). New York: P.F. Collier and Son.

de Munck, V. C. (1996). Love and marriage in a Sri Lankan Muslim community: toward a reevaluation of Dravidian marriage practices. American Ethnologist, 23(4), 698-716.

de Neve, G. (2004). The Workplace and the Neighbourhood: Locating Masculinities in the South Indian Textile Industry. In F. Osella, & C. C. Osella (Eds.), South Asian Masculinities: Context of Change, Sites of Continuities (pp. 45-67). Delhi: Kali for Women (Women Unlimited).

Devere, H. (2005). Friendship. In M. C. Horowitz (Ed.), New dictionary of the history of ideas (pp. 844-846). Detroit, Mich. [u.a.]: Charles Scribner's Sons.

Dickey, S. (2000). Permeable Homes: Domestic Service, Household Space and the Vulnerability of Class Boundaries in Urban India. American Ethnologist, 27(2), 462-489.

Dickey, S. (2010). Anjali's Alliance: Class Mobility in Urban India . In D. P. Mines, & S. Lamb (Eds.), Everyday life in South Asia (pp. 192-205). Bloomington, Ind. [u.a.]: Indiana University Press.

Dickey, S. (2012). The Pleasures and Anxieties of Being in the Middle: Emerging Middle Class in Urban South India. Modern Asian Studies, 46(3), 559 599.

Donner, H. (2008). Domestic goddesses : maternity, globalization and middle-class identity in contemporary India. Aldershot, Hants, England [u.a.]: Ashgate.

Donner, H. (2012). Love and marriage, globally. Anthropology of this century(4).

Dumont, L. (1961). Marriage in India: The Present State of the Question. I. Marriage Alliance in South East India and Ceylon. Contributions to Indian Sociology, 5, 75–90.

Dumont, L. (1964). Marriage in India, the present state of the question: postscript to Part i. Part ii: Nayar and Newar. Contributions to Indian Sociology, 7, 77–98.

Dumont, L. (1980). Homo hierarchicus: the caste system and its implications. Chicago: Univ. of Chicago Press.

Dumont, L. (1986 [1957]). A South Indian subcaste. Social organization and religion of the Pramalai Kallar. Delhi: Oxford Univ. Press.

Eichler, K.-D. (1999). Philosophie der Freundschaft. Leipzig: Reclam-Verlag.

Fernandes, L., & Heller, P. (2006). Hegemonic Aspirations: New Middle Class Politics and India's Democracy in Comparative Perspective. Critical Asian Studies, 38(4), 495-522.

Friedman, S. L. (2005). The Intimacy of State Power: Marriage, Liberation, and Socialist Subjects in Southeastern China. American Ethnologist, 32(2), 312-327.

Fruzzetti, L., Östör, Á., & Barnett, S. (1982). The cultural construction of the person in Bengal and Tamilnadu. In Á. Östör, L. Fruzzetti, & S. Barnett (Eds.), Concepts of person: kinship, caste and marriage in India (pp. 8-30). Delhi: Oxford University Press.

Fuchs, M. (1999). Dalit-Bewegung und ihr Diskurs. In M. Fuchs (Ed.), Kampf um Differenz. Repräsentation, Subjektivität und soziale Bewegungen. Das Beispiel Indien (pp. 168-198). Frankfurt am Main: Suhrkamp.

Fuller, C. J. (1996). Introduction: Caste today. In C. J. Fuller (Ed.), Caste today (pp. 1-31). Delhi [u.a.] : Oxford University Press.

Fuller, C. J. (2003). The renewal of the priesthood: modernity and traditionalism in a South Indian temple. Princeton, NJ [u.a.]: Princeton Univ. Press.

Fuller, C. J., & Narasimhan, H. (2007). Information Technology Professionals and the New-Rich Middle Class in Chennai (Madras). Modern Asian Studies, 41(1), 121–150.

Fuller, C. J., & Narasimhan, H. (2008). Companionate marriage in India: the changing marriage system in a middle-class Brahman subcaste. Journal of the Royal Anthropological Institute, 14(4), 736-754.

Fuller, C. J., & Narasimhan, H. (2014). Tamil Brahmans: The Making of a Middle-Class Caste. Chicago: The University of Chicago Press.

Gaonkar, D. P. (2001). On Alternative Modernities. In Alternative Modernities (pp. 1-23). Durham, NC: Duke Univ. Press.

Gerritsen, R. (2009). Cine-Addictions: Image Trails Running from the Intimate Sphere to the Public Eye. South Asian Visual Culture Series(2), 1-32.

Giddens, A. (1990). The consequences of modernity. Stanford: Stanford University Press.

Giddens, A. (1992). The transformation of intimacy: sexuality, love and eroticism in modern societies. Cambridge: Polity Press.

Gorringe, H. (2005). Untouchable Citizens. Dalit movements and democratisation in Tamil Nadu. New Delhi: Sage Publ.

Gough, K. E. (1956). Brahman Kinship in a Tamil Village. American Anthropologist, 58(5), 826-853.

Grover, S. (2011). Marriage, love, caste & kinship support: lived experiences of the urban poor in India. New Delhi: Social Science Press.

Gupta, A., & Sharma, A. (2006). Globalization and Postcolonial States. Current Anthropology, 47(2), 277-307.

Handler, R., & Linnekin, J. (1984). Tradition, Genuine or Spurious. The Journal of American Folklore, 97(385), 273-290.

Hart, K. (2007). Love by Arrangement: The Ambiguity of 'Spousal Choice' in a Turkish Village. The Journal of the Royal Anthropological Institute, 13(2), 345-362.

Held, D., Mc Grew, A., Goldblatt, D., & Perraton, J. (1999). Global transformations: politics, economics and culture. Cambridge [u.a.]: Polity Press.

Hubermann, J. (2011). Tourism in India: The moral Economy of Gender in Banares. In I. Clark-Decès (Ed.), A companion to the Anthropology of India (pp. 169-185). Malden [u.a.]: Wiley-Blackwell.

Jackson, D. (1990). Unmasking masculinity: a critical autobiography. . London: Unwin Hyman.

Jacobson, D. (1977). Introduction. In D. Jaconson, & S. S. Wadley (Eds.), Women in India (pp. 1-16). New Delhi: Manohar.

Jeffery, P. (2005). Introduction: Hearts, Minds and Pockets . In R. Chopra, & P. Jeffery (Eds.), Educational regimes in contemporary India (pp. 13-38). New Delhi [u.a.]: Sage .

Jeffrey, C. (2010). Timepass: youth, class, and the politics of waiting in India. Stanford, Calif.: Stanford University Press.

Jeffrey, C., Jeffery, P., & Jeffery, R. (2005). When schooling fails : Young men, education and low-caste politics in rural north India. Contributions to Indian Sociology, 39(1), 1-38.

Jeffrey, C., Jeffery, P., & Jeffery, R. (2008). Degrees without freedom? education, masculinities, and unemployment in North India. Stanford: Standford University Press.

Jennings, A. M. (2001). Resistance to Arranged Marriage among Nubian Youth: Ideology and Changing Times. Northeast African Studies, 8(2), 13-22.

Jodhka, S. S., & Prakash, A. (2011). Die indische Mittelschicht:Aufstrebende politische und wirtschaftliche Kultur. KAS Auslandsinformationen, 12, 44-59.

Jolly, M. (1992). Specters oflnauthenticity. The Contemporary Pacific, 4(1), 49-72.

Kakar, S. (2002). The Inner World: a psycho-analytic study of childhood and society in India. Delhi: Oxford University Press.

Kapadia, K. (1993). Marrying Money: Changing Preference and Practice in Tamil Marriage. Contributions to Indian Sociology, 27(1), 25-51.

Karthikeyan, D. (2011, May 2). 'Madurai formula' films and social realities. The Hindu.

Kaviraj, S. (2005). An Outline of a Revisionist Theory of Modernity. European Journal of Sociology, 46(3), 497-526.

Kolenda, P. (1978). Caste in Contemporary India: Beyond Organic Solidarity. Illinois: Waveland Press.

Kolenda, P. (1984). Women as Tribute, women as Flower. Images of Women in Weddings in North and South India. American Ethnologist, 11(1), 98-117.

Krishnan, R. (2008). Imaginary geographies: The makings of 'South' in contemporary Tamil Cinema. In V. Selvaraj (Ed.), Tamil cinema : the cultural politics of India's other film industry (pp. 139-153). London [u.a.]: Routledge.

Kumar, N. (2007). The politics of Gender, Community, and Modernity. Essays on Education in India. New Delhi [u.a.]: Oxford Univ. Press.

Latour, B. (1993). We have never been modern. New York: Harvester Wheatsheaf.

Levinson, B. A. (1996). Social Differences and Schooled Identity at a Mexican Secundaria. In B. A. Levinson, F. D. E., & D. C. Holland (Eds.), The Cultural Production of the Educated Person (pp. 211-238). New York: State University of New York Press.

Levinson, B. A., & Holland, D. (1996). The cultural production of the educated person: an introduction. In B. A. Levinson, D. E. Foley, & D. Holland (Eds.), The cultural production of the educated person (pp. 1-54). New York: State University of New York Press.

Liechty, M. (2003). Suitable modern: making middle-class culture in a new consumer society. Princeton [u.a.] : Princeton Univ. Press.

Lynch, O. M. (1990). Divine passions: the social construction of emotion in India. Berkeley [u.a.] : Univ. of California Press.

Majumdar, R. (2009). Marriage and Modernity. New Delhi: Oxford University Press.

Mandelbaum, D. G. (1970). Continuity and change. Berkeley: University of California Press.

Masquelier, A. (2005). The Scorpion's Sting: Youth, Marriage and the Struggle for Social Maturity in Niger. The Journal of the Royal Anthropological Institute, 11(1), 59-83.

Mathur, P. (1994). Applied Anthropology and challenges of development in India. Calutta: Punthi-Pustak.

Mc Cormack, W. (1958). Sister's daughter marriage in a Mysore village. Man in India, 38(1), 34-48.

Michaels, A. (1998). Der Hinduismus. Geschichte und Gegenwart. München: Beck.

Mines, D. P., & Lamb, S. (2010). Everyday life in South Asia . Bloomington, Ind. [u.a.]: Indiana University Press.

Mines, M. (1994). Private faces, public voices: community and individuality in South India. Berkeley: University of California Press.

Mitchell, A. (2001). Friendship Amongst the Self-Sufficient: Epicurus. Essays in Philosophy: A Biannual Journal, 2(2), Article 5.

Nakassis, C. V. (2013). Youth masculinity, 'style' and the peer group in Tamil Nadu, India. Contributions to Indian Sociology, 47(2), 245-269 .

Naudet, J. (2008). 'Paying back to society' : Upward social mobility among Dalits. Contributions to Indian Sociology, 42(3), 413-441.

Ngo, B. (2002). Contesting "Culture": The Perspectives of Hmong American Female Students on Early Marriage. Anthropology & Education Quarterly, 33(2), 163-188.

Oberdiek, U. (1991). Kontinuität und Wandel: die staatliche Integration der indischen Stämme. München: Trickster.

Osella, C., & Osella, F. (1998). Friendship and Flirting: Micro-Politics in Kerala, South India. The Journal of the Royal Anthropological Institute, 4(2), 189-206.

Osella, C., & Osella, F. (2000). Social mobility in Kerala: modernity and identity in conflict. London [u.a.]: Pluto Press.

Palanithurai, G. (1994). Caste Politics and Society in Tamil Nadu. Delhi: Kanisha Publ.

Parish, S. (1996). Hierarchy and its discontents: culture and the politics of consciousness in caste society. Philadelphia: University of Pennsilvania Press.

Parry, J. (2001). Ankalu's errant wife: sex, marriage and industry in contemporary Chhattisgarh. Modern Asian Studies, 35(4), 783-820.

Rabinow, P. (2008). Marking time: on the Anthropology of the Contemporary. Princeton [u.a.]: Princeton Univ. Press.

Randeria, S. (1996). Hindu- 'Fundamentalismus': Zum Verhältnis von Religion, Geschichte und Identität im modernen Indien. In C. Weiß (Ed.), Religion - Macht - Gewalt: religiöser "Fundamentalismus" und Hindu-Moslem-Konflikte in Südasien (pp. 26-56). Frankfurt am Main: IKO Verlag.

Rao, V. P., & Rao, V. N. (1998). Sex Role Attitudes of College Students in India. In R. Ghadially (Ed.), Women in Indian society: a reader (pp. 109-123). New Delhi [u.a.]: Sage Publ.

Rasmussen, S. J. (2000). Between Several Worlds: Images of Youth and Age in Tuareg Popular Performances. Anthropological Quarterly, 73(3), 133-144.

Reiniche, M. (1996). The Urban Dynamics of Caste: a Case Study from Tamilnadu. In C. J. Fuller (Ed.), Caste Today (pp. 124-149). Delhi: Oxford University Press.

Rivers, W. H. (1914). Kinship and social organisation. London: Constable.

Roche, S. (2014). Domesticating youth: the youth bulge and its socio-political implications in Tajikistan. New York [u.a.]: Berghahn Books.

Rogers, M. (2008). Modernity, 'authenticity', and ambivalence: subaltern masculinities on a South Indian college campus. Journal of the Royal Anthropological Institute, (N.S.)(14), 79-95.

Rosaldo. (1993). Culture and truth: the remaking of social analysis . London: Routledge.

Roulet, M. (1996). Dowry and prestige in north India. Contributions to Indian Sociology, 30(1), 89-107.

Rytter, M. (2012). Between preferences: marriage and mobility among Danish Pakistani youth. The Journal of the Royal Anthropological Institute, 18(3), 572-590.

Sahlins, M. D. (2000). Culture in practice: selected essays. New York: Zone Books.

Schlehe, J. (2003). Formen qualitativer ethnographischer Interviews. In B. Beer (Ed.), Methoden und Techniken der Feldforschung (pp. 71-93). Berlin: Dietrich Reimer Verlag.

Schnegg, M. (2003). Die ethnologische Netzwerkanalyse. In B. Beer (Ed.), Methoden und Techniken der Feldforschung (pp. 209-231). Berlin: Reimer.

Schopenhauer, A. (2015). The Selected Works of Arthur Schopenhauer (Kobo Edition (eBook) ed.). United States of America: Library of Alexandria.

Schrauwers, A. (2000). Three Weddings and a Performance: Marriage, Households, and Development in the Highlands of Central Sulawesi, Indonesia. American Ethnologist, 27(4), 855-876.

Seizer, S. (2005). Stigmas of the Tamil stage: an ethnography of special drama artists in South India. Durham, NC [u.a.]: Duke Univ. Press.

Sekine, Y. (2002). Anthropology of untouchability: "impurity" and "pollution" in a South indian society. London: National Museum of Ethnology.

Seymour, S. (1999). Going out to School: Women's Changing Roles and Aspirations. . In S. Seymour (Ed.), Women, family and child care in India (pp. 179-203). Cambridge [u.a.]: Cambridge University Press.

Skinner, D., & Holland, D. (1996). Schools and the Cultural Production of the Educated person in a Nepalese Hill Community. In The Cultural Production of the Educated Person (pp. 273-299). New York: State University of New York Press.

Skoda, U. (2002). Forever Yours: Mobility and Equilibrium in Indian Marriage. New Delhi: Mosaic Books.

Smith, D. J. (2010). Promiscuous Girls, Good Wives, and Cheating Husbands: Gender Inequality, Transitions to Marriage, and Infidelity in Southeastern Nigeria. Anthropological Quarterly, 83(1), 123-152.

Sökefeld, M. (2003). Strukturierte Interviews und Fragebögen. In B. Beer (Ed.), Methoden und Techniken der Feldforschung (pp. 95-118). Berlin: Dietrich-Reimer Verlag.

Srinivas, M. (1966). Social Change in modern India. New Delhi: Orient Blackswan.

Srinivasan, S. (2014). Development, Gender Discrimination and the Situation of Unmarried Men in Punjab & Tamil Nadu India. 43th Conference on South Asia: Madison.

Strümpell, C. (2006). Wir arbeiten zusammen, wir essen zusammen. Konvivium und soziale Peripherie in einer indischen Werkssiedlung. Münster: Lit Verlag.

Subramanian, N. (1999). Ethnicity and populist mobilization: political parties, citizens, and democracy in South India. New York: Oxford University Press.

Tambiah, S. J. (1958). The Structure of Kinship and its Relationship to Land Possession and Residence in Pata Dumbara, Central Ceylon. The Journal of the Royal Anthropological Institute of Great Britain and Ireland, 88(1), 21-44.

Tenbruck, F. H. (1964). Freundschaft: ein Beitrag zu einer Soziologie der persönlichen Beziehungen. Kölner Zeitschrift für Soziologie und Sozialpsychologie, 16(3), 431-456.

Tomlinson, J. (1999). Globalization and Culture. Chicago: University of Chicago Press.

Trawick, M. (1990). Notes on love in a Tamil family. Berkeley: Univ. of California Press.

Tyagi, H. (2011). Changing Tracks to leave the race. Make your own Destiny, 1(8), 9-23.

Uberoi, P. (2011 a). Foreword. In S. Grover (Ed.), Marriage, love, caste & kinship support: lived experiences of the urban poor in India (pp. ix-xiv). New Delhi: Social Science Press.

Uberoi, P. (2011 b). The sexual character of the Indian middle class: Sex surveys, past and present. In A. Baviskar, & R. Ray (Eds.), Elite and Everyman: The cultural politics of the Indian middle classes (pp. 271-299). London [u.a.]: Routledge.

van Wessel, M. (2004). Talking about consumption: How an Indian Middle Class Dissociates from Middle-Class Life. Cultural Dynamics, 16(1), 93-116.

Varma, P. (1999). The Writing on the Wall. In V. Pavan (Ed.), The great Indian middle class (pp. 170-213). Delhi: Penguin.

Vāsanti. (2006). Cut-outs, caste and cine stars: the world of Tamil politics. New Delhi: Penguin.

Wadley, S. (1991). The powers of Tamil women. New Delhi: Manohar.

Washbrook, D. (1989). Caste, Class and Dominance in Modern Tamil Nadu. In F. Frankel, & R. M.S.A. (Eds.), Dominance and the State Power in India:

Decline of a Social Order (Vol I) (pp. 204-246). Delhi: Oxford University Press.

Wilson, N. A. (2012). He's too Dark, She's too Fat: Middle Class Matchmaking in Tamil South India. Association for Asian Studies: Annual Conference: Sheraton Centre Toronto.

Wilson, N. A. (2013). Confrontation and Compromise: Middle-Class Matchmaking in Twenty-First Century South India. Asian Ethnology, 72(1), 33-53.

Worthman, C. M., & Whiting, J. W. (1987). Social Change in Adolescent Sexual Behavior, Mate Selection, and Premarital Pregnancy Rates in a Kikuyu CommunityAuthor. Ethos, 15(2), 145-165.

Yan, Y. (2005). The Individual and Transformation of Bridewealth in Rural North China. The Journal of the Royal Anthropological Institute, 11(4), 637-658.

Yelvington, K. A., Osella, C., & Filippo, O. (1999). Power/Flirting. The Journal of the Royal Anthropological Institute, 5(3), 457-460.

Zeff, A. (1999). Marriage, film and video in Tamilnadu. Narrative, image, and ideologies of love. Pennsylvania: University of Pennsylvania.

INTERNET SOURCES

Ananda Vikatan. *'நண்பன்' முந்தியது!* December 7, 2011. http://www.vikatan.com/news/cinema/5390.art

Census of India, 2001. *Tamil Nadu: Data Highlights: The scheduled castes*: http://censusindia.gov.in/Tables_Published/SCST/dh_sc_tamilnadu.pdf

Directorate of Census Operations in Tamil Nadu, 2011. http://www.census2011.co.in/census/district/45-madurai.html

India Today Online. *Nanban expected to make record collections*. January 12, 2012. http://indiatoday.intoday.in/story/nanban-expected-to-make-record-collections/1/168432.html

Manas Saran Photography www.manassaran.com/

Planning Commission, Government of India http://planningcommission.nic.in/plans/planrel/fiveyr/welcome.html

MAPS

mkuniversity.org
stepmap.de

Illustrations, tables and maps

Illustration 1: Convivial and western equality 56

Map 1: Location of the field 58

Map 2: Location of the campus 82

Map 3: Campus of Madurai Kamaraj University 82

Table 1: Peer groups 84

Table 2: Expressions of friendship, used among peers 94

Illustration 2: Examples of a-symmetrical relationships 97

Illustration 3: Examples of symmetrical relationships 99

Map 4: Location of the hometowns visited 105

Table 3: Types of marriage assemblers 144

Table 4: List of profile data 148

Table 5: Marriage rituals and central events (example: Paṟaiyar Caste) 207

Abbreviations

AIADMK	All India Anna Dravida Munnetra Kazhagam
BL	Bachelor of Law
BSc	Bachelor of Science
BA	Bachelor of Arts
BC	Backward Class
FC	Forward Castes
IT	Information Technology
IAS	Indian Administrative Service
IPS	Indian Police Service
IFS	Indian Forest Service
MA	Master of Arts
MBA	Master of Business Administration

MBC	Most Backward Class
MLM	Master of Labor Management
MEd	Master of Education
MPhil	Master of Philosophy
MSc	Master of Science
NGO	Non-governmental organization
PG	Post graduate
PhD	Doctor of Philosophy
PK	Piramalai Kaḷḷar
Rs/rs	Indian rupees
RTO	Regional Transport Office
SC	Scheduled Castes
ST	Scheduled Tribes
TC	Transfer Certificate
UG	Under graduation/Undergraduate
UGC	University Grants Commission

Glossary

Expressions in Tamil script

Akamuṭaiyār (அகமுடையார்)	One of the three Tēvar castes (Mukkulattōr)
akkā (அக்கா)	older sister
ammā (அம்மா)	mother
aṇṇaṉ (அண்ணன்)	older brother
aṇṇi (அண்ணி)	older brother's wife
aṉpu (அன்பு)	affection, fondness
appā (அப்பா)	father
appaḷam (அப்பளம்)	papad
attai (அத்தை)	father's sister, mother's brother's wife
avaru (அவரு)	honorific:'he' – form of refering to husband or a respected older authority
cakkaḷātti (சக்களாத்தி)	coll. term for second wife / beloved of ones' own husband
cakkarai poṅkal (சக்கரை பொங்கல்)	sweet rice dish

Cakkiḷiyar (சக்கிளியர்)	caste of the former "Untouchables"
cāmanti (சாமந்தி)	marigold
campaṅki (சம்பங்கி)	tube roses
caṅkalpam (சங்கல்பம்)	mental process of resolution, concentration, usually done before the *puja*
caṉṉiti (சன்னிதி)	altar
caraṇākati (சரணாகதி)	surrender
centamiḻ (செந்தமிழ்)	original (pure) Tamil language
ceṇṭu (செண்டு)	bouquet
Ceṭṭiyār (செட்டியார்)	merchant caste in Tamil Nadu
cīr (சீர்)	form of dowry
cittappā (சித்தப்பா)	uncle, father's younger brother, mother's younger sister's husband
citti (சித்தி)	mother's younger sister, father's younger brother's wife
contam (சொந்தம்)	category of kin (see Clark-Decès 2014: 39)
cukkiraṉ (சுக்கிரன்)	Venus
cumaṅkali (சுமங்கலி)	married woman
hōmam (ஹோமம்)	ritual fire ceremony
jātakam (ஜாதகம்)	horoscope
jāti (ஜாதி)	Indian term for "caste"

jōtiṭar (ஜோதிடர்)	astrologer
kalacam (கலசம்)	a pot of water, cereals and grains to unite positive spirits
kalkaṇṭu (கல்கண்டு)	byproduct from sugar
Kaḷḷar (கள்ளர்)	name of a caste in Tamil Nadu
kalyāṇam (கல்யாணம்)	marriage ritual
kāmam (காமம்)	sexual desire, lust
kaṇavar (கணவர்)	husband
kaṉṉiyatāṉam (கன்னியா தானம்)	ceremony for gifting the virgin
kāppu kaṭṭutal (காப்பு கட்டுதல்)	protection and binding ceremony
karaṇṭi (கரண்டி)	spoon
kātal (காதல்)	romantic love
kaṭalai uruṇṭai (கடலை உருண்டை)	peanut cake
katampam (கதம்பம்)	lit. "mixture" = a bunch of the flowers
kirāmattu paḻakkavaḻakkam (கிராமத்து பழக்கவழக்கம்)	'backward' habits, associated with 'village' attitudes
koḻukkaṭṭai (கொழுக்கட்டை)	steamed rice paste embedded with sweet of coconut, favorite eatable of God Karpaka Vinayakar
Kōṉār (கோனார்)	in Tamil Nadu herder caste
kula teyvam (குல தெய்வம்)	divine ancestry, family god

kulatoḻil (குலதொழில்)	caste specific occupation
kūṭṭu naṭpu / kūṭṭu naṭṭu (கூட்டு நட்பு /கூட்டு நட்டு)	friendship
kūṭṭu pirārtaṉai (கூட்டு பிரார்தனை)	joint prayer
kūṭṭu vaḻipāṭu (கூட்டு வழிபாடு)	joint worship
laṭu (லடு)	Indian sweet
maccāṉ (m.)/ macciṉi (f.) (மச்சான்/மச்சினி)	addressing form between cross cousins, also used among intimate friends
mālai (மாலை)	flower garland
māmā/ māmaṉ (மாமா/மாமன்)	maternal uncle, older cross cousin, older sister's husband
māṉam (மானம்)	indigenous form of dignity
mañcal (மஞ்சல்)	yellow, turmeric
māṅkalya tōṣam (மாங்கல்ய தோஷம்)	hindrance for getting married
māṅkalya tōṣam parikāram (மாங்கல்ய தோஷம் பரிகாரம்)	remedy puja to cure hindrance for marriage
mantai (மந்தை)	central village square
maṇṭapam (மண்டபம்)	hall
māppiḷḷai (மாப்பிள்ளை)	term for groom and younger brother in-law, also used for intimate (inferior) friends
māppiḷḷai vīṭu aṟiya (மாப்பிள்ளை வீடு அறிய)	ceremony for evaluating the house and environment of the groom

Maṟavar (மறவர்)	One of the three Tēvar castes
mariyātai (மரியாதை)	multi-faceted term for expressing respect, courtesy and hommage
mōr (மோர்)	buttermilk
Mukkulattōr (முக்குலத்தோர்)	lit. "people of the three clans", the term refers to the three Tēvar castes Akamuṭaiyār, Maṟavar and Piramalai kaḷḷar
mūṉ mūrtti (மூன் மூர்த்தி)	display of three gods
muṉṉēṟiya (முன்னேறிய)	forward, modern
naṇpar/ naṇpaṉ/ naṇparkaḷ (நண்பர் / நண்பன் /நண்பர்கள்)	friend(s)
Nāṭār (நாடார்)	caste from the down South of Tamil Nadu
nāttaṉār (நாத்தனார்)	husband's sister
navāmsam (நவாம்ஸம்)	planet constellation
nēroḷivāyppu (நேரொளிவாய்ப்பு)	exposure
niccayatārttam (நிச்சயதார்த்தம்)	engagement ceremony
ōtuvār (ஓதுவார்)	priest, chanting Tamil mantras
pācam (பாசம்)	affection
Paḷḷar (பள்ளர்)	caste of the former "Untouchables"
pāl pāyācam (பால் பாயாசம்)	a desert made of milk and cardamom
paṅkāḷi (பங்காளி)	parallel kinsmen

Paṟaiyar (பறையர்)	caste of the former "Untouchables"
parikāram (பரிகாரம்)	remedy
parucam (பருசம்)	ritual for physical contact between both spouses, by exchanging flowers or ring
paṭiccavaṅka (படிச்சவங்க)	educated people
paṭiccavaṅka paḻakkavaḻakkam (படிச்சவங்க பழக்கவழக்கம்)	'forward' attitude, associated with educated background
pāvā (பாவா)	local term for 'friend', frequently used among Naidus, telugu speakers and Piramalai kaḷḷar
periyammā (பெரியம்மா)	mother's older sister
periyappā (பெரியப்பா)	father's older brother
Piḷḷaimār (பிள்ளைமார்)	land-owning caste, mostly from Veḷḷāḷar community
piṉtaṅkiya (பின்தங்கிய)	backward
piṉ taṅkiyanilai (பின் தங்கியநிலை)	backward people
Piramalai kaḷḷar (பிரமலை கள்ளர்)	one of the three Tēvar castes
pōṅka / vāṅka (போங்க /வாங்க)	(honorific) request: "go" / "come"
poṉṉu (பொன்னு)	woman, bride
poṉṉu āḷaikka pōratu (பொன்னு ஆளைக்க போரது)	ceremony, in which the bride leaves the home
Poṉṉu pārkka / peṇ pārkka pōratu (பொன்னு பார்க்க/ பெண் பார்க்க போரது)	'bride-viewing' ceremony

poruttam (பொருத்தம்)	matching
pōṭa	(non honorific): “go away”!
pūcāri (பூசாரி)	local, usually non-Brahmin priest
pū cūṭṭu viḻā (பூ சூட்டு விழா)	flower ceremony
pū maṇavarai (பூ மணவரை)	an arrangement of flowers, adorning an entire wall
racam (ரசம்)	pepper soup
tāli (தாலி)	neck ornament, bound around the neck of the bride to change her status into a married woman
tāḷi kaṭṭu (தாளி கட்டு)	tāli binding ceremony
tampi (தம்பி)	younger brother
taṅkai/ taṅkaicci (தங்கை/தங்கைச்சி)	younger sister
tappāṭṭam (தப்பாட்டம்)	folk dance, accompanied by a percussion instrument
tāra tōṣam (தார தோஷம்)	astrological hurdle to get a bride
tāra tōṣa cumaṅkali pūjai (தார தோஷ சுமங்கலி பூஜை)	ceremony to bestow prayers to cumankali, in order to remove astrological hindrances for marriage
taṟkālattavar (தற்காலத்தவர்)	‘modern self’
tāy māmaṉ (தாய் மாமன்)	maternal uncle
terintavaṅka/ teriñcavaṅka (தெரிந்தவங்க/தெரிஞ்சவங்க)	knowledgeable person, mediator in marriage processes
Tēvar (தேவர்)	lit. ‘god’, local designation for Akamuṭaiyār, Maṟavar and Piramalai kaḷḷar

ṭēy (டேய்)	addressing form for friend
tīpataṭṭu (தீபதட்டு)	lit. 'light', here: plate of small candles as a component of a puja
tō<u>l</u>a(n) / tō<u>l</u>i (தோழ)ன்) /தோழி)	companion (m.f.) / girlfriend
tōṣam (தோஷம்)	Sanskrit term, used in Hindu astrology to indicate any conspicuity in the horoscope
tuṇṭu (துண்டு)	towel
ūr (ஊர்)	home village / native place
vaḷai kāppu (வளை காப்பு)	bangle wearing ceremony
Vaḷḷuvar (வள்ளுவர்)	caste in Tamil Nadu, traditionally preaching and practising astrology, astronomy and medicine
varataṭcaṇai (வரதட்சணை)	material form of dowry
varavē<u>r</u>pu (வரவேற்பு)	reception
veḷaṅkātava<u>n</u> (வெளங்காதவன்)	(coll.) unlucky person
Veḷḷāḷar (வெள்ளாளர்)	an elite agricultural landlord caste in Tamil Nadu
ve<u>rr</u>ilai pākku (வெற்றிலை பாக்கு)	betel leaf and betel nut
vipūti (விபூதி)	sacred ash
Yātavar (யாதவர்)	an originally pastoral caste in India and a category that includes several communities of different names

CURRENT TERMS IN INDIAN ENGLISH

aarti	worship ritual in which fire is offered to the divine in the form of a flame on ghee or camphor
Adhi Sivan	Hindu god, another name for Siva
annadhanam	ritual offering of food
archana / arccaṉai (அர்ச்சனை)	abbreviated puja to invoke individual guidance and blessings
Brahmana	interpretations of the veda
Brahmin	highest varna in Vedic Hinduism / caste
biryani	mixed rice dish from South Asia
chudidar	South Asian garment
Dalit	self-chosen political designation of those castes in India who were formerly considered 'untouchable'
dhal	Indian curry, made of lentils
dhoti	traditional men's garment
Diwali / Tīpāvaḷi (தீபாவளி)	Hindu festival of lights
Ganesh	Hindu god, son of Shiva and Parvati (worshipped as Karpaka Vinayakar)
gopuram / kōpuram (கோபுரம்)	temple tower
gothram	clan
Iyangar	priest of the Vishnavite sect

Krishna	Hindu god (avatar/ incarnation of Vishnu)
Kshatriya	Castes of the second varna, comprising warriors, rulers and kings
kuthu vilakku	oil lamp
mandalam	geometric chart, depicting religious coherences
Meenakshi	decent of the Hindu Goddess Parvati, worshipped mainly by South Indians
panchayat	Local self-government organization at village or small town level in India
Parvati	Hindu goddess, Shiva's wife
prasadam	offerings of holy food in temples or domestic shrines
puja / pūjai (பூஜை)	worship of the deity
puranas	ancient Hindu texts, dating back to 400 – 1000 A.D.
Sadhu / cātu (சாது)	Saint in India
sambar / cāmpār (சாம்பார்)	lentil-based vegetable stew
samskara	life cycle ritual
sangam/ caṅkam (சங்கம்)	academies, associations, societies
Shiva	Hindu god
Shudra	castes of the fourth varna, comprising agriculturalists, farmers, potters, weavers
Siddhar / cittar (சித்தர்)	Saints in Tamil Nadu, usually practicing unorthodox spiritual and medical methods

Vaishya	castes of the third varna, comprising merchants, traders, money lenders and land owners
varna	lit. color, class – also used for classifying all human beings in Hinduism
Veda	body of Sanskrit literature and religious texts in Hinduism, dating back to 1500–500 BC
Vishnavite	religious section worshipping Vishnu
zamindar	ancient aristocrat within the Mogul Empire who held vast tracts of land and control over several kingdoms and provinces

Acknowledgements

This thesis could not have been implemented without the support and engagement of several people and institutions to which I express my deepest gratitude.

First and foremost, I thank all who took the time and trouble to participate in my research. I am particularly indebted to those students and alumni who involved me in their 'circles' and group activities. They not only gave me insights into their own experience of friendship, but let me feel what it means to be one of their tōḻi.

Their engagement was strongly encouraged by professors and lecturers at Madurai Kamaraj University, who allowed me to conduct 'fieldwork' during their class and complemented the findings with their own views. I received invaluable comments from Dr. T. Dharmaraj, Head of the department of folklore and cultural studies, who did not withhold critical remarks and in doing so prevented me from arriving at fallacious conclusions. Moreover, I thank all members of the registrar's office at MKU for permitting me to conduct research within the campus. Essential provisions for implementing the research project were made by Dr. A. Chella Perumal, Head of the Department of Anthropology at Pondicherry University and M.D. Muthukumaraswamy, Head of the National Folklore Support Center (NFSC) in Chennai by affiliating me with their institutions.

I am equally thankful for the support beyond campus borders, which I particularly received from the family members of the graduate students. Parents and siblings eagerly expressed their differentiated views on friendship and let me participate in 'enclosed' family events. Strong efforts have been made by professionals of the wedding industry to explain, evaluate and illustrate contemporary transformations in marriage practices among the middle class in urban Madurai.

Such close access to the field would not have been possible without the hospitality of my host family that not only provided me with accommodation and food, but also involved me to a great extent in their internal family decision making processes with respect to education and marriage. In particular, I thank Yasoda, my host mother for her delicious dishes (I will never forget the legendary *takkāḷi* chutney), Suganth, my host sister for her open talks about her matchmaking process and David, my host brother for his engaged assistance during my research.

Planning and completion of the research project relied on support outside the Indian context. I am grateful to my supervisor Prof. Dr. Gabriele Alex for her useful insights, constructive criticism and her ongoing encouragement. Her guidance and trust was indispensable and also gave me the freedom to elaborate own ideas. Also, I thank my second supervisor Dr. Phil. habil. Heike Oberlin, for her subsequent, rewarding inputs.

For their generous funding, I thank the Landesgraduiertenförderung Baden-Württemberg and the German Academic Exchange Service (DAAD).

I received further encouragement and helpful input from colleagues and doctoral students at the Institute of Social and Cultural Anthropology at Tübingen University, among which I especially emphasize the help of Dr. Susanne Fehlings. Her excellent advice together with shared experiences and amicable support made the writing process much easier for me.

Linguistic and technical 'experts' added the finishing touches to my draft: the editing by Cortnie Shupe, the specifications of Tamil terms by Dr. Thomas Lehmann and the layout review by Daniel Metz refined the script of the thesis into an accurate and well-designed dissertation.

Last, but not least, I turn to my family members and friends. Both the fieldwork and writing process involve inspiration, hard times and reconsideration. Their moral support was essential to my ability to bear this at times exhausting process. Against this background, I am thankful to: my parents, my sister Xenia and 'cousin'-sister Natascha, who always believe in my decisions and accompany me during my ups and downs, and Thomas for his strong trust in me and his patience whenever the writing process turned me into a hectic and stressful companion. Finally, I embrace my own 'female', 'male' and 'mixed-gendered' peer group for delighting in my achievements and cheering me up in troublesome situations. Our joint laughter represents the golden thread of this thesis, which illustrates friendship as a priceless resource.

Social Sciences and Cultural Studies

Marc Wagenbach, Pina Bausch Foundation (eds.)
Inheriting Dance
An Invitation from Pina

2014, 192 p., 29,99 € (DE),
ISBN 978-3-8376-2785-5
E-Book: 26,99 € (DE), ISBN 978-3-8394-2785-9

Carlo Bordoni
Interregnum
Beyond Liquid Modernity

2016, 136 p., 19,99 € (DE),
ISBN 978-3-8376-3515-7
E-Book: 17,99 € (DE), ISBN 978-3-8394-3515-1
EPUB: 17,99 € (DE), ISBN 978-3-8394-3515-1

Maik Fielitz, Laura Lotte Laloire (eds.)
Trouble on the Far Right
Contemporary Right-Wing Strategies
and Practices in Europe

2016, 208 p., 19,99 € (DE),
ISBN 978-3-8376-3720-5
E-Book: 17,99 € (DE), ISBN 978-3-8394-3720-9
EPUB: 17,99 € (DE), ISBN 978-3-3728-3720-9

All print, e-book and open access versions of the titels in our entire list are available in our online shop www.transcript-verlag.de/en!